New Zealand with a Hobbit Botherer

by
John Gisby

with
Annette Gisby as THB

New Zealand With a Hobbit Botherer

New Zealand with a Hobbit Botherer
© John Gisby 2005

ALL RIGHTS RESERVED
No part of this book may be produced in any form, by photocopying or by any electronic or mechanical means, including information storage or retrieval systems, without permission in writing from both the copyright owner and the publisher of this book, except for the minimum words needed for review.

ISBN: 1-4116-5644-X

This edition printed in 2005 by
Lulu Inc.

New Zealand With a Hobbit Botherer

To Annette,

with all my love.

Thanks for not laughing when I said I was going to write a book.

It's okay to laugh when you read it

Thanks also

to Edie and Jack,

to JRR Tolkien for The Book,

to Peter Jackson, Fran Walsh and Philippa Boyens for The Movies

and

to the People of New Zealand for their hospitality.

See you again soon!

New Zealand With a Hobbit Botherer

HOBBIT BOTHERER ON TOUR
2004

New Zealand With a Hobbit Botherer

CONTENTS

	Prologue	I Had A Dream
1	Auckland	Hoops But No Rings
2	Matamata	Calm Down, It's Only A Sheep Paddock
3	Rotorua	Hongi And Hangi
4	Napier	Where's All The Art Deco Gone?
5	Wai-O-Tapu	A Woman Who Turns Out To Be A Geyser
6	Tongariro National Park	Going For A Tramp
7	Wellington	A Beehive And A Chocolate Fish
8	North to South	Sounds Of Green Lipped Mussels
9	Nelson	Knob Jokes And Wearable Art
10	Greymouth	New Zealand's G-Spot
11	The Glaciers	Tears Of The Avalanche Girl
12	Wanaka	Making The Baby Elephant
13	Queenstown, New Zealand	That's No Good, It's Australian
14	Queenstown, Middle Earth	The Lord Of The Rings Bathroom
15	Te Anau	Thousands Of Pinpricks of Light
16	Milford Sound	A Bird With A Rubber Fetish
17	The Catlins	A Surveyor With A Sense Of Humour
18	Dunedin	Get Your Albatross Here
19	Aoraki / Mount Cook	Flour And Water
20	Christchurch	A Hillock In The Middle Of Nowhere
	Epilogue	Another Dream
	Glossary	For People Who Think *Lord of the Rings* Is An Aristocratic Jeweller

PROLOGUE: LONDON

I Had A Dream

Have you ever had the dream where you find yourself at a party dressed in nothing but your underwear? No not *that* dream. Not *that* kind of party. I mean the one where all the other guests, draped in designer labels (and remaining so throughout) whisper smugly amongst themselves, falling silent as you approach. You only catch snippets of what they are saying, "Has he no shame?" "Y fronts are so passé," "Did you see the size of it?" and so on. Eventually you get so fed up that you make for the kitchen to fetch a knife... (Ignore the last sentence if you're not in the habit of watching reruns of *The Shining* and *Psycho* on TV just before falling asleep).

Well this tale begins with a similar dream. The guests are dressed as characters from *Lord of the Rings,* the scraps of earwigged conversation include questions such as, "What was the man doing with the carrot in Bree?", "Who was the horse department assistant for *The Return of the King?*" and "Why did they leave out Tom Bombadil from the book?" but yes, I am still in my underwear. I'll forgive you if you don't wish to dwell on that image for long.

At first I assume it's a party for cast and crew, so naturally I begin a search for Liv Tyler, Cate Blanchett and Miranda Otto. (Note to my wife. This is a dream. I would never, ever seek out these women at a party in real life, even if they were in their underwear too. By the way don't you think that my nose was shorter yesterday?) Two things convince me that this assumption is wrong. Firstly, there is no Liv, no Cate and no Miranda. Nor for that matter are there any other performers I recognise from the movies. Secondly the Dwarves seem to be rather too tall, the Rohirrim rather too rotund and the Elves, it has to be said, rather too ugly to have featured in the movies.

My conclusion about the elves may of course be coloured by the fact that one of their number, sporting a single prosthetic ear, insists on glaring at me suspiciously as I tackle a particularly chewy and rather misshapen mini pitta bread I have discovered on the buffet table.

My second assumption is that it must be a convention of some kind for fans of the movies. That is close... but still no cigar.

New Zealand With a Hobbit Botherer

The truth is finally revealed at the sound of a horn, as a man with a shiny silver bucket on his head encourages Elves, Wizards, Hobbits, Uruk-hai, Orcs, Rangers, Dwarves, Rohirrim, Gondorians and Exhibitionists (glances at yours truly) to sit in a large circle. Briefly I worry that a man-flesh barbecue is planned and that I have been invited along to provide the man-flesh - the Uruk-hai do look rather hungry - but then a cheery-looking, tousle-haired character in shorts, tee shirt and owlish spectacles steps forward. (So I'm not the only one to shun designer clothes from the House of Hobbit). A badge announces the man's name is Jack Peterson. He has the demeanour of a bloke in charge.

"Wilcum ivryone to Hubbit Butherer's Anonymous," he says in a New Zealand accent not easily reproduced on the printed page.

Immediately an Elf in a tight fitting blue shirt and black slacks rises from his seat and leaves, pausing only to mutter irritably at a poster proclaiming *Star Trek Fan Club - Next Week* hanging by the door.

"I see we hiv a new mimber prisunt. Perhups he would like to begin the miting by tilling us why he is hir."

I look around to catch a glimpse of the poor unfortunate who's been singled out and find everyone else catching a glimpse of me. What can I possibly say of interest to a Mordor of Hobbit botherers? (It's a murder of crows, why not a Mordor of Hobbit botherers?)

Finally and tentatively I volunteer, "I have seen *The Return of the King* four times..."

This is the truth. The first time I was totally captivated, enthralled by the story. The second time I admired the beautiful landscapes, the acting, the seamless special effects. The third time I began to get picky, wondering why there was no blood and guts on the bottom of the oliphaunts' feet when they lifted them up after trampling people to death, why Legolas never ran out of arrows and eventually if the movie was showing on a loop which meant it would never end.

The fourth time was some months after the initial release. A local independent cinema were showing the complete trilogy in one day. It made an excellent Valentine's day surprise for my wife and I was able to surreptitiously catch up on some sleep before enjoying a well deserved reward later in the evening and on into the night.

In the dream I think four times is quite impressive (seeing the film!) but my fellow members of the circle clearly do not. There are mutterings of "Fraud! Fraud!" and "Not even double figures!" A group of Uruk-hai in the shadows at the back begin to fire up a barbecue.

With just a hint of desperation I continue, "...but I know someone who has seen it twenty-seven times, bought all the DVDs, cinema and extended versions, and even read Sean Astin's book *There and Back Again* - more than once." This is clearly more impressive, though there are still a few cries of, "A friend, yes of course," and "He's in denial." So I have to come clean.

"Okay. That someone is my wife, Annette. She's taken to collecting DVDs of any films starring Elijah Wood, Orlando Bloom or Viggo Mortensen after seeing them in *Lord of the Rings*. She even claims that *The Calcium Kid* is a watchable movie!"

At the mention of Mr Bloom several of the younger female elves sink to the floor in a faint, sighing "Oooh Orlando," and have to be revived by bringing one of the Rohirrim close by so they catch a nose-tingling whiff of horse manure.

Coming clean about Annette has the desired effect. I am accepted. I am one of the group. I have admitted that I have a problem with *Lord of the Rings* addiction, even if it is addiction by proxy, and now I am ready to hear what the man himself, Jack Peterson, has to say about the matter.

"Think you," he begins. "Thir is a cure. You must furce yurself... er your wife... to rillise that the movies are only funtasy. Trivel to New Zilland and visit where they were shi... er shot. Convince your wife that Hubbits, Ilves and Wizards are not rill."

He turns to reveal a beautiful picture of snow covered mountains reflected in a turquoise lake on the rear of his tee shirt. Below is the legend *Tourism New Zealand*. "My brither, rins a trivil igency," he continues, "I hiv his nimber here."

So that is how I came to be spending a month travelling around New Zealand accompanied by a Hobbit botherer called Annette. A Hobbit botherer eager to stand where Orlando had stood, to see what Viggo had seen and to be given a gold ring just like Elijah had been given.

Dream on.

Incidentally, for those of you who are still wondering what the man was doing with the carrot in Bree, who assisted the horse department for *The Return of the King* and why Tom Bombadil never made it out of the book, the answers are of course, eating it, Angela van der

Weerdhof and weren't the films bum-numbingly long enough already? I wish it to be known that I had to look up the name of the horse assistant. I am *not* the Hobbit botherer. The Hobbit botherer, affectionately shortened to THB, is my wife.

1: AUCKLAND

Hoops But No Rings

There are five main things to consider when selecting an airline for long haul travel on a budget.

(1) Do they fly to the place you want to go?
(2) Do their aircraft fall out of the sky often? (The answer no, they only ever fall out of the sky once is not acceptable).
(3) Is there much leg room in economy?
(4) Is there much leg room in economy?
(5) Is there much leg room in economy?

Of those airlines which scored a yes then a no on the first two questions, Air New Zealand seemed to score best on three, four and five, so we flew with them to Auckland from London, via Sydney. (The diversion to Sydney was for an educational exhibition of *Lord of the Rings* costumes and props. It certainly taught us a thing a two, like don't go to Sydney in early December for an exhibition that starts on Boxing Day).

We made the choice of Air New Zealand despite dire warnings on the internet about the standard of their in-flight entertainment. Before you question that decision, ask yourself this. How many people do you know who would say, "Sure I have acquired a deep vein thrombosis in my leg that might kill me, but it was really worth it to be able to watch Halle Berry in *Catwoman* several times in quick succession on a six inch LCD screen"? Actually if you do know anyone who would say that, get them professional help.

I saw Halle Berry on a rather larger screen appearing now and again from behind the head of the man in the seat in front of me and in my humble opinion this improved *Catwoman* a lot. But not as much as the fact that my headset wasn't working so I couldn't hear any of the dialogue.

Air New Zealand, managed to remain airborne and convey THB and myself over the Atlantic and Pacific oceans without forcing us to sit with our knees tucked under our chins, and left us a few hours to enjoy the departure lounge at Sydney airport before the final leg of our journey to Auckland.

Having toured all the souvenir shops in a vain attempt to swap my remaining Australian dollars for an *Indiana Jones* style leather hat (my dollars were too few and would only run to a *Village People* style leather hat adorned by chains) I had to admit defeat and exchange them for their Kiwi cousins instead. Then I settled down with THB for a game of *Spot the Banker,* a diversion which centres around trying to guess the occupations of fellow passengers.

I pointed to a harassed looking woman waggling her finger at three bored looking children as she lectured then on the finer points of how to eat an ice cream without necessitating a change of clothes. Teacher! THB pointed to an oily haired man in a sharp suit trying to charm an upgrade (or maybe more) out of an unimpressed stewardess. Salesman! I pointed to a furtive looking guy in jeans and a tomato ketchup (or was it) stained tee shirt. Axe-murderer! And so on.

Then THB pointed to a very tall man dressed in a red and black track suit loping across the concourse with the ease of a professional athlete. His clothes featured a drawing of a bearded man with an eye patch peering out from within an inverted triangle. Ophthalmologist? No! Basketball player!

He joined a group of similarly dressed and similarly lofty colleagues. Basketball team!

A short, middle-aged man in thick glasses then sidled up to them and began dispensing advice. "If you manage to put the ball through that hoopy thing more often and let the other team do it less often, I think you will win more games." Basketball fan!

Maybe his comments were a little more incisive than that, I'm no basketball expert, but I don't think the tall guys were impressed. If looks could kill there would have been a set of luggage to remove from the hold before our plane could take off. Luckily before blood could be spilled the giants were marshalled away like naughty kids by an older, shorter, greyer and more stressed looking teacher-substitute. Basketball coach!

To my surprise, when we boarded the plane, the basketball giants were scattered about economy, hunched in their seats like adults having to make do with infants' chairs at a school parents' evening, rather than lounging in first as I assumed sports stars would. Suddenly the room available to a titch like me seemed lavish. And unlike some, I wasn't bothered by autograph hunters on their way back from the toilet for much of the flight. Maybe that was the last time though. You never know how well this book will do.

Auckland airport created a good first impression. It wasn't the usual soulless cavern of steel girders and surly staff that has become the norm nowadays. It was more like someone's living room, expanded to accommodate a handful of shops and the odd extra seat in case a few hundred visitors happened to drop by. And people there were smiling. No really they were. Maybe we'd just turned up at the end of their shift.

The absence of gun-toting police roaming about on the look out for itinerant terrorists was refreshing too. But what if there was an incident? Say the New Zealand ovine rights movement smuggled a flock of sheep into the terminal to protest at the lack of international travel opportunities for our woolly friends, at least when alive. I admit that this sort of behaviour is normally restricted to French farmers, but you never know. Maybe a group of Maori warriors would spring out from hiding (in cupboards, behind doughnut stands, wherever) and whack a few heads with their taiaha (fighting staff). Then the price of lamb in the airport restaurants would fall for a few days.

"Wut mid you wunt to kim to New Zilland?" enquired the cheerful Kiwi on the immigration desk charged with deciding whether we would be allowed into her country.

I should point out here that we had not encountered a small talking bird. Not a feathered one anyway. The word Kiwi is used as an adjective to indicate a person from New Zealand. Apparently the Kiwis prefer that to New Zealander or New Zildish or whatever. I've often thought it would be interesting to extend this idea for use within a country. People from coastal areas could be called gulls, people from cities could be called pigeons, men could be called cocks, women could be called tits... Maybe not.

While I was mulling over the question of avian nomenclature, THB had answered the immigration officer's question, using the magic four words guaranteed, it seems, to get any Kiwi excited. (A clue. They begin with L, O, T and R).

"We saw the *Lord of the Rings* films..." she said, not getting any further before being taken on a verbal tour of filming locations on the

North and South islands, sorted in chronological and then in filmalogical order for good measure. THB took copious notes. Just when I thought we would finally be allowed into the country the duo began to discuss the relative merits of Orlando Bloom and Elijah Wood, firstly as actors then in various other imaginary capacities. Elijah, for example, was judged most likely to make a good toilet brush if held upside down.

The muttering from the queue behind us eventually reached a sufficient volume to coax HB2 back to reality. "Huw lung will you be stiying?" she asked. We requested a month and were allowed six. That's six months in New Zealand, not in the immigration queue waiting to get in.

All the guide books had said that New Zealand was relatively crime free, save for a few thefts from cars in isolated parking spots. Imagine our surprise therefore, when two burly men, having spotted us emerging from the terminal building, began to charge towards us like All Black prop-forwards with an English scrum half in their sights. THB grabbed my hand, as she tends to do in moments of perceived danger. I like to think that it is for comfort and protection but it may be to stop me running away without her.

A few feet away, the men skidded to a halt. Instead of revealing a weapon and demanding my wallet, they adopted the sort of pose that magicians' assistants do after a particularly impressive trick, eliciting applause from a gobsmacked audience. Fortunately they were not wearing spangly tights and feathery headgear. One coaxed our gaze in the direction of a saloon car parked in the distance, the other towards a people carrier. Ah, taxi drivers!

We began to walk towards the car, a people carrier seeming unnecessary for the just the two of us, but the owner of the larger vehicle wasn't giving up that easily. "Same price!" he barked. They stared at each other for a while in a battle of wills. Then Mr Car's head dropped and he slunk away defeated, leaving us no choice but Mr People Carrier to take us to our hotel, *The Airedale* in Auckland city centre.

As we checked in, the first question we were asked was, "Win are you living?" This turned out to be fairly common throughout New Zealand. Note to New Zealand hotel staff. "How many nights are you staying with us?" would be a much more welcoming greeting. And the mathematics necessary to obtain a leaving date, given the current date (look at the newspaper if in any doubt) and the length of stay of a guest, isn't that difficult. Really it isn't.

The room boasted a kitchen at the foot of the bed and a view from the window that would have delighted any aficionado of air conditioning ducts and other functional gubbins. But the bed itself turned out to be comfortable and we had some reading to do. Waiting for us in reception had been a collection of leaflets to rival those which fall out of a Sunday newspaper, provided by our travel agent. Only the leaflets we had described exciting things to do and sights to see, rather than tat to purchase in hope then consign shamefacedly to the cupboard under the sink.

While THB studied the literature provided, I undertook a survey of the number and quality of TV channels available, an important early task on entering any hotel room in a new country. As I surfed through the fare on offer I discovered a sports channel showing basketball. I was just about to surf on, when one of the players caught my eye. That man looked awfully familiar. I looked closer. So did his team mate. So did the team logo, a bearded man with an eye patch in a triangle. I pictured them hunched up in economy seats on an aircraft. That was it. I had travelled to New Zealand with the Hunter Valley Pirates, who were in town to play the New Zealand Breakers.

Now I had a team to follow, the Pirates, and they were winning, basketball suddenly became marginally interesting. I watched the rest of the game with waning excitement as my adopted team snatched defeat from the jaws of victory by 94 points to 106. The commentators seemed to think this was something of a surprise. I didn't. Most new sports teams that I adopt crash and burn in a very similar way.

The obvious place to start exploring Auckland was the Sky Tower. This needle like edifice peered over the older and more restrained town hall opposite *The Adelaide* and promised sumptuous views of the city. At 328 metres high it is Auckland's attempt at the record for the tallest building in that part of the world just outside the bit containing a taller building.

I have a theory that cities build tall towers for the same reason that middle aged men buy red Ferraris. But that may be because I come from a city which boasts the stump like British Telecom Tower (189 metres) as its phallic symbol. Not sure about the red Ferrari theory? Consider this. Auckland felt the need to add a 150 tonne, 96.2 metre mast to the top of the tower specifically to pip the then Sydney Tower in Australia (309 metres) to the honour of being tallest free standing structure in the Southern hemisphere.

You can don overalls and a hard hat and climb to the very top of the mast roped to a guide if you like. But it was very windy the day we were there. And I had the wrong shoes on. And they probably wouldn't have had overalls in my size anyway. And I was starting to get a cold... OK. I admit it. I was scared.

The Sky Tower boasts membership of the World Federation of Great Towers or WFGT as it is known to its friends. That is an impressive sounding organisation with a membership that includes the Empire State Building, New York (443 metres), The CN Tower, Toronto (553 metres), The Ostankino Tower, Moscow (540 metres), Menara KL, Kuala Lumpar (421 metres) and Blackpool Tower, UK (158 metres).

Perhaps there was a typo on the application form when the Blackpool Tower applied to join. "Wow," the WFGT approval committee must have thought, "518 metres. That's a big one." Or perhaps a Wurlitzer Organ and a circus counts for more in the eyes of the WFGT than height alone. London's own Telecom Tower suddenly doesn't seem such a shorty after all.

I imagine that a WFGT inspector tours the world with a clipboard in his hand to keep errant Tower owners in check. "Excuse me Sir. As you've not paid your subscription to The Federation," (pauses in reverence), "this year, we are going to downgrade you from Great to Moderately Impressive." Not that I'm suggesting the Sky Tower would ever suffer such a fate. It is without doubt, a Great Tower.

There are two enclosed viewing platforms below the one in the open air at the very top of the mast, for those people not prone to mistaking pant-wetting terror for fun. That excludes most Kiwis, of course. We paid the extra few dollars to experience the higher one and the panorama that greeted us as we left the glass bottomed lift, enough terror for me by itself, was spectacular.

To one side there was the distant arc of the harbour bridge and dot like ferries departing for the vineyards of Waiheke island, the bird sanctuary of Tiritiri Matangi island or the volcanoes of Rangitoto island. To the other there was a landscape that looked as if someone had covered a collection of Christmas puddings with a green tablecloth, then scattered tiny white buildings all over it. Auckland is a very green city. Twenty one regional parks within easy reach of the city according to the Auckland A to Z.

Only slightly spoiling the view were two black vertical wires dangling past the window opposite the lift exit. Inside, in between them, was a dot matrix sign which read *Next Jumper, 5 minutes*. The minutes counted down as we watched. Were they auctioning knitwear? No. Remember that in New Zealand, jumping off anything tall enough that stands still long enough for a man with some bungy cord to set up a business is a national obsession. Shortly after *1 minute* passed a man appeared outside, yes outside, the window spreadeagled between the dangling wires, mercilessly buffeted by the wind. He halted briefly in front of us to give a cheesy, 'I'm not so sure this was a good idea', smile, before plummeting towards the centre of a large target on the ground below. Welcome to the little known sport of base jumping.

At ground level, reached courtesy of the glass bottomed lift once again rather than a perilous base jump, the cosmopolitan nature of Auckland quickly became apparent. It seemed as if every nationality the world has to offer had leased a small part of Queen Street to ensure passing tourists did not miss out on its own unique cuisine. Every nation but New Zealand. Lamb was on offer sliced from a rotating torso on a spike in Mediterranean kebab shops but not as far as we could see from an authentic Kiwi restaurant.

That was the disappointing thing about Auckland. Red buses and The Houses of Parliament scream London to a visitor, the Statue of Liberty and yellow taxis scream New York, the Eiffel Tower and snooty, self important waiters scream Paris, but nothing Auckland offered seemed to scream Auckland or New Zealand. The city was so cosmopolitan it could have been almost anywhere in the world. Even the Sky Tower itself had that flying saucer skewered by a knitting needle design familiar from Toronto, Las Vegas, Moscow... you get the idea.

On the evening of our first full day in Auckland there was a free Christmas concert in The Domain, a 75 hectare park, Auckland's oldest, developed around the cone of an extinct volcano. Anyone who was anyone in New Zealand showbiz was going to be there to sing a song. A magnificent twenty eight different names were mentioned on the advertising blurb, twenty eight of which we had never heard of. It was hosted by Jeremy Corbett, Kelly Swanson-Roe and Petra Bagust. See what I mean? (Apologies if you are a Kiwi and these people are as well known to you as your own children. Or, if they are your own children, thank you for buying my book, Mr and Mrs Corbett, Swanson-Roe or Bagust). New Zealand celebrity doesn't seem to travel well. Kiri Te Kanawa and Crowded House must have been having the night off.

Incidentally if you haven't heard of Kiri, then don't admit it in New Zealand. The question, "Who is Kiri Te Kanawa?" later on in our trip, nearly resulted in an impromptu lynching for the unfortunate Japanese tourist foolish enough to enquire. (I think the question was actually "What is Kiri Te Kanawa?") Kiwis are fiercely proud of locals made good on a worldwide stage. (Kiri is an opera singer, in case you were wondering, but are now afraid to mention it). Crowded House are also musicians. If you haven't heard any of their songs and are travelling to New Zealand, don't worry. You will.

Back to the Christmas concert in the Domain. We had been looking forward to this all day. A chance to experience Christmas in an unusual setting for us, that is to say mid Summer. After a busy day exploring the city we popped back to the hotel to freshen up and find our glad rags for the evening, but made the mistake of lying down for a few minutes to rest our feet. We woke up to the sound of *Jingle Bells* as the alarm went off for breakfast the next morning. Jet lag has a lot to answer for.

On our second day in Auckland we had to collect the hire car which was to transport us around the North Island. As there was only two of us we had chosen a fairly small model, a Toyota Echo cho cho cho. (Thank you if you laughed at that joke. I tried it out on many people before committing it to computer screen and the only other person who thought it was remotely funny was THB. We're obviously made for each other).

The initial plan was to drive up to Northlands, the bit of New Zealand that sticks out at the top like the arm of a drowning man, to experience the Bay of Islands and Ninety Mile Beach. This was scuppered when we bought a road atlas and discovered just how long such a journey would take. A sixteen and a half hour return trip, that before adding in sightseeing time, did not appeal. So we made do with Kelly Tarlton's Antarctic Experience and Underwater World and Howick Historical Village, still two of the top five attractions of Auckland according to guide books. WFGT fans will be pleased to hear that the Sky Tower makes it into the fabulous five as well.

Kelly Tarlton's was a short drive along the coast from the centre of Auckland, set on a very windy promontory. I have a photograph of THB with horizontal hair which testifies to the strength of the wind.

Kelly was a man who dreamed of allowing the human life of the North Island to view the marine life of the Southern Ocean from the perspective he enjoyed as a diver, without having to get wet or go through the bother of obtaining a PADI certificate. This turned out to be more productive then dreaming of *Lord of the Rings* parties as he eventually designed and built an aquarium around an acrylic tunnel, the sides and roof of which allowed sharks, stingrays and a host of other sea creatures to be viewed from a moving walkway. All that was missing really was a waiter to arrange for the one you selected to be cooked and brought to a candlelit table.

Although the aquarium was certainly interesting, THB and I went through three times, it was not unique. Other transparent tunnels have sprung up in aquaria all around the world. What makes Kelly Tarlton's really special is the Antarctic Experience.

We entered to find a replica of Robert Falcon Scott's Antarctic hut as he would remember it, illustrating the terrible conditions and awful privations that early Antarctic explorers endured. The worst part was the screams and incessant jostling from hoards of rampaging Kiwi school kids. I don't know how Scott managed to stand it. Then, the real highlight. A trip in a snow cat through an Antarctic landscape, maintained through the creation of three tonnes of fresh ice daily, home to a colonies of King and Gentoo penguins. There are few places in the world, without actually visiting Antarctica, that these birds can be viewed so closely. We could have gone round again and again, but unfortunately this was not an option without paying again and again.

Before setting off to Howick we drove along the coast to Mission Bay for lunch, parking beside a mysterious sign with the number 30 on it. A local explained, as if to a particularly dense child, that this was the number of minutes your car was allowed to stay in that spot. A quick lunch then.

Mission Bay offered a wealth of tempting restaurants separated from a beautiful beach by the road and an immaculately kept promenade and park, hotspots for joggers, rollerbladers and frisbee throwers. This was the first of many places in New Zealand that had us thinking, "Yes, we could happily live here." Cue a brief survey of local real estate agents by THB. We ate Italian on the first floor terrace of a restaurant overlooking the waters of the Rangitoto channel. The seafood chowder was fantastic, shooting in to occupy the starter spot in my all time fantasy meal.

The journey from Mission Bay to Howick was our first experience of navigation in New Zealand, since Auckland to Mission Bay had been simply a matter of following the coast. It couldn't be that difficult to find one of the top five attractions in Auckland, even if we were only armed with a postage stamp sized map on the back of a leaflet advertising the historical village, having left our new road atlas in the hotel room. Could it? Yes it could.

Normally countries provide three types of road sign to prevent locals from being continually pestered for directions by floundering tourists. Signs that say:

(1) Congratulations! You're reached a junction. Turn left to get to Tourist Trap. Turn right for Nicetown. Don't go straight on unless you're wearing asbestos underclothes. They barbecue tourists down there.
(2) Don't worry! You're still on the main road, even though it's just got the one lane and is unpaved, and you're still on the way to Tourist Trap. No, you haven't missed a vital turning. Chill out. You're on holiday.
(3) Wow! You are lost aren't you. We don't see many tourists in this neck of the woods. The last one was back in 1994. Or was it '95? He was driving one of those... Oh! You want to get back to the main road? Why didn't you say? Take a left at the end of that track up there, then a right, then another left, straight on for a mile or so, then right again when you see the sheep with the wonky eye...

New Zealand doesn't seem fond of signs of types (2) and (3). Without the reassurance of type (2) signs even the simplest journey is haunted by visions of missed turns and in the absence of type (3) signs there is little hope for those accidentally venturing off the beaten track. On the way to Howick, we accidentally ventured off the beaten track.

We found ourselves circling a network of identical roads lined by identical looking houses, the sort with corrugated iron roofs, that are delivered on the back of a truck. It was like being in a holiday village full of chalets, the only place in Britain that you see single storey dwellings in bulk. Just like when you are stuck in one of those holiday villages, we came up with a plan to escape. A rather desperate plan, but a plan nevertheless. Find another vehicle and follow it.

After twice being led back to their homes by local householders worried that plain clothes cops were on to them, we finally latched onto a truck on its way out of town and made off in the direction of Panmure, which the postage stamp suggested was on the way to Howick. Closer to Howick we had to leave the main highway to get to the Historical Village, and the whole saga began again. Never again did we leave the road map in the hotel room.

Howick Historical Village comprised thirty or so buildings from the 1840-1880 period, the time of the Fencibles, a contraction of the word 'defensible'. The Fencibles were a collection of retired soldiers who were given free passage to New Zealand with their families, a cottage to live in and an acre of land, which became theirs after seven years. All this in return for a few military duties and compulsory attendance of Sunday church services. The accommodation greeting them upon arrival wasn't always quite what they might have been expecting though. The village included a tent of the type presented to early arrivals whose cottages had not yet been built. (Similar things happen nowadays to people buying property in the Spanish Costas or Canary Islands). It also included a raupo, a one room 'cottage' put together from dried bundles of bulrushes collected from local swamps. Waterproof pyjamas were essential for inhabitants of a raupo during bad weather.

In our photo album there is picture of THB sitting outside a raupo. The caption reads 'Our Hotel' but it doesn't really fool anyone, not even those familiar with the standard of budget accommodation in and around London.

There were other more upmarket buildings to explore, these built from wood and ranging from double units for privates (semi detached garden sheds) through single units for sergeants (detached garden sheds) to homesteads for officers (large, handsome and commodious dwellings with 40 acres of land, according to the advertising at the time). Each building was accompanied by a potted history of its inhabitants, many of Irish origin, a feature which really brought the village alive. Tales of great hardship and sorrow were common, such as that of the ship *Clifton* which travelled from Roscommon, Ireland, in 1848 packed with families fleeing the potato famine. Forty six of the hundred and sixty children on board did not survive the journey.

My favourite story was that of Ngamapu, a Maori mail runner who lived in a raupo adjacent to the General Store. He ran between Howick and Auckland from 1848 to 1856 carrying the post, according to an information board we read. I was impressed. To complete that journey on foot in just eight minutes, he must have had a really important appointment in Auckland at seven o'clock in the evening.

That night, our final one in Auckland, Jack Peterson appeared again as I slept. He was not happy. "Hiv you furgotten why you are hir?" he asked, waggling a finger in my direction. He took the lack of a reply from me as a yes, so he answered himself. "To vusit the lucitions whir the *Lord of the Rungs* mivies were shut!" I considered mentioning to him that talking to oneself was generally taken to be the first sign of madness. But where would that leave me, talking to a huffy man prowling around my imagination?

"Git on wuth ut," he said, stomping off to a dusty corner of my brain from where he could keep a watchful eye on me. The problem was that the first visit to a *Lord of the Rings* movie location that we had planned (or so I thought) was in Wellington, five days away. Surely that would do. He wasn't going to keep pestering me every night until then was he?

As it turned out I needn't have worried. THB was sleeping peacefully beside me. True to the appellation given to her for the purposes of this tale, she had hatched a plan to bother Hobbits.

2: MATAMATA

Calm Down, It's Only A Sheep Paddock.

There are those men who claim that women can't read maps. That if a woman shows an interest in the wiggly lines that cover the pages of a road atlas, that interest should be tactfully redirected towards cooking spaghetti. Before I lose half of my potential readership I should point out that I am not one of those men.

I have the utmost confidence in THB's navigation skills bolstered by an uncanny ability to pick the right road in those worrying moments when no part of the map in her hand bears any relation to the surrounding reality. Her only minor failing is a tendency to provide less than helpful instructions to her driver, for instance, "turn down there," (with no pointing finger or nod of the head to indicate where down there is) or, "that was the turning we wanted back there."

When offered the chance to take a turn driving the hire car on the first day in Auckland she had declined saying, "I'll drive on the South Island, where there's less traffic," confirming her position as North Island navigator. That was how she came to be scanning the road atlas the night before we set off for Rotorua from Auckland and how she spotted the little yellow eyes that were to shape much of the rest of our trip.

We drove south from Auckland along the Thermal Explorer Tourist Route, a road that divides the North Island in two, picking its way through a region rich in geological wonders such as limestone caves, bubbling mud pools and hissing geysers. Anxious to reach the tourist hotspot (literally!) of Rotorua we passed through the town of Hamilton without stopping to explore. We also, with more difficulty, resisted the temptation of a side trip to the Waitomo Caves, where visitors are taken by boat on an underground stream to a cavern in which thousands of glow-worms do their best to recreate a starry night sky. We had to wait until Te Anau on the South Island for our glow-worm experience. And so will you.

As we passed through Cambridge we worried that our small Echo cho cho cho (sorry couldn't resist) might be infringing some local by-law that insisted every car must tow a horse box. Other drivers seemed to be obeying this rule to the letter. Clearly this was horse rather than sheep country. Incidentally, isn't it strange that whenever you are following a horse box down the road, even if you are surrounded by stunningly beautiful countryside, your eyes are always mysteriously drawn to the animal's backside looming there in front of you? I can't believe I'm the only one.

It was as we approached Tirau that THB put her Hobbit bothering plan into action by suggesting a small diversion to Matamata. "What's at Matamata?" I asked.

"Well," she said, pausing to flutter her eyelashes and offer her sweetest smile, "there's the remains of the Hobbiton set. Where Frodo, Sam and Bilbo lived in *Lord of the Rings*. It's marked on our map with a little symbol. All the sites in New Zealand where they filmed parts of *Lord of the Rings* are marked with the same symbol. It's a very good map! What are you doing?" Truth to tell, I was trying to deck a smug looking mini version of Jack Peterson who was sitting cross legged on THB's shoulder thumbing his nose at me.

The symbol to which THB referred resembled a small yellow eye half way through a wink. You might think that a yellow eye has more to do with jaundice than *Lord of the Rings*, but I saw it as a reference to the fiery, searchlight-emitting eye used to provide a visual representation of the menacing and ever watchful baddie Sauron in the movies. It sounds a bit naff when written down but works well on film. In fact I saw it wrong.

"It wasn't an eye, it was a golden ring," THB said when she read through the first draft of this book. She found the trusty atlas and showed me the symbol again. Perhaps the oval shape did represent a circular ring viewed from the side. Perhaps a ring would have been a better choice of symbol for *Lord of the Rings* filming locations. While THB watched, I went though the book and changed all 'yellow eye' references to 'golden ring'. Then, when she'd gone away, I changed them back again. I still think that they were really yellow eyes.

Arriving in Matamata we parked the car beside a building resembling a public convenience, at least from the rear, then marched off on foot in search of clues as to where Hobbiton might be. The town was low rise and laid back with, a particular favourite feature of mine, covered walkways running the length of streets to shield window shoppers from the sun in summer and rain in winter. I know malls do that too but, let's face it, they have no soul. The piped muzak is always easy-listening.

We circled the town, then criss-crossed the circle we'd traced, without seeing any sign of anything remotely *Lord of the Rings* related. We gazed through shop windows for signs of life or locals to provide directions, but almost all were closed either because we'd arrived at lunchtime or because it was a Saturday and Kiwis adopt a healthy attitude towards working at weekends. There are better things to do.

Finally a dispirited Hobbit botherer and a man trying to hide his eagerness to get to Rotorua trudged back to their car. The man was muttering, "Gisby one, Peterson nil," at a volume just too low for THB to hear. As they reached the public convenience, now approached from the opposite direction, it became obvious that it was the Matamata Information Centre. It proudly displayed a sign in front advertising trips to the Hobbiton set operated by Rings Scenic Tours. There were places available on a bus leaving in ten minutes. Correction. Gisby nil, Peterson one.

As we sat in the bus, waiting for it to depart, a delicious meaty smell, originating somewhere behind us, wafted past. A few seconds later the bus driver, a cheerful Maori, shouted, much like the giant in *Jack and the Beanstalk*, "Foe Fum, Fee Fie. I can smell the smell of a potato topped pie!" (Actually I put the Foe Fum, Fee Fie bit in for dramatic effect). There were giggles from the back of the bus. "Is someone eating a potato topped pie on my bus?" he boomed, looking back past where we sat. There must have been a nod from behind us because he then added, "Come here!"

A small boy clasping a pie in a paper bag as if it was the last morsel of food he'd ever see edged towards the front of the bus. "Where did you get that?" asked the driver. The boy pointed to a café opposite the Information Office. "Is it good?" The boy nodded. "Can I have a bite?" To accompany this question the driver rolled his eyes and pushed out his tongue as if in mid haka (the tongue poking, eye popping, breast beating, foot stomping challenge issued by Maori warriors and the All Blacks rugby team). The boy fled. Potato topped pies were obviously too good to share with madmen.

The Hobbiton set lies on a working cattle and sheep farm owned by the Alexander family a twenty or so minutes drive outside Matamata. The only way to see it in its full glory is to pay for a ride on the Rings

Scenic bus. People loath to part with their dollars or afraid that they might die of thirst during the course of the tour only make it as far as *The Hobbit's Rest*, an aptly named pub at the entrance to the Alexanders' land. I'll give you one guess which came first, the name of the pub or the *Lord of the Rings* films.

You can just imagine the location scouts, stoked (a local term meaning delighted) at having found the perfect location for Hobbiton, fetching up at the Alexanders' farmhouse one evening to ask permission to build Hobbit holes and film. The response? Probably something along the lines of, "You want to build rabbit holes? We've got enough of those buggers already!" By all accounts the Alexanders hadn't read Tolkein's book at the time.

During the journey to the farm the pie loving bus driver described what we could expect to see. Or rather what we could not expect to see. There would be no Hobbits frolicking in the hills, no wooden beamed Hobbit holes to explore and no giant oak protruding from Bag End. Why did the man not think of a career in sales? But there would be a few Hobbit hole facades, the party field and views of the Kaimai Ranges, considerably underplaying the sight that was to greet us as it turned out.

Our bus passed through the gate to Alexanders' farm (or for the pedantic passed through the gateway, the gate having been opened first) and eased past what had been the vehicle park and animal husbandry area at the time of filming. This was where special good looking stunt sheep, imported for the purposes of the movie, spent their leisure hours. The local ones just didn't cut the mustard, or should that be mint sauce?

Next came the field where the human stars had been fed, watered, dressed and made up. Made up as in encased in prosthetics, not as in conjured from the imagination. Relax Elijah fans, the man IS real. THB fanned herself with the Official Tour Guide, feeling faint as we passed the point where Mr Wood undressed to change after each days Hobbiting. I assume there was some sort of caravan there at the time.

Eventually we were dropped in a hollow beside a wooden lean-to, offered umbrellas if we wanted them (clouds were threatening but fortunately rain never came) and told to wait for our guide, just to heighten the antici...

...pation. The wait was short. She appeared over the top of a grassy rise trailing a departing group, exchanged them for us then led her new charges towards the main attraction. Sports fans will understand the feeling as we crested the rise and caught our first glimpse of Hobbiton.

Remember when as a child you were taken to watch your first professional football / cricket / rugby / baseball / welly whanging game (delete where applicable). With the smell of greasy fast food in your nostrils and the grease of greasy fast food in your hand you climbed the steps leading up to your seat, high in the Gods, the playing area hidden from view until you reached the very top. Suddenly there it was. The vibrant green of the pitch, the virgin white of the markings upon it and the dazzling glare of the floodlights. Did I mention it was an evening game? Never before had green been so green, had white been so white, had fast food been so greasy. You were hooked and followed that one (perennially disappointing) football / cricket / rugby / baseball / welly whanging team for the rest of your life. Non sports fans, see what you have missed out on.

So that was the feeling as we gazed into the hollow before us to see a small blue lake beside Tellytubbyland-like hills, into which were set Hobbit holes, black circles in white facades, like eyes peering out from the hillside. True to the pie lover's promise, the party field and party tree from the beginning of *The Fellowship of the Ring* were there too. All of this with a backdrop of verdant undulating hills and not a hint of the twenty-first or even twentieth century to be seen, even if you had a telescope. The only sounds to be heard were 'seen it all before' baas from wandering sheep and excited squeals from Japanese tourists rushing to take photographs of each other in front of the Hobbiton sign. It was so beautiful, so tranquil. It really was Hobitton.

To those of you thinking "Get a grip Gisby! It's only a sheep paddock after all. You are meant to be the Hobbitophobe here or at least the Hobbitoambivalent," I have to admit that it got to me. Yes I did dance on the party field with THB at the behest of our guide. I did hug the party tree. I'll try to do better in future.

Our guide deserves an honourable mention at this point. Her name was Teresa and she displayed both boundless knowledge and boundless enthusiasm in showing us around the site and answering questions even if her claim that Matamata was the right place to film Hobbiton because it is in the middle of the North Island and Hobbiton is in Middle Earth was a little far fetched. Gold star!

Apparently it is only by a lucky chance that any of the Hobbit holes remained after filming had finished. The intention was to pull down everything and return the site to the sheep, but half way through the demolition there was a storm, conjured up, some might say, by the prayers of the Waikato tourist board, which halted work. During the hiatus, following frantic petitioning, it was decided that what was left could remain. Hobbiton was saved for lots of people to wonder at and lots of other people to wonder what on earth they were wondering at.

The climax of the tour was a visit to Bag End. The steps up to the door and the door opening remain, though behind lurks, not to put too fine a point on it, a hole in the hillside, rather than wooden beams and a welcoming fire as in the movie. The inside shots were done in Wellington and rumour has it that the director Peter Jackson held onto the set for later transportation to some picturesque part of the country for use as a holiday home.

We were told that strange things happen to female tourists while standing atop the Bag End steps. Sometimes they are seized by an uncontrollable urge to kiss the flagstones where Elijah Wood once walked. (He also walked in the sheep field but there does not seem to be a similar urge to kiss that, perhaps because of what sheep may have left behind since). Less frequently they are seized by their accompanying partner and proposed to. Entering into the spirit, I seized THB and proposed that we visit the potato topped pie café in Matamata when we returned to town as I was getting hungry. You'll be pleased to hear, she said yes.

As our bus pulled up outside Matamata Tourist Information Office again, after a wonderful tour which gave us our first real flavour of Middle Zealand or should that be New Earth, I couldn't help mulling over two sources of concern. Firstly I had really enjoyed an afternoon of Hobbit bothering. Was Jack Peterson getting to me? Secondly, and more importantly, the potato topped pie café had closed while we were away.

We set off for Rotorua munching peanut M & Ms from the Matamata Tourist Information Office Gift Shop. I do so love health food.

3: ROTORUA

Hongi And Hangi

When driving around the North Island of New Zealand, there are three ways to tell when you have arrived in Rotorua.

(1) A strange smell of bad eggs becomes apparent in your car. You accuse your passenger(s) of farting but he/she/they deny having done so. Indeed they look back at you accusingly. You open the window to let in some fresh air and the smell gets worse.
(2) Plumes of steam shoot skywards at odd moments from behind buildings to your left, buildings to your right and even from the road in front of you. None of the local people walking along the pavement appear to be at all startled.
(3) Signs pointing to Rotorua that you had become accustomed to seeing beside the road as you drove towards the town now point exclusively to other destinations.

Having checked (1), (2) and (3) to establish we had reached our destination, we pulled into the car park of the *Royal Geyserland Hotel*, swerving to avoid a final spurt of steam from a crack in the tarmac near the entrance.

We had been warned not to be concerned about the rather dated appearance of the place by the travel agent who recommended it. Guests at this establishment pay to look out, not to look at. Spectacular views over Te Whakarewarewa Thermal Reserve are promised from rooms on the upper floors. The trick is to acquire one of those rooms.

"Could we have a geyser view room?" I asked the woman behind the reception desk. I can't remember whether I added please or whether I thought that being prostrate before her would be sufficient. She didn't answer the question but asked one of her own. "You're from London, aren't you, eh?"

"Yes," I admitted. "How did you know?"

"Geezer," she said.

I had always referred to those jets of hot water which spurt from the ground in places where the earth's crust is thin, as geezers. I was saddened to discover that that pronunciation made me sound as if I was auditioning for a gangster movie set in Larndan. "I fort 'e woz a diamond geezer bart I still 'ad ter parnish 'im." (Translation: "I was under the impression that the gentleman was an awfully good chap but despite that fact I was compelled to give him a good dressing down.")

The alternative pronunciation guy-zer seems a bit 'costume drama' to me. "Oh. Mr Fancy. How very presumptuous of you to stroke my elbow as I sit admiring the guy-zer. We have only been engaged for thirty-seven years. What on earth would Mama say?" (Translation: "Jump on me, Fancy. Now!")

For the rest of our stay in Rotorua I tried my utmost to convert to the new way of speaking. The best I ever managed was gee-er-guy-zer.

Our room was on the next to top floor of the hotel, perhaps courtesy of my gangster-like accent, although I wish to emphasise that no mention of deep lakes and concrete footwear was ever made. Opening the door we were faced by a huge picture window through which the magnificent plumes of the *Pohutu* geyser could be seen forming the centrepiece of a vista in which stands of bush were interspersed with shimmering mineral-coated rocks, bubbling mud, beautifully coloured pools and, in the distance, wooden buildings periodically swallowed by scalding fog. A pathway for visitors wound its way through the strange landscape. The promise of spectacular views had been delivered. And then some.

We opened the window for a better view, then quickly closed it again as the sulphurous smell from a collection of mud volcanoes immediately beneath us assaulted our nostrils. It is because of this smell that some uncharitable souls refer to Rotorua as Rottenrua. That night we were lulled to sleep by the gentle plop-plopping of the very same bubbling mud or perhaps by the effects of strange gases leaking into our room. Either way we slept well, at least until 5 o'clock in the morning when the alarm went off to announce that it was time to wake up to watch Arsenal versus Chelsea (a soccer match from England for people from those strange parts of the globe where football refers to a group of men in armour throwing a rugby ball to one another) live on TV. The culture of the old country can't be left completely behind even when on holiday. THB was unimpressed and went back to sleep. Although I haven't managed to educate her in the joys of watching football (or soccer) yet, I have managed to do the job for cricket, which some might consider to be the more difficult task.

The decision where to go the following day was a no-brainer. We just had to visit the thermal wonderland beneath our window. Sorry. I should rephrase that. 'Thermal Wonderland' is the tag line of the rival Wai-O-Tapu geysers and hot pools experience a short way down the Thermal Explorer Highway. How about wonderful thermal-land?

Te Whakarewarewa Thermal Reserve, at least the part closest to our hotel, was operated by The New Zealand Maori Arts and Crafts Institute. As well as allowing the chance to get up close and personal with hot geysers (not geezers) the Institute also offered demonstrations of traditional crafts such as carving and weaving and a midday Maori concert, all taking place within a recreation of a Maori fortified village. There was even a kiwi house, the bird this time, note the lack of a capital K. The kiwi was to provide me with my biggest shock of the day.

I have developed a personal scale for describing the size of birds (in the ornithological sense rather than the late 60s or early 70s sexist sense) which works in a similar way to Mho's scale for the hardness of rocks. For those who think Mho runs a bar frequented by Carl, Lenny, Barney and Homer in *The Simpsons*, I'll explain. Mho's scale ranges from one to ten and gives examples of rocks appropriate to each number along the way. 'Mummy's boy' talc is at number one and 'knuckledusters and tattoos' diamond is at number ten. The Gisby scale for birds (as I shall modestly call it) runs as follows:

(1)	Humming Bird	Minute
(2)	Wren	Teeny
(3)	Budgie	Tiny
(4)	Starling	Small
(5)	Pigeon	Medium
(6)	Seagull	Large
(7)	Chicken	Family Meal
(8)	Turkey	Family Meal with Leftovers for Sandwiches
(9)	Penguin	Whopping
(10)	Ostrich	Get a Bigger Pot, a Much Bigger Pot

Remembering a book I read when I was young which described a kiwi as a "nocturnal flightless bird the size of a wren" I confidently expected to see a number two hopping about the kiwi house floor once my eyes had become accustomed to the darkness. Imagine my surprise when a number seven marched out from behind a tree stump looking like a hairy football (spherical variety) on three legs. It turned out that one of the 'legs' was its long pink snout sniffing out food on the ground. The book I'd read had obviously been written by someone who'd eaten a whole kiwi once and didn't want to own up to how greedy he was. "I can write anything I like," he thought, "No-one will actually sail to New Zealand to check the facts, then come back to spill the beans. Shall I give it a long green tail with a purple pom-pom on the end?" Note the word sail. It was a book written in the days before the hoi-polloi like me could afford to travel by air.

We continued our walk into the park past pools of bubbling mud known as the play things of Koko (Ngamokaiakoko), pausing only to note how much like an Eastern European military prison our hotel looked from the rear, before heading geyser-wards. The geyser, or rather collection of geysers, was spectacular. The continuous performance of the *Prince of Wales Feathers* sending boiling water skywards to rain down upon silica coated rocks before running down to steaming lake was only eclipsed by the twice as tall but more occasional spurts of *Pohutu*.

THB experimented with the movie mode of our new digital camera to capture the dancing plumes of steam. It also captured the hiss of the geysers and the ever so slightly annoyed "Shh," of THB herself as I enquired, "Is it working? Is it working?" I didn't realise that the thing recorded sound as well as pictures.

Having enjoyed a pleasant walk through a landscape unlike anything we'd seen before, careful to heed warnings to keep to the marked paths and so avoid experiencing jets of steam shooting up our legs, we returned to the Maori village to join fifty or so others gathered on a patch of manicured grass in front of the Meeting House (Te Aronui a Rua) awaiting the midday show.

Our master, or rather mistress, of ceremonies was a slightly built, traditionally dressed, Maori woman from the Mary Poppins mould in that she encouraged us to enjoy ourselves but also made us aware that there were rules to be obeyed within the Marae (meeting area). And we would obey them. She even said that we could call her Mary, making the rather patronising but probably accurate assumption that we wouldn't be able to pronounce her Maori name.

The experience began with a ceremony of welcome (Powhiri) but before this could start we had to nominate a chief to represent the interests of our newly formed tribe (iwi) and presumably to be the first one killed if the iwi we were visiting didn't like the look of us. A volunteer was duly selected by Mary, an elderly gentleman with a grey beard who looked as if he would treat the whole thing with due reverence and who, if the worst came to the worst, had already had a good long life.

We were then ushered back to stand in a line slightly behind our chief, to show him respect. There were no exceptions. Mary would not accept mere infirmity as an excuse for remaining in front of the chief and refused to continue until an elderly woman with a walking stick had been coaxed away from her position on a bench in front of Chief Greybeard. Finally she began a eerie wailing song saying something like, "Hello. We have arrived. Can we come in?" to our prospective hosts. They replied in a similar vein with, again in loose translation, "We saw you coming ages ago. You can't creep up on us. Wait there. We're sending a warrior to suss you out." So out he came.

Sporting ferocious looking tattoos (moko) and dressed only in a Maori grass skirt (except for underpants to cover his modesty during more energetic movements) he hopped and skipped towards us in a graceful and sweeping arc, fixing our chief in a wide eyed stare. After an impressive display of taiaha (fighting stick) twirling clearly designed to say, "Don't mess with me, mate!" he advanced and placed a small branch, a symbol of peace, on the ground before Greybeard. Greybeard's moment of glory had arrived. He edged forward, mindful of the taiaha and wishing to remain alive to see his grandchildren again, then picked up the branch. Finally, after a brief hongi (pressing of noses) with the warrior, we were free to enter the Meeting House.

Our chief had a front row seat waiting him, courtesy of his elevated status, but for the rest of us it was a free for all. This meant that the orderly line of Greybeard's people advancing over the grass behind him quickly became a V as those on the outside, furthest from Mary's withering gaze, sought to steal a march. Inside, as it turned out, there was plenty of room for all.

The show featured Maori action songs (waiata-a-ringa), poi dances (in which balls on strings were twirled in in intricate patterns at ferocious speed without decapitating neighbouring dancers), stick games (tititorea, in which short sticks were thrown between players at pace and with venom, and usually caught at the other end, testing hand and eye coordination) and the famous haka or posture dance. Maori stick games should be a required part of the training regime of all relay runners. Then there would be no more dropped batons.

Rotorua was a much bigger town than we'd expected, even featuring attractions to coax dollars from those tourists not impressed by hot water, bad smells and Maori culture. These included displays of all things farmy and particularly sheepy in the Agrodome, the Skyline Gondala to whisk people up Mount Ngongotaha for views over the town and finally the zorb, Rotorua's own contribution to the New Zealand panoply of 'so you think life isn't scary enough' rides. A zorb is a transparent inflatable ball which people climb into, then roll down the side of a hill. Pity the poor zorb operator who has to clean up the inside of the ball between punters.

What the town didn't seem to offer is the chance to eat out after about eight o'clock in the evening. Maybe we were looking in the wrong places but THB, the trusty Echo cho cho cho (penultimate time) and myself toured the place on our first evening looking for that uniquely Rotoruan dining experience but found only a steakhouse chain that was open. The food was good and plentiful but we were chased out before dessert by a watch tapping waitress at about ten to nine. Does everyone zorb during the day, so they don't feel up to eating in the evening? On our second evening we solved the problem of finding somewhere to eat by means of a hangi.

Picked up from our hotel by coach and taken across town to a tour office come gift shop, we had to hangi around there until a full complement of hungry people had been gathered. Then we were sorted into new coaches and began our journey to the Tamaki Maori Village.

I say we travelled by coach because our mode of transport certainly looked like a coach. It was a long metal vehicle with windows along the sides, seats down the middle and a pair of wheels at the front and back. You know the sort of thing. Our driver, however, seemed to think it was a canoe and urged us to propel it along using imaginary paddles, in synchronisation, in the centre aisle.

He taught us three useful Maori phrases, kia ora, which means hello, thank you, can I have an orange drink? and seemingly lots more besides, waka which means canoe, our supposed mode of transport and uh! (pronounced as if you are a karate master about to go through a pile of bricks with your bare hand) which we were instructed should accompany every stroke of our imaginary paddles. A short distance along the road we veered alarmingly onto the verge but this was corrected by the people on the left hand side of the waka putting in a little more effort.

Once the novelty of paddling had worn off the driver asked where we all came from and received a hearty "Walengireausamerifiji!" in reply. He then tried a different tack, asking in turn "Is there anyone from England?", "Is there anyone from America?", "Is there anyone from Australia?" and so on, making each nationality sing a song from their country before moving on. THB refused to answer "Yes," to "Is there anyone from Ireland?" for fear of having to sing *Danny Boy* on her own. Incidentally most nationalities proudly sung their national anthem but the English sung *Roll Out The Barrel*. Make of that what you will. It wasn't my personal choice, but I did join in with the few words I knew. "Roll", "Out" and "The Barrel".

Just before we arrived at the village, a chief was selected to represent our interests. A reluctant Welsh gentleman called Evan was volunteered by his wife. The driver, eager to avoid conscription, accepted her offer. Personally, had we been going to confront another tribe for real, I would have much preferred Evan's wife to be our chief, she being the more fearsome of the two, but we were told that the Maori do not allow women to be chiefs. Our new chief had a grey beard. Can you see a pattern emerging?

The last thing the driver said as he dropped us off was "Don't forget the number ninety-eight. That is the number of your waka." He pointed to the figure ninety-eight on a piece of paper stuck to the front window of the bus. "The number of the waka that will take you home at the end of the evening." After a short pause he added, "If you can't remember the number ninety-eight, remember the number twenty-nine fifty. That is the cost of a taxi ride back to Rotorua."

We waited in a small arena outside the village's wooden fortifications for five other wakas to appear, each with its own chief, then the ceremony of welcome began. The gathering dusk made the wailing cries of the Maori women within, warning of our arrival, seem particularly eerie and the sudden appearance of a group of tattooed warriors quite chilling. We felt more involved in this ceremony, not present as mere spectators, than we did in the earlier one at Rotowhio Marae. The warm up act on the waka had obviously worked. The approach of the Maori warrior to present the branch of peace to the assembled chiefs was not as spectacular as the sweep across the grass in the morning though. Space was more limited at Tamaki.

Once we had gained entry to the village we passed through a small wood in which a series of traditional Maori dwellings had been faithfully recreated. In front of these, by firelight, poi dances, stick games, mock taiaha fights and crafts such as carving and weaving were being demonstrated. Then we made our way to the Meeting House for a Maori concert, presented by the Rangiatea culture group with a little more humour, and perhaps a little less authenticity, than that enjoyed earlier.

"Kia ora," bellowed one of warriors from the stage.

A few muttered kia oras came from audience in reply.

"Kia ora means hello. Say kia ora!" he encouraged.

"Kia ora!" came the reply, louder this time.

"Welcome to our Marae. Say Marae!"

"Marae!"

"We now going to play some music using a traditional Maori instrument, agitar. Say agitar!"

"Agitar!" We were really getting into our stride now.

A second Maori warrior sauntered onto the stage playing a guitar.

You'll have noticed that I've not mentioned food yet, nor explained what a hangi actually is. "How much longer do I have to wait?" you might be thinking. My stomach was asking much the same question as the evening wore on, until we were finally ushered into the wharekai (food house) and the feast of chicken, lamb, fish and vegetables all cooked underground in a pit using hot stones, commenced. Hangi is the word used to describe this traditional Maori method of cooking.

The meal was delicious and gave us our first taste of kumara, the New Zealand sweet potato. We shared a table with a family from the USA on the last day of a whistle stop tour of the world before leaving for home. Maybe if you come from a big country such as America it seems reasonable that three days is enough to see a small one like New Zealand. They seemed bemused by the less than traditional Maori dessert of treacle pudding and custard. The custard in particular, a seething yellow mass steaming in a cauldron on the buffet table, was regarded with suspicion.

"What IS that?" asked the mother, deciding that culinary matters were her domain, as I helped myself to lashings of the stuff, skin and all.

Unable to believe that there was in existence a family from an English speaking country who had never encountered custard, I assumed the question was a rhetorical comment on the perceived quality of the hangied variety and didn't answer straight away. Apparently not. She looked as if she was expecting a reply.

"Custard," I said, because that's what it was.

She thought for a moment, tried the word out for herself, "Cuss-Turd," then turned to her family with a wry 'I'm not making much headway with these foreigners' look. Not to be defeated, she tried a new tack, "What flavour is it?" (A sensible enough question before eating something you believe has 'turd' in its name).

That threw me. Custard is custard flavoured isn't it? Fortunately THB saved me. "Vanilla," she said. All those years of eating custard and I have to travel half way around the world to discover it is vanilla flavoured. From my wife. What next? Are oranges really smoky bacon flavoured? The foundations of my world had taken a knock. And the Americans never even sampled the cuss-turd.

Before leaving the subject of food I ought to issue a warning about the New Zealand sausage. It looks like a normal, meaty or beany (for the vegetarians amongst us) sausage but tastes of... well absolutely nothing really. There must be a machine somewhere, invented by a Kiwi having a day off from sheep shearing, that extracts even the last vestige of taste from any food passed through it. What use would such a machine be? None. Unless the inventor had a brother in Parliament who could usher through a law that all sausages made in New Zealand had to be processed by the machine before consumption due to Health and Safety. Then the inventor would make money, his brother would get a cut and everyone would be happy, apart from sausage connoisseurs.

All this is speculation, of course. The real reason for the blandness of New Zealand sausages was discovered by THB, by chance, later on in our trip. You have to read on now to discover the horrible truth.

After the feast we toured a few shops selling Maori arts and crafts before returning to waka ninety-eight. As a shopping-o-phobe I'm normally fairly cynical about the obligatory stroll through the gift shop to reach the exit of any tourist site but this time it was different. It felt more like an enjoyable browse in a gallery than a hard sell. The works of art which caught our eye in this particular gallery were Maori greenstone carvings.

Greenstone in the common name for the semi precious rock nephrite which is related to jade and highly valued by the Maori who call it pounamu. It is a beautiful stone but also very hard and very tough, making it suitable for use in making tools and weapons. Maybe it was a comfort when struck a fatal blow by a Maori club to contemplate the beauty of the stone from which it was made as you breathed your last. Or maybe not.

Nowadays greenstone is used to make jewellery such as hand carved pendants in traditional Maori designs, each with special spiritual meaning. The Maori had no written language so carving was used as a method of story telling. I bought THB a roimata, a spiral shape representing eternity, so she's stuck with me forever. Sadly she didn't buy me one in return so I shall have to watch out if we ever find ourselves in close proximity to Orlando Bloom, Elijah Wood or Viggo Mortensen. Apparently a gift of greenstone is never yours to own completely but is expected, one day, to make its way back to the Maori people from whom it came. I don't know if that applies to pendants purchased in a Maori gift shop. Perhaps we can expect a Maori warrior to knock on our door one day to say, "About that pounamu you have Mrs Gisby..."

After a full day of sightseeing without the slightest hint of Hobbit bothering I fully expected a dischuffed Jack Peterson to amble out from behind my cerebellum during the night. This he did, finger wagging and tut-tutting mercilessly as he approached. But I was ready for him this time.

"We have been experiencing Maori culture," I said. "Wasn't the war-like posturing of the Uruk-hai before the Battle of Helms Deep inspired by the Maori haka?" (THB sometimes accuses me of not listening to her words of wisdom from the passenger seat during long car journeys. My knowledge of this *Lord of the Rings* behind the scenes fact proves her wrong. It also proves that there wasn't any football commentary on the car radio the day she revealed it to me).

Jack Peterson looked surprised but not ready to concede defeat. Not ready to agree that I hadn't been neglecting my appointed task.

"And I think they missed a trick in not filming at Rotorua," I continued. "The hissing geysers, the bubbling mud, the stench of bad eggs. It would have made an excellent Mordor."

Now he looked impressed.

"I'm imprissed," he said. (Close enough). "You hiv mide much bitter prugress thun I dired hope. Kip it up."

What did he mean? It was THB we were supposed to be treating here, not me. Wasn't it?

4: NAPIER

Where's All The Art Deco Gone?

Napier, on the eastern Hawkes bay coast of the North Island and the ultimate destination of the Thermal Explorer Highway, is a town with a tragic past. On a hot and humid day in February 1931 an earthquake measuring 7.9 on the Richter scale combined with the raging fires that followed it, devastated the town. Faced with the choice of decamping to Rottenrua or rebuilding, the redoubtable Naperians fetched their hammers and nails, hods and hard hats and set to work. The result was, and still is, a time capsule of art deco architecture, a place destined to be a highlight of the New Zealand tour for me if not for THB. (No *Lord of the Rings* connections, you see). To understand why it is that we never got there, you have to know a little about the way my brain is wired.

I have always had a problem with names that begin with the same letter of the alphabet and contain the same number of syllables. I'll happily enjoy a book featuring the characters Jill, Jackie and Jennifer but I'll quickly put down one involving Kylie, Kelly and Karen in a state of confusion. Was Kelly the one with the pet ferret who found the body in the cupboard? Or was that Kylie? Was Karen the policewoman with the crush on the man with the wooden leg who fancied Kelly? Or was that Kylie? Who is Kylie anyway? You get the idea. THB, who is a writer, (novels available at reasonable prices, see adverts at the end of this book) now tries to make sure that all of her characters' names begin with different letters just so I'll be able to follow the plot.

Bearing this in mind, perhaps you can understand why, intending to visit the Art Deco wonders of Napier, I booked a three night stay in Nelson, three hundred or so kilometres away, as the kiwi doesn't fly, at the top of the South Island.

More about Nelson (or as THB now calls it, Not Napier) later on.

As a post script to this part of the story, the day after I committed these words to computer screen a friend, Stephen, phoned to invite THB and me to a summer proms concert. "Featuring orchestral arrangements of fifties hits like *Diana*," he read from the advertising pamphlet. "Yes," I enthused, "I remember that one." I broke into something vaguely resembling song.

"She just stood there laughing. (Maniacal laugh)
I felt the knife in my hand and she laughed no more."

Think more Sensational Alex Harvey Band than Tom Jones for my rendition. No knickers were thrown my way, not even from THB. Stephen sighed. "That song was *Delilah*," he said.

5: WAI-O-TAPU AND TAUPO

A Woman Who Turns Out To Be A Geyser.

Leaving Rotorua, as with almost every place we stayed in New Zealand, we wished we could stay longer, to do more things, to see more sights, to bother more Hobbits. We had seen nothing of Lake Rotorua and nothing of the buried village, a casualty of the eruption of the Tarawera volcano in 1886 which also claimed the fabulous 'pink and white terraces' formed from silica deposits and described at the time as the eighth wonder of the world. We hadn't even zorbed. Not all bad news then.

On the road south towards Tongariro National Park, our next overnight stop, we spotted a sign for the Waimangu Thermal Valley. We resisted. There was a long journey ahead. Then we passed a sign for the Kerosene Creek Thermal Area. We resisted. There was a long journey ahead. Finally a sign for the Wai-O-Tapu (Sacred Waters) Thermal Wonderland. We gave in. After all we had no idea where our next geothermal area was coming from. Until we looked at the road atlas and saw The Hidden Valley, Craters of the Moon, Broadlands Road Geothermal Scenic Reserve...

"Do you want to see Lady Knox Geyser?" asked the man at the visitor centre. "That would be Lord Knox would it?" I replied. He looked bemused, so I added. "Lady Knox's Geezer. That would be Lord Knox." Jokes lose something when you have to explain them.

He ignored my attempt at humour and advised, poker faced, "She goes off at ten-fifteen. You'll have to be quick." So we departed at a run. Well, to be truthful, a purposeful walk. Once we'd left, I imagine he picked up a walkie-talkie to speak to his colleague down at the geyser. "Hey Dave. There's a smart arse English bloke coming your way. Can you hurry things up a bit so the bugger misses the action?"

For the few minutes it took us to get from visitor centre to geyser, I was mightily impressed by what I was about to see. Lady Knox was so predictable that she could be relied upon to perform at exactly the same time every day, ten-fifteen, without fail. I'd read in books about geysers like that. True wonders of nature. If only we human beings could get buses to run that reliably.

Then my illusions were shattered. We reached the geyser just in time to join the assembled crowd as they watched Dave pour soap flakes into the vent to encourage Lady Knox along. It was all a fake! I find it is much more satisfying when a Lady climaxes naturally without having to resort to artificial methods of stimulation, don't you?

Lady Knox Geyser was discovered by accident one day in the early nineteen hundreds by some convicts on bush clearing and tree planting duty. As they washed their clothes in one of the many hot pools in the area, liberally sprinkling soap flakes about, they were surprised by the unexpected appearance of a jet of hot water shooting towards the heavens. The eponymous Lady Constance Knox, daughter of a New Zealand Governor, came along for a look a few years later and the phenomenon was given her name, probably by some toady looking for a leg up the greasy political pole. For myself, I'm not sure that 'Lady Knox Geyser' is a better name than 'Scalded Convict Geyser' for example.

The geyser is not the foremost attraction at Wai-O-Tapu. That honour goes to the collapsed craters, rainbow hued pools and stunning views on offer in the main park. A looping path took us on a three kilometre trek through manuka scrub which parted regularly to reveal a hellish landscape of steaming sulphur tinged craters, followed by bubbling lakes coloured bright red, orange, yellow, green and purple by minerals dissolved underground then carried to the surface and finally waterfalls and panoramic views over Lake Ngakoro (The Grandfather). The path pinched in on itself to give the weary a chance to cop out at the one and a half and two kilometre marks. We ploughed on despite the baking heat from both sun and steam and it was well worth the effort. Te Whakarewarewa may have the best geysers but Wai-O-Tapu wins hands down on everything else.

Wai-O-Tapu was one of the rare places in New Zealand where other people walked at the same slow 'enjoy the scenery' pace as THB and I rather than forging ahead with 'outta my way' velocity. I think this says more about the determination of backpackers to bag the best bunk at the next hostel than it does about any lack of sights to admire. At no other place did we get as many offers of, "I'll take a picture of you together, if you take a picture of us together." (One of the perils of going on holiday as a couple used to be that your holiday snaps made it look as if you couldn't stand the sight of each other. There couldn't be any photos of you together because one of you had to be behind the camera. Thank goodness for cheap cameras with timers. Now your holiday snaps can show you smiling together at a drunken angle. The camera has to rest on a log, rock, wall, sheep or whatever surface you can find at the right height and that surface is rarely, if ever, perfectly horizontal. "Tripods!" I hear you say. "I couldn't be arsed to carry one," is my riposte).

We headed south from Wai-O-Tapu towards Taupo, but were sidetracked once more by a sign for Huka Falls, New Zealand's most visited natural attraction according to their publicity. Considering the competition in the 'natural things to see in New Zealand' stakes the Falls just had to be good. Or perhaps they just had a good agent. As it turned out, they were spectacular.

At Huka the mighty Waikato river squeezes into a narrow tree-lined gorge on its way north and is then forced over a ten metre cliff. More than two hundred and twenty thousand litres of water make the drop each second finishing up in a 'great mass of foam,' which gives the Falls their Maori name, Hukanui. Lucky visitors get to see a kayaker making the descent with the river. Unlucky visitors are that kayaker.

From the road, the town of Taupo, south of Huka Falls, presented itself as a collection of single storey shops and holiday homes, a laid back tourist town that didn't have to try too hard for attention courtesy of the natural wonders, Lake Taupo, the Waikato River and numerous Geothermal Areas, which surround it. It should have tried harder if it wanted to snare us as we left the Thermal Explorer Tourist Route and drove onwards down State Highway 1, hugging the eastern shore of Lake Taupo, without stopping.

Lake Taupo is New Zealand's largest lake by surface area, covering 616 square kilometres. I have to be precise in what I mean by 'largest' here as New Zealand lakes are as competitive as cities with tall towers. Others may lay claim to 'largest by volume of water' and 'largest by length of shore line' not to mention other categories like 'deepest', 'bluest' (a bit subjective) and 'most contrived claim to fame-est'.

Taupo is a fairly recent addition to the New Zealand landscape, formed as recently as 181 AD by the collapse of a volcano following a massive eruption which ejected one hundred cubic kilometres of material up to fifty kilometres high, turning the skies blood red as far away as Rome. Lake Te Anau on the South Island must have been really cheesed off at the arrival of this upstart, beating it down in the pecking order to second largest lake (by surface area).

'Most tranquil' and 'island most like a surfacing whale' (at least from the angle we saw it) are two other titles for which Lake Taupo could realistically hope to compete. Its character was very different from that of lakes such as Hawea, Wanaka, Wakatipu and Te Anau, hemmed in by starkly beautiful mountains, we were to encounter on the South Island. Lake Taupo offered wide open space and a feeling of peace, with no hint of claustrophobic threat from encircling, snow-topped peaks. Mind you the fine sunny weather might have helped. That turned out to be in shorter supply further south.

At the head of Lake Taupo sat Turangi, transformed in the nineteen sixties from a rural Maori fishing village to a (then) modern town, designed to house an influx of people needed to work on the Tongariro Power Development, a hydro electric scheme often cited as one of the world's most environmentally friendly. Nowadays Turangi styles itself as 'Trout Fishing Capital Of The World'. Since it is illegal in New Zealand to sell trout in restaurants, or even to farm them, the only way to get one to eat is to catch it yourself. Those available to catch are wild and streetwise as opposed to namby-pamby and ready to throw themselves on your hook. This, I'm told is the attraction.

THB and I stopped in an almost deserted windswept car park next to a small shopping mall in the centre of town. "The mall was draughty, shaded and depressingly characterless," I quote from a stunningly honest web site I found, designed to entice people into the area to stay. We were briefly attracted by a sign saying, 'New World' but this turned out to be a New Zealand supermarket chain. Hungry and still hankering after a potato topped pie, we finally found a small cafe. With corrugated metal walls it was difficult to tell whether it had been designed in a 'run down chic' contemporary style or whether it was actually run down. Let's give it the benefit of the doubt and say designer chic.

The choice of pies was prodigious, though sadly potato topped had sold out long ago. I tried steak and cheese and THB tried steak, both of which were very tasty and both of which, to our surprise, contained generous helpings of carrot. A lunchtime pie was to become something of a ritual during our trip but wherever we ate and whatever the type of pie we chose we always found unadvertised carrot in the filling. I suspect that this is a New Zealand government ploy to make sure its citizens can see in the dark to fight off any foreign sheep rustlers attempting to strike by night. There are even subliminal messages in the *Lord of the Rings* films. When the Hobbits tumble down an earthy bank running away from Farmer Maggot, what do they fall on and break in half? A carrot! As the camera pans through the streets of Bree, there is a man (Peter Jackson, the film's director, in a cameo role) munching on what? A carrot! What is that in the top right hand corner of the New Zealand flag? No there's not a carrot there yet, but give it time.

No longer hungry, and well equipped in case our car's headlights failed, we made off down State Highways 47 and 48 into the wilderness of Tongariro National Park and towards our final destination for the day, Whakapapa village.

Those of you who were paying attention during the bus trip to the hangi (thank you for that) may remember that waka means canoe and be tempted to translate Whakapapa as 'Father's canoe'. I'm afraid it doesn't work like that. This Whaka has a letter H in it. Whakapapa can be loosely translated as genealogy or lineage but it means much more than simply that to Maori people. It embraces the belief that a person cannot move forward without knowing where they came from, that without a starting point there is no direction. Our direction over the next couple of days in Whakapapa was determined largely by little yellow eyes printed in our road atlas.

Was that a grumpy voice in my head saying, "Abit tim too!"

6: TONGARIRO NATIONAL PARK

Going For A Tramp

Most normal people, those who do not suffer Hobbit bothering tendencies, visit Tongariro National Park for one of two reasons. They come either to ski (usually in the winter months as a dusting of snow is advantageous where this activity is concerned) or to go for a tramp. Some readers may be shocked that the latter activity is allowed to go on. For their benefit I should point out that to 'go for a tramp' in this context does not mean to 'make an unprovoked attack on an unfortunate gentleman, down on his luck, who is sleeping rough'. In New Zealand it means to 'go for a hike'.

For us, well for THB in particular, the attraction of Tongariro National Park was little yellow eyes dotted about the place on our road atlas like olives on a pizza. Remembering Matamata and Hobbiton, I was quite looking forward to visiting the filming locations, though I wouldn't have admitted it to Jack Peterson. That was until I saw the names of some of the places in Middle Earth that were represented. The Plains of Gorgoroth, Mount Doom and Emyn Muil were the most evil, depressing, soulless and deliberately unHobbitonlike places visited by the characters in the movies. And we were going to have the pleasure of spending two nights in their vicinity.

Our base was the *Skotel Alpine Resort*, the highest hotel in New Zealand. This is in terms of distance above sea level and not in terms of consumption of illicit substances, you understand. It was a rambling collection of wooden buildings set on the slopes of Mount Ruapehu just below the altitude where scrubland turns to bare rock and just above the altitude of the more upmarket but less up-high *Grand Chateau*. Comfortingly the *Skotel* had been chosen by experts as the place in Whakapapa least likely to be swallowed up by a lava flow. Hence it was the mustering point for locals in case of volcanic activity. Less comfortingly, Mt Ruapehu had last erupted just ten years before our visit, as photographs dotted about the hotel testified.

We were given a single room chalet with sliding glass doors at the foot of the bed leading out onto a small wooden deck. The doors faced north east giving a spectacular view across a wide expanse of tussock to a grey conical peak with white fingers of snow reaching down its sides, all set against a (temporarily) cloudless blue sky. This was Mount Ngauruhoe (no I can't pronounce it either) better known to Hobbit botherers as Mount Doom. Who'd have thought that the geysers and mud pools view from our hotel at Rotorua would be trumped at our very next stop.

That evening we ate in the *Skotel* Restaurant. Prices were refreshingly uninflated considering the captive nature of the hungry punters. Where else were we going to eat more than half way up a mountain? THB and I were seated next to a tropical fish tank, which was interesting at first, then increasingly disconcerting as one inhabitant spent the whole meal treading water (or whatever the fishy equivalent is) staring at my 'Catch Of The Day' with a mournful expression on its face. I could imagine a thought bubble above its head. "Mummy. Mummy. You're looking awfully thin Mummy. I can see your bones." Sensibly THB had chosen the lamb.

While we ate, an older couple were seated at the table next to us. Both looked shattered, hardly able to lift a knife and fork, let alone eat, such was their exhaustion.

"Have you done it?" the waitress asked them, rather impertinently in my opinion. They managed a weak smile. "Yes. It took us nine hours though. We didn't have the clothes that we usually wear, but we thought we'd give it a go anyway."

Subtle questioning in the bar afterwards revealed that they were talking about the famed Tongariro Crossing, often cited as the best one day walk in New Zealand, passing over lava flows, past geothermal areas, skirting blue and emerald lakes and finally heading across tussock strewn mountainside. The Crossing, giving the opportunity to view the Plains of Gorgoroth from *Lord of the Rings*, had been our plan for the following day. Oh all right, it had been my plan, with the Plains of Gorgoroth as a sweetener to get THB interested.

THB and I are not seasoned trampers. Nor are we occasional trampers. We are more walk to shops once in while if the car is being fixed-ers. So it was a little nervously that we made our way to the Whakapapa visitors centre early(ish) the next day to sort out a few minor details before setting off. Things like how we should get to the start point of The Crossing without having to retrace our steps after the walk to pick up the car, how we should avoid getting lost on the way and what facilities were available en-route to revive us in case of difficulties. The answers to these questions appeared to be, "the bus has left already", "don't go" and "it might rain."

We were a little discouraged.

We then glanced at a poster advertising six essentials to carry with you if tempted to try one of the longer tramps around Whakapapa. At seven or eight hours The Crossing certainly fell into that category.

(1) Raincoat and overtrousers.
Our coats were back at the *Skotel*, but they were heavy, not easily luggable for eight hours on the off chance of rain. And as for overtrousers, who on earth takes them on holiday? I always wear shorts.
(2) Sturdy boots.
Would trainers do instead? Probably not.
(3) Food and lots to drink.
Half a bottle of mineral water?
(4) Maps.
That's what we were in the Visitors Centre for. Give us some credit.
(5) Sunglasses and Sunscreen.
Yes and yes. Things were looking up.
(6) First aid kit.
No. Things were looking down again.

If we really needed all that stuff, we quickly realised we would also require:

(7) A backpack to carry it in.

We had a suitcase with wheels and a collapsible handle back at the hotel, but somehow that didn't seem to fit the bill.

Those were just the essentials. The poster went on to advise about when it would be necessary to carry a compass, an ice axe, crampons...

We were now more than a little discouraged.

I decided to offer THB a get out. Although I would have been quite willing and able to tackle The Crossing myself, you have to believe that, maybe I should have put in a little more preparation to ensure that THB would be comfortable.

"Would you like to try the Taranaki Falls walk instead?" I said.
"OK," she replied.

I just caught this word from behind her as she left the Visitors Centre at a run, in case I changed my mind. I don't think I have ever been so relieved... sorry, that should have read disappointed.

The Taranaki Falls walk was a gentle six kilometre loop on a well marked and well maintained track starting and finishing just beyond the deck of our hotel room. We set off confidently into the tussock and after a short while Whakapapa Village, the *Skotel* and *Grand Chateau* merged into the landscape leaving us alone in a windswept wilderness with Mount Ngauruhoe brooding before us and the speckled peak of Mount Ruapehu behind, dark spots of rock poking out here and there through its glistening cap of snow.

The path led on through a small wood, out over barer rocky land, crossing several gullies, then on to the top of the Falls. We met no more than a handful of people on the way, most of them more energetic, offering a cheery "Hello" to fellow trampers as they overtook us. The exception was a sprightly grey-haired woman hiking towards us, against the flow, with hunched determination. She looked horrified as I said "Hello" and hurried off as if I'd threatened to steal her walking stick, despite attempts by THB to placate her. Even if I'd wanted the stick, and truth to tell it was nothing special, I don't think I could have caught her to take it.

The Taranaki Falls are formed where the Wairere Stream gushes over the edge of an ancient lava flow and down a twenty metre drop to splash into a turquoise pool. Well worth the tramp in our opinion, but we are dyed in the wool waterfallophiles. Our path crossed the stream and passed down the gorge it had carved, through a forest of beech, then out onto the tussock and alpine shrubland once more. After three very pleasant hours we arrived back at the *Skotel*.

Three hours was fifty percent longer than the time advertised for the Taranaki Falls walk. Of course it would have been quicker without pauses to take in the views, but that would have defeated much of the point of doing it. On that basis The Tongariro Crossing might have taken us twelve hours. And yes we would have needed those coats. The distinctive patter of rain on leaf had not escaped our notice as we passed through the beech forest.

Congratulating ourselves on having made the correct decision, but vowing to return, better prepared, to tackle The Crossing one day, we made for the car. I had had my way with the tramp and now THB wanted to do some serious Hobbit bothering. (For those people who were shocked at the concept of 'going for a tramp' earlier, perhaps I ought to rephrase 'I had had my way with the tramp' as "I had got to go on a scenic walk").

Our first Hobbit bothering excursion was the relatively short one up Bruce Road beyond Whakapapa Village to the Whakapapa Ski Field. The place had that dreary, lifeless feel of a tourist spot out of season. Probably because it was a dreary and lifeless tourist spot out of season. The road even looped around at the bottom of the chair lift as if to say, "You don't want to stop here, do you? I'll take you back down." But THB did want to stop.

There was no snow where we parked, along with just one other car and a motor home, just a persistent annoying drizzle. You've guessed correctly, the coats were still in a suitcase at the *Skotel*. There must have been some snow further up the mountain though, because once in a while a weary and bedraggled looking hard-core snow boarder passed us by as we stood among a group of brown wooden huts, themselves huddled among brown pointy rocks, getting wet. In fact it was the rocks we had come to see and that all pervasive feeling of cold and despair that we had come to experience, for this place had been Emyn Muil in the *Lord of the Rings* movies.

If you have seen the films, you will remember the Hobbits Frodo and Sam, trolling endlessly about a desolate landscape of 'razor sharp rocks' on their way to Mount Doom. That was Emyn Muil and the Whakapapa Ski Field, out of season, was that landscape. If you haven't seen the films you probably think Emyn Muil is a Welsh donkey. You're making up your own stories now aren't you?

The only thing that was missing from the authentic Emyn Muil experience was the mist that descended as the Hobbit trolling scenes were being filmed, just to add that extra touch of misery to proceedings. As I was counting my blessings I thought I saw someone or something lurking beside the hire car, maybe seeking some respite in its silver paintwork from the relentless brownness of the surroundings. I soon realised that with that tee shirt, those hairy legs poking out from baggy shorts and those spectacles, there was only one figment of my imagination it could be. The figment grinned the malevolent grin of its namesake Mr Nicholson in *The Shining*, then clicked its fingers. The mist descended.

THB was ecstatic but I was only that much colder and that much wetter. Thank you very much, Mr Peterson.

"Pardon?" said THB.

I didn't realise I'd said it out loud.

Eventually I managed to drag her into a café with the promise of a steak (and unadvertised carrot) pie, thankful that Orlando Bloom didn't feature in any of the Emyn Muil scenes otherwise she'd still have been among the rocks today, buried under a substantial layer of snow due to the onset of winter.

I tried the café's special of deliciously warming pumpkin and kumara soup. It had orange bits in it. Suspiciously carroty tasting orange bits.

Our hunger sated and our clothes wrung out, we headed off to the south side of Mount Ruapehu, in search of Mangawhero Falls, marked with a little yellow eye and the legend Ithilien in our road atlas. The journey took us through the quiet, pretty town of Ohakune with its bright wooden chalets, skiing accessory shops and (double take here) giant carrot. I've heard of people turning orange through too high a carotene intake but never hallucinating vegetables the size of trees, balanced on their pointy ends by the side of the road. Mind you, as Mr Peterson would testify, I had a history when it came to imagining things.

"What is that?" asked THB as we passed the vegetable by. Panic over. She had seen it too.

Ohakune is a market gardening centre with good rail links for the distribution of produce, a late growing season and cold snowy winters to kill off pests. It styles itself as 'New Zealand's Carrot Capital' and even has an annual carrot festival in which people parade down the street dressed as carrots, eat carrot cake and enter carrot throwing competitions. (I am assured that it's just throwing and not throwing up). I have to admit that I wasn't even aware that a country needed a carrot capital. I don't remember any schoolteacher ever saying to me, "Very good Gisby. The capital of Peru is Lima. But what is its carrot capital?" It is a sobering thought that every pie and soup recipe in New Zealand would have to be changed if the carrot weevils around Ohakune ever realised that wearing overcoats in the winter keeps the cold out.

After Ohakune, the narrow and wooded Ohakune Mountain Road led us up towards the Turoa Ski Field, past huts where you could stop in the snow to have chains fitted to your tyres, deserted in summery December. There were several false alarms in our search for Mangawhero Falls, moments when the trees parted momentarily and we spotted a green sign with yellow writing, the sort used in New Zealand to indicate, "Hey! There's something here worth stopping to look at." When you do stop you may find a spectacular view, a waterfall or a lake. Or you may find the world's largest carrot field.

Having experienced repeated disappointment in her quest for Ithilien, the normally cheery THB was ready to give in to despair (I blame an overdose of Emyn Muil in the morning) but I wouldn't be defeated and drove on. I could just imagine a nocturnal whinge from Jack Peterson if I turned back to Ohakune without sighting the Falls. "You wunt all thut way ind still didn't fund it? Dun't you wunt your wife to git bitter?"

Eventually we reached a dusty lay-by with a sign indicating that a waterfall was a short walk away. I don't remember it actually saying Mangawhero Falls but it was obvious that we were in the right place when we saw the characteristic stream of water split into two by a stubborn rock, like the tusks of a walrus, just before tumbling into a small blue pool far below. Guidebooks say that spectacular icicles form at the Falls in the winter. I suspect they also formed on the extremities of Andy Serkis who frolicked in the water above the falls as Smeagol shortly after the New Zealand fire brigade had washed away a fall of snow so that *Lord of the Rings* filming could take place.

The following day we were due to drive to Wellington, New Zealand's non carrot capital and Hobbit botherer heaven, boasting a host of *Lord of the Rings* filming locations, including the studios where special sets were built and indoor filming was done, Weta Workshop where the special effects were put together and the home of Peter Jackson, the films' director. THB should have been excited, keen to be off and amongst it, but in fact she was subdued after a sleepless night. A gusty wind had whistled across the tussock during the hours of darkness, causing our chalet to creak like a galleon in mid ocean under full sail. It kept her awake, but I didn't hear a thing.

Before we left Whakapapa, fortified by the some of the best

omelettes we'd ever tasted courtesy of the *Skotel* chef, we attempted a final tramp from a car park beside Bruce Road to Tawhai Falls, ten minutes away through mountain toatoa and beech forest. I had suggested attempting the longer two hour Whakapapanui Walk, maybe extended to four or five hours if we got confused with signs for the Whakapapaiti Track, but one look from a tired THB convinced me it was a suggestion I should not pursue any further. Not unless I wished to receive a forceful suggestion of my own in return. Perhaps involving carrots.

The shorter tramp was probably best as it minimised the chance for thieves to help themselves to our worldly possessions from the hire car parked on its own beside a sign saying "Tawhai Falls, 20 minutes, return via same track." Translation: "They are going to be away for at least 20 minutes. Help yourself." For the record, the Tawhai Falls, viewed in the middle distance through a gap in the trees, were impressive, different in character, wider and more voluminous then either the Taranaki Falls or the Mangawhero Falls.

The trip to Wellington took us to Wanganui, our arrival badly timed with respect to the schedule of the Wanganui river steamer to THB's relief, then down the eastern coast of the North Island through Bulls ("Where do you come from?" "Bulls!" "All right, I only asked.") and on to olde-worlde Foxton where we stopped for a break. I remember Foxton for its picturesque windmill and the worst cappucino I have ever tasted. I didn't specify foulness as a requirement when I ordered it, but I did say yes when the waitress asked if I'd like to try one with cinnamon. That may have been where the problem started. THB remembers Foxton for the Doll Museum, advertised with increasing enthusiasm along the road side as we approached town, then closed when we finally arrived. Truth to tell it looked as if it had been closed for a couple of decades.

It was around about this time that we missed the opportunity to visit the famous hill just outside Porangahau which claims the longest place name in New Zealand. It would have meant a long trek across the foot of the North Island through Palmerston North towards Hawkes Bay to get there. If only we'd had time I'm sure it would have been worth it to have been photographed beside a sign which read Taumatawhakatangihangakoauauotamateaturipukakapikimaungahoronukupokaiwhenuakitanatahu. This translates approximately as "The place where Tamatea, the man with the bony knees, who slid, climbed and swallowed mountains, known as landeater, sat and played his flute to his beloved".

The names of some places in Britain can be translated in a similar way.

(1) "The town where Wobbledagger, with the quill pen, crafted instruments of torture to be used on school children hundreds of years after he died." (Stratford-Upon-Avon)
(2) "The home of Robin, an early wood elf, who earned a living helping passing noblemen carry their heavy gold and jewels." (Nottingham)
(3) "The place where travelling giants abandoned a game of dominoes before heading east on large bicycles." (Stonehenge)
(4) "The place where a wheel fell of one of the bicycles." (London Eye)
(5) "The lake where a large man in a rubber suit goes swimming from time to time to keep the Scottish tourist industry ticking over." (Loch Ness)

THB was more interested in a couple of sites closer to Foxton than Taumatawhakaetcetera. Yellow eyes on our road atlas indicated Trollshaw Forest and Osgiliath Wood, but there were no sign of roads or paths to lead us there. She wasn't quite sure where and when Trollshaw Forest featured in the films anyway. So in the end we pushed on though Levin, and Waikanae, then alongside the Hutt River into Wellington (which translates as 'Rubber Boot') and the *Bay Plaza Hotel*.

7: WELLINGTON

A Beehive And A Chocolate Fish

If a hotel thinks you are a really important person, in the league of Kiri Te Kanawa or Peter Jackson perhaps, they will set down a red carpet to welcome you to their establishment. The *Bay Plaza Hotel* in Wellington afforded us an even greater honour. They put out the white sheets.

As we made our entrance we could see that every surface was covered, from the lobby floor and the sofas provided for the comfort of waiting guests to the reception desk itself. As an extra touch the management had also contrived to provide an uplifting smell of fresh paint for our pleasure. In Britain this is a privilege usually only accorded to royalty. Indeed it is believed that the Queen thinks the whole world smells of fresh paint, because whenever she decides to visit a place there is always a man with a paintbrush, a pot of paint and a tired arm a few hundred metres in front of her.

We picked our way to the reception desk rather like people crossing a cow pasture in their best shoes, just in case there were of dollops of wet paint lurking on the dustsheets. The receptionist offered a nervous 'it's my first day' smile as we approached, checked her hair for white spots in a mirror on the wall behind her, then asked, "Win are you living?"

After the formalities of checking in had been completed and we had been allocated a room next to the lifts (a location dubbed Murder Central in the American TV crime series CSI as it offers both ease of escape and only one neighbour to overhear screams) it was time to try out the receptionist's local knowledge. Since our faithful road atlas displayed no fewer than eleven yellow eyes on its Wellington page we had decided to take an organised *Lord of the Rings* tour, if one was available, to maximise seeing time and minimise seeking time. To this end THB enquired, "Do you know if there are tours of *Lords of the Rings* filluming locations operating?" (Sadly THB is losing her Irish accent after living in London for cough, cough years with me, but the word film is one that remains defiantly Irish).

"No," came the receptionist's reply. In fact it came rather too quickly without passing through her brain first, suggesting that what she meant was something like, "I've finished checking you in now, so go to your room and stop bugging me with questions that weren't covered in the training manual. I need a lie down. This job is only temporary anyway until I make it into the movies. *King Kong* is shooting here, you know, and they're auditioning for extras. But I'm allergic to gorillas so I can't go. Even though I'm prettier than that Naomi Wattshername. Miaow. Life's soooo unfair." Its amazing what a single word can convey.

As we peered behind a few dustsheets, trying to find the hotel's lifts, there was a stage whisper from the office behind the reception desk. "Look in the paper," it said.

The receptionist repeated, "Look in the paper." Only more loudly and in our direction.

We were about to ask which paper and maybe, if we felt we had the time and patience, where we could buy a copy, when the whisper added. "No YOU, look in the paper."

"Which paper?" the receptionist asked the wall behind her. Now she was speaking in a stage whisper too.

"On the end of the desk," came the disembodied reply.

For a moment I thought we were going to get, "Which desk?" but the receptionist was on top of that one and retrieved a listings sheet from a pile on the far end of the reception desk. She skimmed through it to show willing but found nothing to help us.

"Nothing," she said, with just a hint of 'I told you so' in her voice.

It was at this point that the whisper took human form, obviously deciding it was time to put both receptionist in training and punters out of their misery. The form was a besuited middle-aged woman not the tousle haired, bespectacled man in shorts by the name of Peterson I had half expected.

"There are usually walks advertised in here," she said, subjecting the paper to another brief study, "And there's also the Rover Ring Tour..." (A pause while she sized us up, working out whether we were Rover Ring Tour type people) "...but that's very pricey and it lasts a WHOLE DAY." The concept that a person might want to spend more than half an hour Hobbit bothering was clearly one she couldn't quite grasp. That made two of us then.

As THB and I waited to discover whether further information might be forthcoming the ex-whisperer glanced down at our entry in the hotel register, then her face lit up. Suddenly everything made sense. "You're from England," she said. (Apparently that explained our eccentric idea of fun). "You can afford 150 dollars each!" I wasn't aware that Dick Whittington had retired to New Zealand to become a geography teacher after his stint as Lord Mayor, but clearly someone had told this Kiwi that London's streets were paved with gold.

We left for Wellington's Information Office to make our booking clutching a photocopy of a flyer which promised visions of The Outer Shire, Race To The Ferry, Dunharrow, Bree, Minas Tirith, Helms Deep, River Anduin, Fords of Isen, Rivendell and Isengard (THB recognised most of those names even if I didn't) and also a picnic lunch (the part which sounded best to me). It turned out that places on the tour were available the very next day, which was lucky because that was the only full day in Wellington that we had.

On the way back to our hotel from the Information Office we discovered that it was late opening at The Museum of New Zealand or Te Papa Tongarewa, a striking modern building on the Wellington waterfront. So that was where we spent three enthralling hours, nowhere near long enough to do it justice, until hunger finally defeated us and we left to find a restaurant. Wellington residents will tell you that Te Papa is Maori for 'Our Place'. Auckland residents, however, emphasise the alternative translation of 'Buttocks'. Take your choice.

Forget the old fashioned concept of a museum where people shuffle around for a couple of hours silently peering into dingy glass cases because they feel it is something they ought to do. Te Papa is a colourful, interactive, enjoyable experience set out over five levels, covering all aspects of New Zealand history and culture. What do I remember most? The moa, earthquakes and bell-bottomed trousers.

Moa were flightless birds native to New Zealand and eaten to extinction three hundred or so years ago. The smallest species was about the size of a turkey. If you got six or seven of those turkeys to stand on each others heads, you would have an idea of how high the largest species *Dinornis giganteus* was at the shoulders. You would also have an act to guarantee you a job in the circus.

Acrobatic turkeys were not needed in Te Papa as a life size model of *Dinornis giganteus* battling an eagle had been thoughtfully provided. Encountering this tableau had a profound effect on me as it necessitated a revision of the Gisby scale for birds introduced in the Rotorua chapter. Please add just underneath ostrich at number ten:

(11)   Moa   Get The Camera! They're Meant To Be Extinct.

Incidentally moa is properly pronounced as in "That cake was nice, can I have some moa?" and not, "That grass needs cutting, fetch the lawn moa."

The Te Papa earthquake exposition in the Awesome Forces gallery was fascinating, especially for someone who comes from a country that is a couch potato seismically speaking. New Zealand is hyperactive, recording over 10,500 earthquakes each year. Only, if that is the right word, between 100 and 150 of these are violent enough to be felt by the Kiwi in the street, or the home or the sheep paddock. That is about one every three days. Fortunately we were in Wellington, which sits above five major fault lines, for the other two.

You'll be pleased to hear that THB and I didn't miss out on experiencing an earthquake altogether though, thanks to Te Papa's earthquake house which simulates an aftershock of the Edgecumbe earthquake, magnitude 6.6 on the Richter scale, of 2nd March 1987. This quake resulted in just the one death, a heart attack victim, largely because a foreshock a few minutes earlier had cut power, encouraging people to wander outside before the biggie hit. There were injuries though, one woman being felled by a bull thrown into the air by the force of the jolt. It is a strange and interesting country that breeds giant birds that don't fly and domestic cattle that do.

Te Papa's bell-bottomed trousers came as part of a special exhibition on New Zealand in the 1970s, called 'Out On The Street'. Focusing on the growing assertion of women's rights, Maori rights and New Zealand's own right not to be nannied by 'Mother England' during the decade it also documented the swirly orange and brown fixated fashions of the time. For an hour or so our conversation consisted of phrases like, "Hey, my parents used to have wallpaper like that," "Hey, I used to wear trousers like that," (still would if I thought I could get away with it) and "Hey, those colours are hurting my eyes."

On our way back to the hotel we passed our first *Lord of the Rings* landmark in the Wellington area. It looked like an upmarket theatre transformed into a cinema (in England it would probably have gone through Bingo Hall in between) but THB regarded it open-mouthed. "That's the Embassy," she said excitedly. I was trying to work out why the British Embassy would cause such delight (was THB hankering after news from the old country or missing long conversations about the weather?) when she explained "It's the cinema which hosted the world premier of *The Return of the King*."

The story goes that Wellington really did become Middle Earth on that day as the cast of the film paraded through town down streets temporarily renamed Frodo Road, Gandalf Drive and the like. This was to the annoyance of wandering tourists whose street maps were rendered temporarily useless. If you visit the Embassy today you can rest your rear in the very place where your favourite actor or actress rested theirs. In most cases you are guided to the appropriate seat by a small plaque glued to its back. If you are a Legolas fan, however, it is a small plaque held in place with industrial strength rivets. The cinema has a problem with kleptomaniac teenage girls and disappearing 'Orlando Bloom's.

We watched the film *Hero* at the Embassy, although to THB's dismay 'Orlando Bloom', the seat, had already been taken. Never mind, her crowbar had been confiscated on the way in anyway. She had to make do with 'Viggo Mortensen' and I sat next to her, on 'Viggo Mortensen's sword'. A devoted method actor, Viggo never departed from character during filming and, so the legend goes, took his sword everywhere with him. Which brings us neatly around to the *Lord of the Rings* Tour.

Dan and Andy picked us up from our hotel lobby in a 4WD (four wheel drive) mini van early the next day. The division of labour between them seemed very unequal. Dan was charged with the driving, fetching and carrying and most of the talking while Andy sat with his feet on the dashboard, chipping in with *Lord of the Rings* facts once in a while. Usually these turned out to be *Lord of the Rings* fictions as either Dan or (making a strong bid for teacher's pet) THB corrected him.

As Andy didn't seem to know much and didn't seem to do much, we reached the obvious conclusion that he was the boss. This illusion was to be shattered a short way into the tour when Andy confused Rohirrim and Gondorians for about the third time and was told by Dan, in half exasperation and half amusement, "You'll have to read the book again before we let you out on your own!" I'm still not sure whether Andy was really a trainee or part of a very entertaining double act.

We were given a short tour of Wellington's hotels, picking up another couple, Paul and Mary (Paul from England and Mary from the Philippines, Peter couldn't make it) and two Japanese girls, Oki and Kyoko, on the way. (No they didn't put their left legs in, their left legs out...) Then we were off briefly downmarket to a backpacker hostel to pick up a German girl, Christa, with red spiky hair and a liking for punk fashion. And so the cosmopolitan nine was completed. Sadly there was no po-faced elf lurking about to dub us 'The Fellowship of the Rover Ring Tour'. Probably off auditioning for *The Matrix*.

Our first stop was Mount Victoria, for wonderful views of the city to the northwest, the airport to the southeast and the Miramar Peninsula to the east, then a guided walk through its beautiful forested greenbelt. Even I recognised the spot where Dan eventually brought us to a halt. We were on a narrow path with trees ether side of us, their branches intertwined above our heads, casting spooky shadows on the ground. It was the place where, in *The Fellowship of the Ring*, Frodo cried, "Get off the road!" to warn his friends Sam, Merry and Pippin of the approach of a sinister Black Rider. The place where the four frightened Hobbits cowered in hiding among the tangled roots of a giant (polystyrene) tree.

As we recalled the scene and stifled our laughter as Christa toppled backwards down an incline having stepped back too far while trying to capture the perfect photograph, Dan shouted, "Get off the road!" A nice touch, referring back to the film. "Get off the road!" he shouted again, more urgently. It was just in time to save us from a speeding mountain biker. Walking on Mount Victoria can be hazardous as it is criss-crossed by mountain bike tracks. It was used for the mountain bike world championships in 1998.

From Mount Victoria we were taken to a grassy hill offering views over Wellington airport and purely by chance, if you looked in the opposite direction, over the Three Foot Six studios on the Miramar peninsula where *Lord of the Rings* filming took place. We were told that it was not unknown for security staff patrolling the area to confiscate cameras from people photographing the studios. Lucky then that we were really only interested in the aeroplanes. And that, your honour, is the case for the defence.

The Three Foot Six studios themselves bore an uncanny resemblance to an old paint factory (probably because they were an old paint factory) as we discovered when driving slowly past them on our way to Seatoun. Efforts not to look like gawping tourists and so avoid getting moved on were hampered by girlie shrieks from the more hard core fans amongst us (THB, Oki and Kyoko take a bow) when they spotted some weatherbeaten logs in the studio yard that could once have been part of an Ent.

Seatoun was a fairly exclusive suburb with a pretty beach offering views across Chaffers Passage, the inlet to Wellington harbour through which ferries pass on their way to and from the South Island. It is home to Peter Jackson and also to the famous Chocolate Fish Café where *Lord of the Rings* actors gathered after a hard days filming to swap stories of Peter Jackson's dedication to his art (he made you do how many takes?) and possibly to air their clothes to remove the smell of paint.

If you are not a Kiwi the concept of a chocolate fish might need some explaining. It is a delicacy prepared by coating the head of a local fish, the Madei-Tup, with molten chocolate. The chocolate is then allowed to set and its template cut away, leaving a receptacle in the shape of a fish head. From this cup it customary to drink a broth formed by boiling the remainder of the Madei-Tup in sheep's urine. How far did you get before you realised I was joking? A chocolate fish is actually a marshmallow in the shape of a sea creature beginning with the letter F covered in, you've guessed it, a confectionary beginning with the letter C. The Madei-Tup? Yes, I made it up.

Patrons of the Chocolate Fish can take the air, enjoy a wonderful sea view and share their snacks with marauding seabirds (if they are not sufficiently vigilant) in a small beachside enclosure on the far side of the road from the café itself. This means that waiters have to run the gauntlet of passing cars to take orders and deliver food and drinks. Drivers are warned of this hazard through a 'Waiters Crossing' sign that has become something of a tourist attraction in its own right. THB and I enjoyed a coffee and a cake in the enclosure accompanied by a patrolling seagull. It had obviously decided that persuasion rather than intimidation was the way to get our food, adopting an, "I'm soooo hungry" look rather than a "Feed me or else I'll peck you" look. It was still soooo hungry when we departed.

The plan on leaving Seatoun was to make our way north-east to Kaitoke Regional Park for a picnic lunch. Before we consign the Miramar Peninsula and the east of Wellington to the been there, seen that, bought the tee shirt part of the book though, three other sights demand a mention. These are the surfing beach, Gollum and the stairlifts. (No, Gollum and the stairlifts is not a rock band).

Before drawing our attention to Wellington's premier surfing beach at Lyall Bay, Dan made sure there were no Aussies in our fellowship. Apparently Aussies tend to sit wide eyed and open mouthed when they see the size of the white topped waves speeding in to shore, sometimes completely engulfing people's ankles. Then they start to laugh. Not as loudly as they do when you tell them the England cricket team are going to win 'The Ashes' but almost. (Note that this was written before September 2005. The Aussies have stopped laughing now. Thank you, Freddie Flintoff).

Dan also encouraged us to squint through the fence surrounding the airport as we skirted past it, promising a *Lord of the Rings* moment. The long-sighted amongst us managed to spot a gigantic Gollum reaching down from the top of the terminal building and clutching a equally gigantic golden ring. His first home was the top of the Embassy Theatre for the *The Return of the King* premier but I suppose he couldn't be left there permanently for fear of causing traffic accidents in Kent Terrace. ("What the hell's that?" says driver, craning neck. Crash!) Instead he now terrifies small children as they enter New Zealand. I suppose it limbers them up for base jumping, bungy jumping, zorbing...

The site of the third sight clamouring for a mention was Oriental Bay, where we perused some of Wellington's most expensive real estate clinging desperately to the hillside. The owners of this real estate are not the sort of people who can be bothered to walk up steps from the road to their front door after returning home with the shopping. Many have solved the problem by installing outdoor stairlifts of the sort used indoors by elderly people in Britain. The ones that take you up to bed so slowly that by the time you get there it's time to get up.

In Britain the term 'joyriding' refers to the act of stealing some unfortunate's car and driving it around quiet (at least until you arrived) residential streets, wearing a baseball cap backwards. In Wellington it means hot-wiring some rich guy's stairlift and riding it up and down all night. All right then, up only. It would take a particularly speedy model to get up and down in the one night.

And so it was off to Kaitoke Regional Park, stopping on the way to view some not particularly picturesque earthworks and a couple of concrete mixers at Dry Creek Quarry. I racked my brains but could not remember a *Lord of the Rings* scene featuring such vehicles. Maybe it was in a super extended edition. Most of our fellowship had reached the 'okay we've seen it so can we move on now' stage before THB, sneaking in to steal Dan's thunder, revealed that this was where sets for the fortress of Helm's Deep and the city of Minas Tirith were built, used, then thoroughly dismantled.

Everyone scanned the scene for evidence that anything more interesting than quarrying had ever taken place in the quarry and found none whatsoever. The blow was softened by Dan conjuring up pictures of terrified motorists being overtaken in the dead of night by bus loads of Uruk-hai en-route from make up to set and telling tales of in-fighting between haughty, foreign models, hired to played elves, and just about everyone else during lulls in the filming. Apparently these pointy-eared pretty-boys wormed their way well up the nasal orifices of the 'stand none of that nonsense' locals hired to play other Middle Earth races. That was Dan's story.

The balance should be redressed by mentioning another Rover Ring guide, Nathan, who took THB and I on a repeat tour the year after our introduction to New Zealand. (Look out for *Hobbit Botherers Two: Return To Aotearoa* if the sales of the book you are reading are encouraging enough!) Nathan is a Kiwi who passed the rigorous tests necessary to become a movie elf (not simply a matter of being tall, thin and able to pass for a girl on a dark night) and rose up through the ranks to become a banner carrier at Helms Deep. His performance as a guide included posing on a grassy mound, ready to unleash death (or a maybe just a nasty bruise) from a child's plastic bow, while sporting a blonde (obviously female) wig and Dumbo-like prosthetic ears. This parody of elves in general and one Blooming elf in particular could not have been contemplated by the sort of 'I'm better than you' model described by Dan. Rest assured, there was at least one friendly, fun-loving elf at Helms Deep.

Kaitoke Regional Park itself was the location chosen to become Rivendell, a beautiful and tranquil refuge for the elves among trees and waterfalls. The place must have had some hidden flaw though, since the pointy-eared ones spent an awful lot of time in the movies planning a move far away 'Into The West'. Once more Dan's eloquence was required to put a pretty but not obviously *Lord of the Rings* related site (apart from the sign erected to allow park rangers to do their job without having to give directions to Rivendell every few minutes) into its movie context.

After a splendid picnic lunch the paying members of the fellowship departed for a rainforest walk along the loop of the swingbridge track while Dan and Andy did the washing up. We'll never know whether Andy washed, dried or simply watched, but I know which one I'd bet on.

Christa, a seasoned tramper, headed off at a fast pace not to be seen again until we returned to the mini van. THB and I, fresh from recent tramping practise in Tongariro, took up second place. We were closely followed by Oki and Kyoko, then Paul and Mary far, far behind. Paul was even less well designed for tramping than me.

A short way along the track we heard what we thought was a waterfall in the trees and set off on a side path to investigate. Oki and Kyoko were obviously shocked. A conversation in Japanese followed, drifting through the trees behind us. I think the gist of it was...

"The British couple have left the path!" (Shock, horror).
"They will get lost." (Concern).
"Shall we go on or follow them to point out the error of their ways?" (Indecision).
"If we follow them, we will get lost too." (Growing concern).
"Maybe we are lost and they have gone the right way." (Full blown worry).
"We should follow them, then we will not be lost." (Wrong choice).

As they stepped in among the trees we stepped out, having not found any trace of a waterfall. So a new Japanese conversation began.

"The British couple are back." (Confusion).
"What were they doing among those trees?" (Shock, horror).

At the end of the swingbridge track was the eponymous swingbridge, a walkway across the Hutt River able to take a maximum of two people at a time. Dan and Andy were stationed at one end to ensure the rule was obeyed. I can confirm that the bridge was well named. It swung prodigiously as I made my way across alternating between slow progress on tiptoe and a fast 'get it over with' run, unsure which was the best way to progress. As I sat down on the far side to recover, THB enjoyed views of the grey pebbled banks of the Hutt, where Theodred's almost dead body was found in *The Two Towers*. It was claimed that he was killed by Orcs but I have my suspicions he fell off the swingbridge.

On the way back to the city we stopped for another view of the Hutt River, a site where the movie Fellowship were filmed canoeing down the mighty Anduin, and also at Harcourt Park, which masqueraded as Isengard. This was the Isengard where Gandalf and Sauraman walked on the grass together in chummy fashion just before the former found out that the latter, to borrow from a different series of films, had gone over to the dark side. Watch out for THB's sequel to this book, if we ever travel to Tunisia, *Tatooin With A Wookie Worrier*.

Harcourt Park also introduced us to a new sport, surprisingly sedate where New Zealand is concerned, frisbee golf. Dotted about the park were small metal cages supported on poles, not designed to snare squirrels but to catch flying frisbees. Players take the game very seriously, even carrying a collection of different discs, some designed to cover long distances and others for accuracy in putting. I can just imagine entering a sports shop in England and asking, "Have you got a putting frisbee?"

The reply would probably be "We don't sell Frisbees. And there's no need to swear!"

Back at our hotel, after thanking Dan for an interesting and entertaining trip (highly recommended if you find yourself with a day to spare in Wellington) we set off to do the two must dos we had not yet done, The Beehive and The Botanic Gardens.

Quiz question. Why is the New Zealand parliament building in Wellington known as The Beehive?

(1) Because the politicians inside work hard, like bees.
(2) Because the politicians' words are sweet, like honey.
(3) Because the building is oddly shaped, like a beehive.

Congratulations if you picked number three. If you picked number one, how many votes did you get at the last election? You are a politician, aren't you?

The Beehive is in fact only part of the parliament complex, an earlier, more traditional stone and colonnades government building having been started in the early nineteen-hundreds but never completed. New Zealand obviously has higher priorities than a bunch of politicians. It occupies the space earmarked for the southern wing of the original design and has become something of a Wellington icon, the must take photograph when you are there. We took the photo, commented on the need for a coat of paint, and moved on.

The Botanic Gardens, an area of protected forest and plant collections, sit on a hill behind the city and are reached, at least by the energetically challenged, using a cable car. The short cable car ride is itself part of the Wellington experience, we told ourselves, as THB and I decided not to walk up the hill. Emerging from the cable car to beautiful sunset views over the city we discovered that The Botanic Gardens closed at dusk.

That evening was our last in the North Island. Just as we were falling asleep ready for an early start to catch the ferry in the morning, I heard the door of the hotel room creak open. A shadowy figure entered. A squat shadowy figure either wearing baggy shorts or with strangely shaped legs that suddenly thinned at the knee. In silhouette it was difficult to tell. Spots of light from the window reflected in large, round glasses finally gave away the figure's identity. I waited for Jack Peterson to speak, but he simply placed a sheet of paper on the desk at the foot of the bed and left.

The title at the top of the paper read:

Hobbit Botherers Anonymous
Half Term Report

Good. I wanted to see how THB was doing. As far as I could see, visiting Hobbiton, Mount Doom, Emyn Muil, The Wooded Road, Rivendell and Isengard... sorry that should be Matamata, Mount Ngauruhoe, Whakapapa ski fields, Mount Victoria, Kaitoke Regional Park and Harcourt Park... had only reduced THB's ability to distinguish between real New Zealand and fictional Middle Earth still further. Luckily that would never happen to me.

The report turned out to be rather disappointing...

Knowledge Of People..C
Can distinguish Hobbit from Elf but still confuses Eomer, Eowyn and Elrond.
Knowledge Of Locations..D
Thinks Kaitoke Park is where people go for a sing along. Must do better.
Locations Visited...B
Dragged kicking and screaming to many North Island filming locations.
Enthusiasm..D
See "kicking and screaming" above. Unfortunate tendency to take the piss.
Resemblance To Lord of the Rings Character............................B
Short, fat and hairy. Embryonic Hobbit. Sadly no taste for pipeweed.

...None of this appeared to relate to THB in any way, except maybe the part about pipeweed. (In order to save my marriage I should emphasise that the short, fat and hairy bit is particularly irrelevant). Obviously Peterson was working on more than one case and had dropped off some other Hobbit botherer's report by mistake. I rushed from the room to catch him and give it back, but he was gone.

I could hear chuckling from inside the lift though.

8: NORTH TO SOUTH

Sounds Of Green Lipped Mussels

Saying that THB is prone to travel sickness is a little like saying it is a long swim from London to New York. The statement is true but doesn't quite tell the whole story. I have known her to feel queasy on just about every mode of transport known to man, including a bicycle, but boats are without doubt her nemesis. She even turns green if someone stands in front of her on dry land and sways gently from side to side while whistling a hornpipe. (I have tried this once or twice in the spirit of experimentation). So it was with some trepidation that we began our journey to the ferry terminal the next morning on our way to the South Island. This trepidation was enhanced by a forecast of choppy seas in the local newspaper (THB had been monitoring weather forecasts closely for days in anticipation of the boat trip) and by the memory of a television programme we had watched just before leaving Britain.

Television in Britain has become infected with the sort of programmes that celebrate the one in a million horrors that can arise in everyday situations, but usually don't. The usually don't bit tends to be glossed over. These are the programmes with attention grabbing titles like "When Bungalows Attack!", "Vegetables That Kill!" and "Cats And Dogs Go Bad!" (Come to think of it the last one might have been a documentary about the benefits refrigeration has brought to restaurateurs in some parts of Asia).

The particular programme that was worrying THB had been entitled "New Zealand Turns Nasty!" (or something like that) and featured, among tales of terrible earthquakes and volcanic eruptions, which she took in her stride, the story of the sinking of the TEV Wahine in Wellington harbour during a massive storm in 1968.

The Wahine hit a reef in turbulent seas, then drifted for two hours, even after her anchors were dropped. They finally held off Seatoun beach, where efforts to bring the ship under control with tugs failed and she eventually foundered, made unstable by water sloshing about her car deck. Of the 734 people aboard 44 passengers, six crew members and one stowaway perished. They are remembered by a monument built from debris from the ship on the shore at Seatoun.

As THB and I dropped the Echo cho cho cho (last time) off at the ferry terminal, hire cars obviously prone to sea sickness as well as THB since they are not allowed to cross between New Zealand's main islands, we were pleased to note that although the day was overcast it was not at all windy. There was no great storm imminent. At least that's how it seemed until the man checking in our bags said, "The ferry will be sailing two hours late today due to bad weather on the incoming trip." He said that after he'd taken our bags, so THB was trapped with two hours to sit and think about the Wahine. Cue another game of *Spot the Banker*.

When we finally boarded the ferry we grabbed a couple of seats amidships (less movement close to the centre of gravity, so the theory goes) and settled down to endure and enjoy the journey respectively. As the ferry juddered into motion an announcement came over the tannoy to the effect that, "The sea is going to be a bit lumpy. If you feel the need to chunder, use a bag and not the carpet. If you do chunder on the carpet a steward will come around and rub your nose in it." Point made, I think.

For those of you unfamiliar with the verb 'to chunder' it is a Kiwi expression meaning 'to vomit'. All foreign visitors are tested on their knowledge of 'KiwiSpeak' phrases on the way into New Zealand and if they don't know the meaning of at least half the ones they're presented with, then it's back on the plane. So how would you do with, greasies, hottie, judder bar, savs and pavs, wop-wops, hollywood, scroggin, scarfie, cocky, fitter and turner, long drop, piker, other side, mountain oysters and tinbum? Answers when we get closer to Nelson.

On hearing the tannoy announcement a small boy sitting next to me sprang up to grab a sick bag. A look in his eye said, "I've met the chunder steward before and I don't want to meet him again." As he checked the bag's integrity his mother offered some advice on its correct usage. I was surprised to hear that there was much more subtlety to this than simply, "Open up and chunder in". (You may want to skip the next few lines if you are eating).

"Hold it close to your face," she said, making as if to treat him for hyperventilation. "So that you don't miss." Fair enough, so far. She relaxed her grip on the bag as the child began to turn blue, and continued, "That's okay if its thick and chunky. If it's thin and watery you should hold the bag further away." He looked puzzled. "To avoid splash back," she explained. Yuk! Luckily THB had already fallen asleep with her head on my shoulder, otherwise a bag would have been filled before we left the harbour.

The boy soon departed, mother in tow, in the direction of the ship's shop. He was replaced by a female backpacker who promptly fell asleep with her head on the shoulder not already occupied by THB. I find that this is not an uncommon phenomenon. My shoulders seem to hold the same attraction for female heads as a wheelbarrow load of manure does for flies. On more than one occasion on a long haul flight a strange woman has fallen asleep resting on my shoulder. Not the same strange woman each time, you understand. When it happens there is always the same dilemma to be faced. To wake or not to wake? That is the question.

First there is the 'wake' option. She's in the midst of a wonderful dream, dancing through fields of sweet smelling flowers with Orlando Bloom, then just as he begins to... she's jerked back to reality by yours truly. She's not happy and I have to suffer her 'if only they could kill' looks for the rest of the trip.

The alternative is the 'not to wake' option. Note that this is only available in the absence of drool. Any trace of drool and the 'wake' option immediately comes into effect. Left to sleep she eventually wakes up of her own accord and is embarrassed to find her head on a stranger's shoulder. She wonders what's been going on while she's been asleep and I have to suffer 'don't you come near me again' looks for the rest of the trip.

It's a no win situation, but I usually go for the 'not to wake' option. After all I know I'd be annoyed if some bozo disturbed me while I was dreaming, lets say, of Miranda Otto...

...sorry, I was miles away there. Remind me, what was I talking about?

The ferry sailed across an almost glasslike Cook Strait, with no hint of the bad weather or chundersome seas that had been threatened, and on into the Marlborough Sounds, a maze of crinkly-edged islands with rocky cliffs rising from the sea towards lush green summits. Ideally I would have rushed onto deck to breathe in the view as we sailed towards Picton, it is not uncommon to spot leaping dolphins, but the best I could manage was to turn my head slowly and catch the occasional glimpse of the islands through salt encrusted windows. The remainder of my body was numb by that time from lack of movement, afraid as I was to wake the sleeping beauties.

In the end they woke together just as the ferry began to manoeuvre into its berth and a "Thank you for sailing with us. The exit's that way. Goodbye," announcement came over the ship's tannoy. I was rewarded for my forbearance in impersonating a pillow for three hours with a 'don't you come near me again, you perve' look from one of them and a 'what have you been doing with her' look from the other. Thank you, dear reader, for allowing me to set the record straight.

Outside the ferry terminal at Picton we were greeted by a sweep of glass fronted buildings, mostly car rental offices, that looked as if they'd been put up in a hurry a few hours before. We joined the queue outside one and shuffled forward as the same conversation was repeated over and over in front of us.

"We'd like to hire a car please."

"Have you made a booking?"

"Er... No."

"I'm afraid we only have cars for people who've made a booking. Next!"

Note to hire car companies in New Zealand. Have a few extra unbooked vehicles handy when the ferry comes in. There is a gap in the market.

"We'd like to hire a car please."

"Have you made a booking?"

"Yes."

It was all the man behind the desk could do to prevent himself stepping forward and hugging us. Finally a pair of punters who played by the rules. It had been worth getting out of bed that morning after all.

He guided us through a mound of paperwork, then finally parted with the keys to a Mitsubishi Colt that was parked, so it seemed, on the other side of Picton. Not that far away then. Still, one of us had to go and fetch it in the drizzly rain while the other waited with the luggage in a dry office. Now seemed the perfect time to remind THB of her offer to take over the driving on the South Island.

Unfortunately for me she was ready with a pitiful 'I'm still suffering from sea sickness, if you were a kind husband you'd understand' look, backed up by a couple of 'heroine in a costume drama about to expire' coughs. I like to think I'm a kind husband, who certainly does understand (when he is beaten) so I set off into the drizzle.

The Colt was silver and from the outside looked much the same as the Echo (see I told you it was the last time) before it. Inside was a different story. First of all the Colt had a strange plastic paddle sticking out from the side of the steering wheel. It featured markings indicating positions for Reverse, Park, Drive, Drive with more oomph to go up unsealed mountain roads (not that you are encouraged to do that in a hire car) and so on. An automatic, I deduced. But it also had three foot pedals. All automatics I'd ever encountered had just two foot pedals, the brake and the gas. They didn't need a third pedal, usually the clutch in manual cars. So what was the Colt's third pedal for?

Various options went through my mind. Ejector seat? Machine guns? Self destruct? (Yes, I have probably seen too many *James Bond* movies in my time). I decided to ignore it and try to drive back to the hire-car office using what I assumed were the brake and the gas. But the Colt wasn't having any of that and just sat there beeping angrily whatever I did. (The next couple of weeks were to teach me that this was the standard response of the Colt to any action at all by its driver). Eventually I had to leave the wretched machine and trudge back to the office, carless and wet, to seek advice.

The car hire man made a prodigious effort not to laugh as I told him of my predicament and even volunteered to fetch the car himself before giving me a quick driving lesson. This may, of course, have been a ploy to allow him some time to giggle alone. His instruction revealed that the mysterious third foot pedal was what I would call the handbrake, the one that stops your car hurtling backwards down hills under the influence of gravity while you are away. Only now the handbrake was a footbrake. But not THE footbrake, the one you use to prevent you flattening errant sheep as you drive along country roads. I'm glad that's clear.

The pantomime with the hire car had convinced THB that perhaps she would not be driving on the South Island after all. So I was behind the wheel again as we set off for Nelson.

A choice of two routes presented itself for first part of our journey, Picton to Havelock. It was either along the winding Queen Charlotte Drive, a back road hugging the coast and promising stunning views over the Marlborough Sounds, or a longer U shaped diversion through Blenheim (rather harshly described as devoid of either tourist attractions of charm in our guide book) and Renwick on State Highways 1, 63 and 6. THB selected the latter, rough and winding roads being something she thought she could not sanction in her queasy, post boat trip, state. Knowing who would get the job of cleaning up the Colt if her breakfast did decide to make an unscheduled reappearance, I agreed.

So we spurned scenic views and were rewarded with... scenic views. In New Zealand you can't get away from them. The diversion to Blenheim and Renwick took us through wine country, lush countryside with signs offering vineyard tours or wine tastings at every turn eventually giving way to rolling hills and distant mountains punctuated by the occasional tranquil hamlet. Perhaps hamlet is too grand a word to describe a handful of wooden houses huddled beneath forested hills. Maybe 'bend in the road' would fit the bill better.

We stopped at one such place, Waikikamukau I think it was called, to capture on film (well on memory card) the tranquil beauty of low clouds skulking like naughty schoolchildren in 'greens of all hues' hills. Two girls watched in obvious puzzlement, scanning the horizon to see what we had seen (a two headed sheep or alien spacecraft maybe) then collapsed in fits of giggles when they realised there was nothing there apart from the view. A view they had seen every day of their lives and would leave behind without a thought as soon as they could for the bright lights of Picton and beyond.

Havelock was slightly bigger than Waikikamukau, as befits a place that styles itself 'The Green-lipped Mussel Capital of the World'. No false modesty here, not just 'Capital of New Zealand' but 'Capital of the World'. We spent a short time there (for that's all it took) stretching our legs and searching for a giant green-lipped mussel to rival Ohakune's carrot. Sadly we didn't find one. Instead, as we made our way down State Highway 6 to Nelson (Not Napier), we contented ourselves with speculating as to how the mussels came to have green lips. A predilection for munching seaweed or sipping lime juice, a tendency for the mussel's lips to be the last part to ripen and a secret conspiracy between the local tourist office and a paint manufacturer and were some of the less outlandish theories we came up with.

State Highway 6 passed through Canvastown, a historic gold mining town where miners used to pitch their tents, then Pelorus Bridge and Rai Valley, where modern day campers and hikers pitch their tents. We stopped at a dairy, a roadside shop that opens every day and sells everything, for a midday steak and cheese pie, which we decided to eat al fresco. There was silence as we munched except for the distant baa of a sheep, the approaching baa of a sheep, the close up baa of a sheep, then finally the close up baa of many sheep. We had become an attraction in our own right. I can only guess as to what the creatures were saying...

"Hey look Woolma, what are they eating?"

"It's soft and brown inside."

"I can only think of one thing that's soft and brown and I wouldn't eat that."

"Humans are so disgusting. Baa baa ric even."

From Rai Valley it was on through beautiful mountain forest, past Gentle Annie (a wonderfully named peak) and down the coast towards Nelson. As we approached the city I explained to THB how American country singer Willie Nelson had visited New Zealand on tour and impressed the locals so much that they named a town after him. She almost believed me until I went on to suggest that Queenstown had acquired its name in a similar way after a concert by Freddie Mercury, Brain May, Roger Taylor and John Deacon.

In truth Nelson is named after Admiral Lord Nelson, famous for his victory at the Battle of Trafalgar in 1805 and for the apocryphal dying words, "Kiss me, Hardy." His actual final words, whispered as he lay thirsty, hot and in pain, dying from a sniper's shot, were "Drink, drink! Fan, fan! Rub, rub!" By a strange coincidence those were also my words to THB after completing a long tramp in sunny Abel Tasman National Park the following day. More of that in the next chapter.

For those of you still worrying over the 'KiwiSpeak' phrases I listed earlier on, it is time to worry no longer. Here are the translations. For those of you who had forgotten all about them, its still worth giving the translations a look. They may save you a long and frustrating search for the beautiful bend in the road named Waikikamukau on a future trip to New Zealand.

Greasies	Fish and chips.
Hottie	Hot water bottle. Deduct a point if you said "attractive person".
Judder bar	Speed bump.
Savs and Pavs	Saveloys and Pavlova. Typical Kiwi party fare along with endless supplies of piss (beer).
Wop-wops	An out of the way place, the back end of beyond.
Hollywood	A faked sporting injury.
Scroggin	Trail mix made of nuts, raisins, more nuts, more raisins.
Scarfie	University student.
Cocky	Farmer.
Fitter and Turner	A bad cook, who fits food into pots and turns it to shit. (My personal favourite phrase, being one myself).
Long Drop	An outdoor toilet, basically a shack over a hole in the ground, often minus the shack.
Piker	A person not tough enough to get going, when the going gets tough.
Mountain Oysters	Lamb's testicles.
Other Side	Australia, as in the other side of the water. Deduct a point for anything vaguely psychic.
Tinbum	A lucky person.
Waikikamukau	Not a real town but a generic Kiwi term for a back end of beyond place. It is pronounced "Why kick a moo cow?"

You'll be stoked if you knew more than half that lot, mate. Piece of piss, eh? If you didn't, then don't pack a sad. She'll be all right. I was only joking about the 'KiwiSpeak' test to get into New Zealand. They'll let you in even though, lets face it, you couldn't see the road to the dunny if it had red flags on it. I'm a bit of dag, eh?

Dunny	A toilet.

9: NELSON

Knob Jokes And Wearable Art

Nelson is the sunniest place in New Zealand. That's in terms of sunshine hours, reputedly 2500 each year, rather than sunshine intensity. Some other proud, if somewhat frazzled, conurbation probably lays claim to the intensity crown. But what use is sunshine without beaches? Nelson has those too, sand stretching into the distance with hardly another soul in sight. Before I sound too much like a holiday brochure I should point out that there is also wind. A good deal of it in our three day experience. Hence the lack of souls on the beach.

Our hotel, the *Rutherford*, shared its name with New Zealand's Nobel prize winning chemist Ernest Rutherford, born in Brightwater just 20 kilometres away. As THB and I approached from its rear it looked rather boxy and uninteresting but this impression was soon corrected by a modern glass front, a spacious, marble lobby and a free room upgrade. That's the way to persuade a writer not to bad mouth your establishment.

The *Rutherford* nestled in Trafalgar Square, a quiet leafy oasis compared to its tourist, traffic and pigeon packed namesake in London. The square didn't feature a stone column with a statue of Nelson on top but rather a cathedral with an unconventional tower, one that looked more like the scaffolding erected at the start of building project than the finished article when the scaffolding is taken down. You might think that that Nelson's cathedral, set on a hill in beautiful grounds, was enough of a tourist attraction for one small square, but you'd be wrong. There was another draw, especially attractive to Hobbit botherers.

"Jens Hansen!" shouted THB excitedly, not more than a handful of steps away from the hotel as we set off on a quest for an evening meal. Three questions sprang immediately to mind.

(1) Who was Jens Hansen?
I assumed he was connected in some way to a certain film series you may have heard of with an aristocrat and finger furniture in its title. Maybe he played a bit part like 'Orc who

met a sticky end at the point of a Legolas arrow'. That would narrow it down to a few hundred people.
(2) Where was Jens Hansen?
I scanned the square for a gentleman with a Germanic look besieged by Hobbit botherers and exercising his autograph signing hand, but there was none. There was no-one else to be seen at all apart from two un-Jens-like women window shopping at a goldsmith's.
(3) Would THB provide the answers to questions (1) and (2)?
In the case of (1), yes. In the case of (2), no. But as it turned out, it didn't really matter about (2).

"He made the ring," THB explained.
"Oh. You mean he played Sauron," I said, paddling the shallow depths of my *Lord of the Rings* knowledge.
"No. In real life, he made the ring. He's a goldsmith."
Actually Jens and his son Thorkild designed and made over forty rings suitable for different sized fingers and different types of shot. There was even an eight inch diameter one, made from steel then gold plated, featured in the series' prologue. This we read on a poster displayed in the shop's window. The same poster also tempted passing Hobbit botherers (or 'discerning individuals' as they were described) with the chance to possess their own replica ring, crafted to Jens and Thorkild's original design. There was no mention of whether the precious item would be suffused with evil, designed to gradually corrupt its owner, sapping their spirit and wasting their body, as the one in the movies did. Somehow I doubted it, but THB, imagination in overdrive as befits a writer of fiction, wasn't willing to take the chance. Together we discerned that it was time to leave the shop and find somewhere to eat.
The one disappointment of our trip to New Zealand up until Nelson had been the food. Don't get me wrong, our meals hadn't exactly been terrible, just a little bland and unadventurous, with the glorious exceptions of the hangi and Mission Bay chowder. In Nelson and nearby Richmond we had no such problems, enjoying some of the best Thai, Mexican and Italian food we had ever tasted (not all in the one night). Still nothing typically Kiwi though. Do they really export ALL the lamb?

Nelson is surrounded by National Parks and Forest Parks in the same way that Orlando Bloom is surrounded by teenage girls whenever he appears in public. The difference is that the parks are generally quiet and peaceful and the teenage girls aren't. To the west of Nelson are New Zealand's smallest and largest National Parks, Abel Tasman and the giant Karurangi respectively, to the east Mount Richmond Forest Park and to the south Nelson Lakes National Park. The pedants among you may shout "Ha! That's not surrounded. What about north?" Well north of Nelson is Warawara Forest, 650 or so kilometres away on the North Island with a lot of Tasman Sea in between, but it is north. "Ha! Don't get picky with me."

THB's yellow eye survey of our road atlas, now customary in any new town, revealed three filming locations within excursion distance of Nelson, labelled Eregion Hills, Chetwood Forest and Dimrill Dale in *Lord of the Rings* speak. Except for Eregion Hills these were rugged, out of the way places used for arty shots of characters travelling from somewhere where interesting stuff had just happened to somewhere else where interesting stuff was about to happen. Eregion Hills, on the other hand, was a rugged, out of the way place where interesting stuff did happen, Frodo was caught by the Nazgul on Weathertop. Sounds painful eh?

Beside the Chetwood Forest yellow eye, on the fringes of Abel Tasman National Park, lurked an undulating orange snake, indicating an unpaved road. Eregion Hills and Dimrill Dale, both in Karurangi National Park, had no such serpentine neighbours, suggesting that very long tramps or helicopter hire would be required to visit them. Decision made. It was off to Abel Tasman National Park on our first full day in the Nelson area.

Abel Tasman National Park covers a piece of headland jutting out between Golden Bay and Tasman Bay to the north-west of Nelson. It is reached by a road in the shape of a left handed tick, skirting the bottom of Tasman Bay and passing a collection of difficult to resist distractions in the form of picturesque islands and beaches on the way. Our journey along this thoroughfare was memorable for longest, most mind numbingly straight piece of tarmac we'd ever encountered. THB and I could have tied the steering wheel in place, placed a brick on the gas pedal and retired to the back seat for a while to enjoy a picnic (or some other form of entertainment) in perfect safety. I doubt the car's insurers would have been happy though.

No vehicles are allowed in the National Park itself. The idea is that you leave you car at one of its extremities and go tramping or kayaking. Alternatively, if you are short of time or just plain lazy, you catch one of the water taxis which ply their trade between sandy coves along the coastal path. Although the lazy category was made for us, we tramped. There is no arguing with THB's wariness of waterborne transport.

We parked the car at the southern end of the coastal track, beside the Park Café and several empty tour buses, then began a stroll across the Marahau Estuary, alternate stretches of sand and boardwalk beneath our feet and cheery greetings from fellow trampers (coming the other way and so nearing the end of their journey) in our ears. One group, a man and woman with several trailing children and an infant in a pushchair, expanded on the theme of a simple hello with, "Have you seen a hat?" The infant's headgear had blown away and the concerned parents were trying to retrieve it. In whimsical mood (unusual, but the sun was out and I was on holiday) I toyed with the answer, "Yes. It's one of those cloth things you put on your head isn't it?" but THB got in first with a simple, "No, sorry." Just as well really, we were outnumbered.

On the far side of the estuary an information board marked the entrance to the park proper. Underneath the park's name it showed pictures of a stick man striding purposefully left, a stick man with a rucksack striding purposefully left behind him, a stick man on a bicycle crossed out, a camp fire crossed out and a dog crossed out. After some deliberation THB and I decided this meant that if you chased a man into the park because he had stolen your bicycle, set fire to it and then set his dog on you, all of which he wasn't really allowed to do, you should make sure that you were carrying a something large to hit him with in your rucksack.

The path hugged the undulating coast, shaded by kunuka and fuchsia trees which occasionally parted to reveal the green humps of Fisherman and Adele Islands and beyond them, across the sparkling blue water of Tasman Bay, grey mountains capped with snow. On the side away from the sea, cascading hills were covered by bush in deep-pile emerald green. The path wound alternately out around headlands then back into rocky coves each boasting its own secluded beach complete with fallen tree, bleached white by the sun, to be used by weary trampers as a seat during rest stops.

The bleached tree was a standard feature of beaches on the South Island, always artistically placed to offer the perfect snapshot when surveying it or the perfect view when resting your backside upon it. A government aesthete must be employed to tour the country's beaches to make sure all the trees are placed correctly. That man, or woman, has an enviable job.

Surprisingly few of our fellow trampers joined us for stops at Porter's Beach, Stu's Lookout, Tinline Bay and Guilbert Point. I like to think that it was not the sweat that I had worked up during our hike that kept them from joining us but the grim determination to keep to a schedule forced by the water taxi timetable. The local bird life seemed to be happy to spend time in our company though, a succession of brightly coloured number twos, threes and fours on the Gisby scale flitting in and out of the trees.

I can report that birds from New Zealand (flying variety) are as dim as their British cousins when it comes to encountering humans walking along a path. They land a few metres in front of you, get worried as you approach, hop a few metres further down the path away from you to safety, get worried as you approach again, hop a few metres away from you again, and so on. It never occurs to them to hop to one side instead and let you walk past them.

Mind you, imagine the scene when God is dolling out gifts to all the different creatures on Earth and asks the birds, "Would you like to be able to soar high in the sky and shit on every other animal below you if the mood takes you, or would you like a brain that lets you to work out the best direction to hop in?" I'm not so sure they made the wrong choice.

After a couple of hours of tramping we turned around somewhere between Guilbert Point and Appletree Bay about half way to the first major overnight stop for serious trampers, Anchorage. I had secretly hoped to be able to complete the advertised four hour hike to Anchorage, by which time THB would have been sufficiently worn out for a water taxi ride back to Marahau to seem attractive, but she was one step ahead. No change there then. With hindsight I have to admit that four hours for a walk to Alaska did seem a tad optimistic.

We arrived back at the car park, hot and weary, longing to sit back and savour the air conditioning of the Colt. Unfortunately for us said vehicle had other ideas. Starved of attention while we had been away tramping, abandoned by its erstwhile tour bus companions and left in the sun, it had decided to do exactly what a fractious two year old would do. It threw a tantrum.

As THB and I got in, sat down and turned the key in the ignition we were greeted by a plaintive cry.

"Beep! Beep! Beep!"

Fair enough, the driver's door was still open. I closed it.

"Beep! Beep! Beep!"

I didn't have my seatbelt on. Not that I thought I needed a seat belt to sit in a car park and (hopefully sometime before I died) enjoy my vehicle's air conditioning. But I humoured the whinging Colt and pulled the seat belt around me.

"Beep! Beep! Beep!"

Oh all right. I put it on properly.

"Beep! Beep! Beep!"

Now it had me flummoxed. What was its problem? I decided the only thing to do was to get out of the car and start the whole getting in process again, this time closing the doors and belting up before trying to turn the key in the ignition. THB and I did exactly that and the key would not turn. I tried gentle wiggling, two handed twisting, abject pleading, forceful swearing and various combinations of the four, all to no avail. It would not budge. I was on the verge of disappearing into the bush to return with a sturdy branch to give the useless heap of scrap a good thrashing (in the fashion of Basil Fawlty) when THB coaxed me off to the Park Café for a calming bowl of pumpkin and kumara (and carrot) soup. When we returned to the car it worked without a hitch, obviously happy that it had made its point.

The tantrum was to be repeated twice more during our tour of the South Island, each time ending with the Colt refusing to start. Two theories come to mind as to why this might have happened.

(1) It was some sort of security feature designed to stop owners losing their precious Mitsubishi Colt to thieves.

(2) It was some sort of security feature designed to stop owners getting rid of their wretched Mitsubishi Colt (and so gaining relief from its incessant nannying beep) by allowing the thing to be stolen.

My favourite was (2).

After Abel Tasman we continued north along State Highway 60 up onto Takaka Hill to search out the location used for Chetwood Forest in the *Lord of the Rings* movies and so give THB her fix for the day. Every few minutes we stopped to enjoy a spectacular view over tree topped hills and green patchwork fields towards the town of Motueka and across Tasman Bay to those distant snow capped mountains once more. Then we climbed a little higher and the scenery became even more spectacular, if a little further away.

As we approached the top of the hill the landscape grew rockier, grass edging out bushes and trees as the predominant form of vegetation. We passed a sign for the Ngarua Caves then turned right along an unsealed gravel road, or metal road as the Kiwis call it, towards the location indicated on our road atlas. Even now we are unsure whether we actually found the right place. We didn't know where Chetwood Forest featured in the movies (actually it's in between Bree and Rivendell in *The Fellowship of the Ring*) so couldn't really search out the precise spot where filming took place. It was worth the trip though, not only for the wonderful mountain views but also for the satisfaction of hearing the regular clunk of stone on Colt bodywork. As it turned out there was another metal road leading down to the Ngarua Caves from State Highway 60, so we paid them a visit too on the way back to Nelson, just to show the Colt who was really in charge.

No-one knows who first discovered the Ngarua Caves, but in an area dotted with sinkholes it is not difficult to imagine a possible scenario. It is the late nineteenth century and a man is out walking his pet kiwi on a cold winter's evening. In a vain effort to keep warm he stamps his feet. A few seconds later he finds himself underground examining newly acquired bruises by the meagre light filtering down from a tiny circle far above his head. "How lucky I am," he thinks, "that I have a bird as a pet. A bird that can fly out of this hole and summon help." Then he thinks some more. "Oh bugger!"

Early visitors to the caves interpreted the tourist code 'take nothing but pictures, leave nothing but footprints' rather idiosyncratically as 'take nothing but stalactites and moa bones, leave nothing but your name carved in the wall'. To prevent irrevocable damage, they were closed from 1905 to 1970 (the caves, not the visitors) when walkways and lighting were installed and guided tours began.

Our tour, some thirty five years later, was the last of the day. It was conducted by a man enthusiastic about the history of the caves, more enthusiastic about the archaeological remains to be found within by Indiana Jones wannabes (he was one) and extremely enthusiastic about the meal awaiting him at the tour's end. As four of us took photographs of the wonderful limestone curtains and phalluses of all shapes and sizes hanging from the cave roof (out of reach of light fingered early visitors) he took the cameraless spouses aside and whispered a heartfelt "Don't worry. They'll get fed up soon."

THB was enticed into the caves by a weatherworn still from *The Fellowship of the Ring* on a board at the end of the metal road leading down to the entrance. Don't get fooled by that. The caves are spectacular in their own right, but have no discernable connection to *Lord of the Rings* apart from the fact that they are in New Zealand and (just to remind you in case you nodded off at a vital moment while reading this epic) the *Lord of the Rings* movies were filmed in that fine country.

Having spent an hour or so admiring phallic limestone formations we continued the theme as we drove back into Nelson by following a roadside sign pointing the way to Paddy's Knob. How could we resist? It turned out to be a hill with a lookout point at the top offering not even the most tenuous anatomical connection to a male of Irish descent. (If you can't work out why there should be such a connection and you are over eighteen try typing knob into an internet search engine. If you are under eighteen you have probably already done that and have moved on to imagining conversations like, "Have you seen Paddy's Knob?" "Yes. He should get his trousers mended.") Before you pass judgement on the Kiwis for their provocative use of the word knob to describe a rise in the land (Paddy's Knob is far from being an isolated incident) you should consider what such a geographical feature might be called in Britain. Mount Paddy is hardly any better is it?

Enough of knob jokes. It's now time for some culture.

Rio de Janiero is famous for Carnivale, New Orleans for Mardi Gras and Nelson for WOW, the World of Wearable Arts Festival, which culminates in an awards show each September where garments ranging from the bizarre to the even more bizarre, each created especially for the occasion, are paraded on stage and judged in a variety of categories. The beauty of the competition is that anyone can enter as long as they have a sufficiently inventive mind and a talent for needlework, collage, origami, structural engineering or welding depending on the material selected for the garment and the strength of the model's shoulders destined to bear it.

The World of Wearable Art and Collectable Cars Museum is well worth a visit to marvel at some of the most outrageous and most successful entries over the event's seventeen year history, even though it is located in Quarantine Road. THB and I survived a visit without catching anything untoward. The exhibition gets a bit po-faced at times, when it tries to drag a deep spiritual meaning kicking and screaming from each design, but fortunately the idea that the whole thing is just a bit of fun refuses to lie down for very long.

I went in expecting to endure the Wearable Art exhibits and enjoy the collectable cars but it turned out to be the other way around. What use is standing around and looking at a classic car? You want to get in and marvel at how uncomfortable its seats are, how unwieldy its controls are and how daft it is that you'd still trade its great grandchild sitting on your drive (and possibly your own great grandchildren too) to own it. Well I do anyway. There were too many forbidding rope barriers at the Collectable Cars Museum for my liking.

THB went in expecting to endure the collectable cars and enjoy the Wearable Art exhibits but in the end it was another facet of the museum that she would remember most. Are you thinking that there must have been a *Lord of the Rings* connection? Got it in one!

In the sort of unprepossessing corner of the museum's entrance hall usually reserved for a rubbish bin we discovered a polished marble cube balanced on a metal stool. Upon the cube sat a roughly hewn chunk of grey rock, the stage for a giant gold (plated) ring. It was the Jens Hansen original used in the prologue of the *Lord of the Rings* movies, stealing into the World of Wearable Art with, I feel, somewhat dubious credentials. Although certainly an example of the metalworker's art, at eight inches in diameter it isn't wearable except by an elephant maybe. Perhaps that is the loophole. It isn't the World of Humanly Wearable Arts.

Since there was no-one else interested in the artefact and no "keep off" signs we tried slipping our arms through its centre to see if we were transported into a nightmarish world where fearsome characters lurked ready to do us harm. After all that is what happened to anyone foolish enough to don the ring in the movies. And so we were...

THB was greeted by Orlando Bloom as Legolas who wanted her to go with him Into The West. That wouldn't be a nightmare for THB you might think (especially if you are young and female) but remember the preferred mode of transport of the Elves is a boat. Aaaargh!

I was greeted by Jack Peterson. "I hiv sin the future," he said. "You hiv still to visit the Pullars of the Kings, Ithillien, Amon Hen, Ford of Bruinen, Pelennor Fields, Edoras," there were many more places on his list, "bifore you cin live this country." Aaaargh!

THB and I being suckers for exotic animals, we couldn't contemplate leaving Nelson without a visit to Natureland, set in a stand of refreshingly shady trees beside Tahunanui Beach. It turned out to be more of a petting zoo with pretensions than the grand sounding 'Zoological Park' we'd seen advertised but it did pass my test of a REAL zoo, the presence of a penguin. Natureland featured just the one, in temporary residence while recovering from illness. It also boasted George, the most clearly spoken cockatoo we'd ever encountered (Kiwi and avian accents seemingly very compatible), a host of hungry ducks waddling in our wake wherever we went and, the star of the show, the tuatara.

A tuatara grows up to 50 or 60 centimetres in length and has a lizard like head, a lizard like body and a lizard like tail. Normally such features are a fairly good indication that a creature is, in fact, a lizard but this does not work with the tuatara. "If it isn't a lizard, what is it?" you might be tempted to enquire. In fact it is the unique survivor of a group of reptiles that wandered around at the time of the dinosaurs, now known as *Sphenodontia* having been renamed from *Rhynchocephalia* at the time of the tuatara'a discovery. You did ask.

Information boards proclaimed that this living fossil, only found in New Zealand, had not changed for 225 million years. That being so, its clothes must really smell, explaining the need for another claim to fame, its ability to hold its breath for nearly an hour at a time. The tuatara has a third eye used to absorb ultra violet light when it is young but it does not have a penis. Personally that is not a trade I would be prepared to make.

I'm sure that the breath holding, extra eyed, non lizard, memberless nature of the tuatara will lodge in my brain ready for retrieval at some later date in response to a general knowledge quiz question. It will probably find space alongside the fact that the largest otter in the world is about the size of Kylie Minogue. Thank you Portsmouth Sea Life Centre for ensuring that while most men think of something else when Kylie is mentioned, I think of otters.

As we set off from the *Rutherford* hotel on the morning of our third day in Nelson, bursting with the best cooked breakfast so far encountered on our trip (the sausages tasted like sausages), we passed South Street, a time capsule of sixteen wooden working class cottages built in the 1860s and still inhabited today. The effect of a trip back in time was only slightly spoilt by parked cars and an abundance of green wheelie bins. It must have been rubbish collection day. Then it was off down State Highway 6 towards Nelson Lakes National Park, Murchison and finally Greymouth.

Nelson Lakes National Park is a region of mountains, deep valleys gauged by long departed glaciers and, of course, water features such as Lake Rotoroa (not to be confused with farty smelling Rotorua) and Lake Rotoiti without which the place would have to be renamed Nelson Lacks. Surprisingly these lakes seem to spurn the sort of epithets (biggest, deepest, widest, wettest) so beloved by other members of the inland expanse of water club such as Taupo and Te Anau. The nearest Rotoroa and Rotoiti got to boastfulness was the rather pathetic 'largest lakes in the area' spotted on an information board. 'Most shaped like a map of South America' for Rotoiti and 'Most phallic' for Rotoroa are my alternative and, dare I say, more tourist friendly suggestions. If eventually adopted, a free trip to New Zealand for the author and his wife for the naming ceremony would be much appreciated.

Eagerly subjecting the Colt to another unsealed road, on the basis that we'd almost certainly lost our deposit on the wretched thing already, we made our way to the northernmost tip of Lake Rotoroa for a brief taste of the Nelson Lakes experience. There we found a lonely wooden shelter and a life size carving of a Maori warrior guarding a path to the water's edge. The shelter was adorned by posters warning about the dangers of giardia.

Contrary to my initial thoughts, giardia is neither an airport in New York nor the Irish police force (both of which some might say should carry a warning) but a parasite that can be picked up in New Zealand's wilder places by drinking water which has been contaminated as a result of itinerant wildlife or trampers failing to follow instructions on how to defecate in the bushes responsibly. It wallows happily in your intestine for a week or so then rewards your hospitality with generous gifts such as stomach cramps, nausea and diarrhoea, the latter encouraging you to defecate irresponsibly yourself and so further the beastie's travels.

The lake itself was an eerie sight, nestling between ranges of thickly forested mountains bathed in bright sunshine to our right and showered in torrential rain from brooding grey clouds to our left. We watched as its surface became increasingly rippled by a stiffening breeze as the storm edged towards us, the only people on the shore. I suspect everyone else had read the weather forecast.

"Shall we go now?" THB asked, eying the approaching clouds and sheets of precipitation. I was preoccupied, photographing the sort of wooden landing stage from which unknown actresses are dragged kicking and screaming by sea monsters in horror movies. "Its going to rain," she pointed out. I was now after the perfect shot of a pair of oystercatchers on the lake shore. "Can I have the car keys?" was her final gambit. As a result THB stayed dry while I got soaked. The photos were good though.

From Lake Rotoroa we followed State Highway 6 through Murchison and the picturesque Buller River gorge, a rich prospecting area until the easy gold became exhausted. Now it is tramping, rafting, kayaking and fishing country, offering outdoorsy tourists the chance to become exhausted instead. We intended to continue to Westport, then down the coast past the famed pancake rocks at Punakaiki (more of them later) but the rain, pouring incessantly since Rotoroa, drained our enthusiasm for getting out and amongst more scenery that day, so we took the more direct road through Reefton to our overnight stop, Greymouth, instead.

The Reefton route is also the one favoured by the railway between Westport and Greymouth, the tracks meandering along beside the road, switching sides now and again to confront the unwary tourist with a succession of level crossings. I was that unwary tourist.

In Britain, where I am used to driving, level crossings have bells which sound, lights which flash and barriers which descend to stop all but the most determined motorists from venturing into the path of an oncoming train. In New Zealand there is none of that, just unguarded railway tracks crossing the road. In my mind there were two possible strategies for dealing with this:

(1) Approach the crossing slowly, carefully looking out for trains in both directions, as far as overgrown foliage and buildings would allow.
(2) Step on the gas and take your chance, since more speed means less time actually on the crossing, so less time in danger.

My personal method was a nod towards (1) at first, then an engine roaring, wheel spinning, THB scaring, full blown dose of (2) until safely across the tracks.

We never actually encountered a train during one of these procedures but passed a couple, while driving well within the speed limit, as they trundled along between crossings. Having witnessed their sedate 'we'll get there eventually' pace, we realised that (2) was probably unnecessary. A family picnicking on the railway lines and sighting a train would probably have time to pack away their goodies, fold the cloth, unfold it and fold it again properly, then beat a leisurely retreat all before it finally reached them. Even if it hit a tardy picknicker it probably wouldn't have enough momentum to do any damage. Despite that, I didn't ever stop (2)ing. It was too much fun.

As we followed the Grey River (or Mawheraui to give it its less drab Maori name) to the coast, the rain finally ceased, although the sky remained determinedly overcast. Maybe Greymouth wouldn't turn out to be "The West Coast's most dispiriting town," as our guide book described it. Maybe our travel agent in Britain had been wrong to beg us to drive from Nelson to Fox Glacier in one day without an overnight rest in Greymouth. Maybe we should have listened to people who knew what they were talking about.

10: GREYMOUTH

New Zealand's G-Spot

The northern hemisphere's largest island was discovered by a Viking named Gunnbjörn Ulf-Krakuson around 930 AD when he was blown off course while travelling between Norway and Iceland. (Bear with me, this is relevant). He proudly named the land Gunnbjarnarsker, or Gunnbjörn's Skerries, a mouthful of a moniker which clung tenaciously to the land for fifty or so years until Erik the Red decided it was ripe for colonisation. But how could Erik persuade people to travel to a frozen land lacking even the saving grace of penguins? His masterstroke was to ditch Gunnbjarnarsker in favour of Greenland, reasoning that "men would be more likely to be drawn there if it had an attractive name."

Why am I telling this tale? I was just thinking that if dreary sounding Greymouth had boasted a man of Erik's vision and mendacity in its early days it might now be a thriving tourist destination known as Sunnybeach or Rainingbeer. Instead it was named after a river named after Governor George Grey and never looked forward. It's lucky that the eponymous governor wasn't called George Footand. The honest but perhaps a little unimaginative townspeople of the time would undoubtedly have called their home Footandmouth.

Our home for one night was to be the *Kingsgate Hotel*, which offered us a friendly welcome in what seemed to be a recently refurbished reception area and accommodation in what seemed to be an unrefurbished since the time of George Grey, bedroom. Outside the door a rectangle had been cut into the carpet, bordered with wooden batten, then filled with gravel. We guessed it was an attempt at something different decor-wise, and the hotel is to be applauded for that, but it was still a little disconcerting to emerge from our room and find what looked like a meticulously tended grave outside the door.

The morbid effect was somewhat lessened by the presence of a half inflated (or half deflated if you are a pessimist by nature) football set upon the gravel. At first THB and I thought it was a child's toy discarded by one of our neighbours, but it remained in exactly the same place throughout our stay. Surely the staff would have cleared away an unwanted plaything? Finally we decided it had to be art. Remember we had been to WOW in Nelson just the previous day. We were ready to believe anything was art.

Having arrived in the late afternoon THB and I set off from the *Kingsgate* around five o'clock in an attempt to sample as many of Greymouth's delights as possible before dinner. We saw the flood defences. We saw the station. We saw a couple of blocks of single storey shops either about to close for the evening or closed long ago for ever. And that was it. At five-fifteen we were ready to eat.

Sadly for us, Greymouth wasn't quite ready to provide us with food at so early an hour. We were caught in the lull between shop closing and eatery opening, presumably provided to allow hedonistic tourists a few minutes to catch their breath. THB and I caught ours searching for Greymouth's cinema and hoping that something vaguely interesting was showing that evening. The search was helped by a smiling local who pointed east along Mackay Street and offered the advice, "Check your eyesight," when asked for directions. We found the pointing useful but the words unnecessarily harsh until we reached our destination, "next to the *i*-site" (or tourist information office) and realised what our guide had actually said.

The film on offer was *My House in Umbria* an art house movie about the relationships which develop between a rag bag of characters thrown together after a terrorist attack. Not immediately attractive but the alternative was an evening on the streets of Greymouth in the drizzle. We tried to book two tickets in case they sold out.

"It's not on until eight o'clock," the woman manning (or should that be womanning?) the box office advised.

"That's okay, we want seats for the eight o'clock performance."

"You'll be all right if you come back at seven forty-five," she said, totally failing to grasp the concept of advance booking.

We must have looked perplexed because she added, "Don't worry. There are hundreds of seats and there will only be thirty people watching the film."

And there were. Exactly thirty, including us and three backpackers with smelly feet in the row before us. I counted during a slow(er) part of the movie. The backpackers had removed their shoes to luxuriate in two hours of warmth acquired for the price of a cinema ticket and were hatching plans to remain where they were all night rather than freezing in their hostel. The *Kingsgate* might have had its foibles but at least it was warm. Bathroom excluded.

But I'm getting ahead of myself. The movie was preceded by dinner in a restaurant, well more of a bar that did food really, chosen above its culinary rivals on the basis of three carefully considered criteria.

(1) It was the first eating establishment we came to.
(2) It was open.
(3) We were hungry.

Another point of note was that it had lamb on the menu, but we wiped that off before ordering.

Faithful to my national stereotype, I chose a roast dinner. (There is some sort of recessive gene in the make up of an Englishman that expresses itself in the form of fierce cravings for meat and two veg. when on foreign soil. Hence the proliferation of cafés named after English football teams in Spanish holiday resorts, offering piping hot roasts beneath the midday sun. Really unfortunate Englishmen get the tomato ketchup gene as well).

I was presented with a delicious slab of lamb accompanied by vegetables that could be eaten through a straw. I know I'm English, but even in England the 'boil vegetables until khaki' school of food preparation has been in decline since the 1970s. I forgave the microwave operator, or chef as he probably styled himself, knowing that in all likelihood the unfortunate individual hadn't got long to live. There were no carrots on my plate. The boys from Ohakune would be on their way already with big sticks and possibly a horse's head.

In case my words, so far, have given you the impression that Greymouth has nothing to offer visiting tourists, apart from ample opportunity to whinge and a greater appreciation of other places they visit, I thought I would list the ten best things about the town to try to redress the balance. Sadly, in consultation with THB, I could only come up with nine, possibly because we only stayed in Greymouth for one night. Hey! We only stayed for one night. That makes ten.

(1) Greymouth lies at the end of the scenic four and a half hour Tranz-Alpine rail journey from Christchurch through Arthur's Pass. Strangely the timetable is arranged to allow people to get

out of Christchurch for the day to visit Greymouth, rather than to get out of Greymouth for the day to visit Christchurch. I would have thought that the demand would have been the other way around.

(2) Greymouth claims to be the biggest town on the South Island's West Coast, a boast along the same lines as 'tallest tree in a bonsai forest'. It also styles itself as 'The Heart of the Coast' on carrier bags dispensed by the *i*-site, picturing smiling tourists beneath a blazing sun. If I compared the town to part of the human body, it wouldn't be the heart. It wouldn't even be the mouth, grey or otherwise. It would be something located at the opposite end of the alimentary canal.

(3) Greymouth is a 'year round' destination. No need to worry when it will rain. There's a sort of apologetic drizzle all the time.

(4) Greymouth is the home of Dragon's Cave through which you can sail on subterranean waters and even down subterranean waterfalls while clinging to a rubber tube. If this adventure had been better advertised while we were in town they might have had a taker. Maybe even two takers, as THB would surely have overcome her fear of water based transport to make sure I didn't journey through the intriguingly named 'love tunnel' without her. I only found out about Dragon's Cave rafting from a website after returning home. It is a site worth visiting simply to see Greymouth described as New Zealand's G-spot.

(5) Greymouth offered the best CD bargain bin we encountered in New Zealand. Although most of its contents seemed to be aimed at the sort of people who consider James Last to be a little bit racy, there was a Meat Loaf album lurking amongst the dross, probably ordered for someone's granny and returned like 'A Bat Out Of Hell' when it was found not to offer cookery tips. Just ten NZ dollars and the Colt's CD player was providing 'Paradise By The Dashboard Light'.

(6) Greymouth comes recommended by none other than Billy Connolly. During his excellent, *World Tour of New Zealand*, he speaks fondly of the town, but if you watch the show carefully you never actually see him leave the seat of his motor tricycle while he's there. His encouraging words were one of the reasons a stop in Greymouth featured on our varied

itinerary. Thanks a lot Billy.

(7) Greymouth features interesting (comparatively speaking) stone statues of a dolphin and a burly fisherman in a sou'wester and waterproofs on top of the defensive wall which protects the town from the ire of the River Grey, presumably sparked by the theft of its name.

(8) Greymouth provided THB and me with the biggest laugh of our whole New Zealand trip. We were walking along the path beside the statues and happened to glance back towards town. A huge banner draped across the upper stories of our hotel proclaimed, "Stay Ten Nights, Get The Eleventh Night Free!" Now that is optimism. "Stay Ten Nights In Greymouth, Get A Free Brain Examination," would be closer to the mark.

(9) Greymouth offers no *Lord of the Rings* filming locations to visit. THB did not see this as a plus point. She scoured our road atlas in search of yellow eyes but found none on the Greymouth page and only one on adjacent pages, that at Franz Josef Glacier further south, labelled 'Lighting of the Beacons'. THB was keen to move on, so on we moved.

Before heading south to our next overnight stop at Fox Glacier we headed forty or so kilometres north to visit the famed Pancake Rocks at Punakaiki, reluctantly forsaken on the trip down to Greymouth from Nelson because of bad weather.

The rocks are limestone formations which resemble columns of stacked pancakes, hence their name. A fenced path meandered amongst them offering impressive views of the stacks themselves and of rocky inlets between them filled with seething white foam. The occasional soaking, courtesy of geyser like spurts of water from blowholes dotted about the site, was an added bonus. THB accomplished some quite prodigious leaps in response to the loud booms, echoes of water meeting rock in caverns far below, which accompanied each shower.

According to a board at the Punakaiki site, no-one knows how the pancake stacks were formed. This is quite surprising since down the coast towards Hokitika there is another board, pointing the way back to Punakaiki, which describes in great detail the laying down of different rock strata and their subsequent erosion by wind, water and spray. Maybe some ancient feud means that that Punakaikians and the Hokitikans don't speak to each other. Or perhaps the Punakaikians should simply get out more.

As a storm that had been threatening all morning finally hit Punakaiki, to the dismay of all except hardened blowhole aficionados (blowholes perform best in bad weather) we began our journey south, along State Highway 6 and back through Greymouth. Then it was straight down the coast to Hokitika for a midday pie, past a string of deserted pebble and driftwood strewn beaches relentlessly pounded by angry waves.

Hokitika seemed a much more upbeat place that its northern neighbour, a clean, bright and busy little town, boasting a large Christmas tree, decorations hanging from lamp posts, an incongruous clock tower in the centre of the main road through town and a tussock lined beach complete with artistically placed fallen tree trunk. Like others we had seen, the trunk was bleached white. I would have added 'by the sun' to the end of that sentence but it is a little difficult to believe that the West Coast ever sees enough sun to accomplish such a task.

Our stop in Hokitika had been prompted by leaflets advertising the presence of the 'National Kiwi Centre' in town. After a short and fruitless search for a large modern purpose built kiwiarium, possibly in the shape of the bird itself (after Ohakune's carrot anything was possible) we came across the 'National Centre' in the back of a shop just off the main street.

It turned out that although there were indeed 'kiwi' inside and the shop was sort of 'central', the word 'national' in the name of the establishment was there more for decoration than anything else. Never mind, 'Two Out Of Three Ain't Bad'. Yes we had been listening to Meat Loaf on the way down from Punakaiki.

Feeling just a little cheated, THB and I paid our entrance fee and wandered into the darkness of the room which housed the kiwi habitat. Details of the establishment's name were quickly forgotten as our eyes became accustomed to the low levels of light and we spotted two number six or sevens on the Gisby scale engaged in what seemed to be a frank exchange of views. We couldn't quite work out whether they were two birds of the same sex not getting along or two birds of opposite sexes, one of which wanted to get along rather more closely than the other one did. In the end they stomped off to opposite ends of the enclosure for a spot of loud and bad-tempered foraging. Rumour had it that there was a third bird to be seen. Clearly it recognised a time to keep a low profile when it saw one.

South of Hokitika, State Highway 6 skirted the Southern Alps, majestic peaks soaring above a grey ribbon of tarmac. At least that's what the road atlas indicated. A view through the Colt's rain spattered windows revealed little more than verdant forest peeping out from beneath sullen grey cloud. We drove through a succession of small settlements including the old gold town of Ross, then Harihari (not populated by shaven headed people in orange robes) and finally Whataroa.

Harihari's claim to fame is that it is the place where Guy Menzies landed on completing the first flight across the Tasman Sea from Australia. He emerged from his plane to fall head first into a swamp accompanied by enthusiastic cheers from assembled locals. Whateroa was the cry from the crowd as Steven Redgrave won his fifth gold medal in successive Olympic Games but is also the only place in New Zealand where Kotuku (White Heron) come to nest.

The smallest conurbation encountered on the road from Hokitika was Pukekura, not even qualifying as a bend in the road since the road through it was straight. It boasted a population of two busy people who ran the Bushman's Centre, featuring displays of New Zealand bush craft, and the wonderfully named Puke Pub, the only place I have ever seen offering Possum Pie for the epicurean delight of patrons. Visitors were assured that to eat a possum was to do New Zealand an environmental favour as these unwelcome Aussie immigrants destroy native forest, endanger native wildlife and spread tuberculosis to cattle and deer. After finding out about the tuberculosis, Possum Pie suddenly didn't seem quite so appetising.

According to our guide book the Bushman's Centre also offered knife-throwing lessons and a giant model of a sand fly (a rival for the Ohakune carrot) to tempt would be passers-by into becoming curious comers-in. Sadly neither seemed to be available on the day of our visit. I suspect that THB would have spurned the opportunity to become a knife thrower's assistant anyway. Especially if I was the thrower. "I'll do anything for love, but I won't do that," would have been her response. After all, she'd been listening to Meat Loaf too.

State Highway 6 finally led us into the village of Franz Josef Glacier, which we passed through with fingers crossed, hoping that the weather might ease the following day so that we could return and actually see something. Then we arrived at our next overnight stop, the pretty (even in the rain) alpinesque village of Fox Glacier and the *Te Weheka Inn*.

New Zealand With a Hobbit Botherer

Matamata: *Conclusive proof that Hobbits drive white vans?*

Mount Ngauruhoe: *Got a ring to destroy? That's the place to go.*

New Zealand With a Hobbit Botherer

Wellington:
Chocolate Fish Café.

Lady Knox Geyser:
After soap flakes applied.

Ngarua Caves:
Never did get fed up.

Christchurch:
Art or giant rubbish bin?

Fox Glacier: *Albert to its old friends.*

Queenstown: *The author and THB try a new sport. Yeah right!*

Beech forest near Glenorchy: *Boromir should have stayed in the boat.*

Deer Park Heights: *A mountain tarn on the way to Helm's Deep.*

Arrowtown: *Where Isildur was attacked by Orcs and lost the ring.*

Milford Sound: *But no sight.*

Niagara Falls: *The New Zealand version.*

Taiaroa Head, Dunedin: *Is that an albatross? No.*

New Zealand With a Hobbit Botherer

Moeraki Boulders: *Marbles anyone?*

Mount Cook National Park: *Move that cloud, someone.*

Lake Pukaki: *A black and white version of my screen saver.*

Mount Sunday: *Edoras, the hillock in the middle of nowhere.*

11: THE GLACIERS

Tears Of The Avalanche Girl

There are three conjectures concerning the origin of the Franz Josef and Fox glaciers, the poetic Maori theory, the pedantic Pakeha (non Maori) theory and the plainly fanciful, "Peter Jackson, who is God, needed a location for filming The Lighting Of The Beacons in *The Return Of The King*, so he created one," theory. At the risk of reawakening an irritating figment of my imagination last encountered on the North Island, I'll concentrate on the first two.

According to the Maori, it is all down to a beautiful girl called Hinehukatere who had a penchant for climbing in the Southern Alps and persuaded her lover, Tawe, to join her one day. As so often happens in tales that begin happily with two young lovers, tragedy followed. Tawe fell to his death and Hinehukatere's floods of tears became the two glaciers, known in Maori as Ka Roimata o Hinehukatere or The Tears of the Avalanche Girl.

How can the Pakeha beat that? Imagine standing in a walk-in freezer with someone piling ice cream on the top of your head. Eventually there comes a point when gravity takes over and lumps of rum 'n' raisin begin to slide down your face. (Keep your mouth closed. This is a serious scientific demonstration, not a free dessert). Now replace your head by a mountain, the ice cream by compacted snow and let the whole thing take place in super slow motion. That's how the glaciers really work.

There is, of course, one way to discover beyond all doubt which of the competing theories is correct. It involves hiking up onto one of the glaciers, preferably with a guide to avoid tumbling down a crevasse, then falling onto your knees and licking the ice. Note that if the ice closest to you has a yellowish or brownish tinge, it is probably best to lick elsewhere.

If the ice tastes fresh, then the Pakeha theory must be right. If it tastes salty (and isn't yellow) then it must have been formed from tears, so hats off to the Maori... unless, of course, a hiking group the previous day spilt the condiments from their picnic. Bugger. Nothing's ever straightforward.

We arrived at the *Te Weheka Inn* in the early evening, grabbed the last parking spot in the bays beneath the main building, and set off to explore our home for the night. The inn was a fairly new addition to the landscape of Fox Glacier (the town) built to a design that mostly screamed 'ski lodge' with the occasional whisper of 'medieval castle' where stone momentarily interrupted timber and glass. The quirky effect was enough to earn the description 'boutique hotel' in literature for Kiwi consumption, a sobriquet which apparently indicates a certain cachet, a certain style and a certain reluctance to let riff-raff check in. It does not, as I initially thought, indicate the presence of a shop selling dodgy sixties fashions. Bearing the no riff-raff rule in mind, THB and I approached the reception desk for our entrance interview with some trepidation.

We needn't have worried. The girl staffing reception was keen to please, completing check in with courteous efficiency and without ever asking win we were living. She then passed us on to a slightly nervous colleague whose job it was to escort us to our room (making sure we used and admired the hotel's lift rather than resorting to the stairs) and then to introduce us personally to every item inside it.

"These are the beds." (For sleeping in).

"These are the windows." (For looking out of. Open curtains first.)

"This is the light." (Press little button and darkness goes away).

"This is the bathroom." (Er... I'm sure you know what to do in there).

If we'd been in the USA we'd have assumed she was killing time before the ceremonial offering of the gratuity, but this was New Zealand, a land where tips are not expected, although recipients tend to be so entertainingly gobsmacked when you make the effort, it's well worth doing so now and again.

The only explanation for the nervousness and painstaking attention to detail of our guide was that she suspected we were hotel inspectors. One thing would clinch it for sure. If we were inspectors we would have to find something wrong with the room to check how the staff dealt with it.

She was just about to launch into...

"This is the ceiling." (For stopping the people in the room above falling on your head).

...when THB ventured, "There are twin beds. Have you got a double room available?" (THB likes there to be a very short distance between her elbow and my ribs when I start snoring).

Struggling to combat mounting panic, our guide tried to call reception, politely asking permission to use the phone in our room. But no-one answered the phone. With visions of hard-earned stars having to be removed from the hotel's advertising material she beat a hasty retreat in search of reinforcements, promising to return in five minutes and urging us to enjoy our (hopefully temporary) room while she was away. We did our best, but it is difficult to fully enjoy a bedroom in just five minutes.

When she returned, we happily exchanged 'twin room with village view' for 'double room with car park view' enjoyed a reprise of the "This is the unidentified stain on the carpet" speech, then set off to explore the village between rain showers.

Fox Glacier township was a place that was 99% geared up to feeding, watering, sleeping and visually stimulating (with natural wonders rather than dancing girls, I hasten to point out) its visitors. Actually THB and I saw no evidence that this figure was not 100%, but presumably there must be a few xenophobic Foxes or Glacierians (if that is what you call people from Fox Glacier) who devote themselves to the West Coast's other speciality areas of timber, cattle and moss. Yes, you did read that correctly. Cattle and moss, not cattle and moos.

Moss deserves a special mention because it seems unlikely, at least to a travelling Londoner, that anyone could make a living selling stuff that lawn owners do their best to exterminate. But West Coast Sphagnum moss, dug by hand from natural swamp land, is special. It has moisture retaining and antibacterial properties which make it sound like a skin cream but, more importantly, act as a first rate medium for plant propagation. It is highly valued, particularly by orchid growers in Japan.

So people do make a living selling stuff that gardeners pay good money to get rid of. And what is more, they sell it back to gardeners. I had always thought that people whose idea of fun was digging and weeding were a perverse lot. Point proven?

Fox Glacier shamed Greymouth not only in terms of the number of eating establishments open in the early evening but also in terms of the length of the queues to enter said establishments. THB and I finally managed to bag a table in a pizzeria from which delicious smells were wafting, having joined a line which looked daunting at first but turned out to consist of just two large parties, both of which spurned the small table which we nabbed. The food was delicious and excellent value for money. Worth its wait in the cold, you might say.

The evening's entertainment, according to my plans, was to feature a visit to Fox Glacier's glow-worm forest. I imagined a romantic walk, hand-in-hand with THB, beneath a thousand pin points of light in the canopy above our heads. Sadly, THB simply imagined having to dodge material falling towards her head from the leaves, never knowing whether the incoming were innocuous water droplets or ravening beasties. (THB regards anything small with more legs than a dog as a ravening beastie. Mind you, she also has her doubts about dogs). Never mind, I still had the Te Anua glow-worms to look forward to. Only three chapters to go now!

Speaking of imaginary beasties, it was that night that my very own chose to make a reappearance.

"This unn hus gut a gist lunge," Jack Peterson pointed out, not very helpfully as I was trying to fall asleep and already in the ideal location for doing this, namely a bed.

"Uh," I replied, with polite disinterest.

"Thuy hiv a tilivision," he continued.

"Uhh."

"Thuy might hive a DVD pliyer..."

"Uhhh."

"...Ind win you wir in Auckland, you bught yur wife the *The Return of the King* spicial extindid DVD, for Chrustmis."

Even in my dozy state, I saw where this was going.

"It's not Christmas yet!" I pointed out in a tone sufficiently haughty to send him scuttling back to my subconscious.

"I know. But there's only three days to go," said a half asleep THB.

The next morning dawned drier than its predecessor although there was still a persistent grey 'you wait 'til you get out in the open somewhere and I'll chuck it down' threat in the sky. That didn't dampen our spirits as we planned a glacier viewing day and it certainly didn't dampen the spirits of our cheery host at the *Te Weheka Inn* as he evangelised about the area over breakfast and offered us enough suggestions of things to do to fill a fortnight, illustrated by photographs of himself doing them. This travelogue was only interrupted by visits to the kitchen to fetch more coffee and toast.

After breakfast we thanked the *Te Weheka Inn* staff for their helpfulness and hospitality and began to load the Colt with our luggage. They seemed genuinely surprised by this compliment. Maybe they were still expecting us to reveal ourselves as hotel inspectors and present them with a list of things to put right. As we left they were still puzzling over the hotel register. So who were the REAL inspectors? Which room had they been put in? Had they been seriously neglected in favour of the two impostors (glances towards our departing backs) from the other side of the world?

The drive from Fox Glacier (the village) to the car park at Fox glacier (the icy tourist attraction) along Glacier Road (imaginative eh?) took only a few minutes. The walk from car park to glacier face, through a misty boulder strewn valley, fording a couple of beautifully clear brooks on the way, took three quarters of an hour. Lazy tourists may wonder why the car park wasn't built closer to the glacier face. Truth to tell, it was.

Over recent decades (despite a brief hiatus in the nineteen eighties and early nineties) ice has been melting at the glacier face faster than snow has been falling high in the mountains, being compacted and finally barging its way down to the rainforest at the coast, encouraged by gravity. (Being a Pakeha, I am working on the Pakeha theory here). This has prompted a gradual withdrawal of the glacier face from its point of furthest reach, marked by rocky debris left behind on its retreat. Visitors have to climb over this mound of debris, or terminal moraine, on leaving the car park, to get their first sight of the distant ice wall.

The walk through the glacial valley, sandwiched between cliffs of grey and occasional pink, generously clad in trees of green and moss of yellowish brown (well it looked sort of mossy, I'm not a horticulturist remember) would have been a wonderful experience even without the dangling (metaphorical) carrot of the glacier face growing larger and larger before us as we progressed. Standing in front of the wall of ice itself, when we finally reached it, was awe inspiring. It was also proof of the veracity of our guide book which had wittered on, rather fancifully so I thought, about the blueness of the glacier's ice. How could that be? I'd seen snow before and it had always been white, at least when fresh, before the grime of London had had a chance to turn it a mushy grey. I'd fallen over in the stuff and had never ever got up looking like a Smurf. If ice was blue (to use a Kiwi expression) my arse was a red cabbage.

When we reached the glacier's face, it was beautiful. (Actually it was probably beautiful before we reached it, but we weren't there to check). It was shimmering white, where exposed to what little sun was to be had, peppered grey with rocky debris gathered on its downward journey, deepest black inside a mouth like cave at its base and... well all right, a fresh turquoise blue in its gentle folds and shady crevices. Excuse me while I go and trim the leaves of my arse.

The glacier was so impressive, we wanted more, and more was what Glacier View Road seemed to promise. According to our two dimensional road atlas it ran parallel to Glacier Road (the one leading to the car park) but in reality it sprung off into a third dimension, following the ridge of the southernmost wall of the glacial valley. We anticipated spectacular views of the upper reaches of the glacier as we drove upward waiting for a break in the trees. At last a gap presented itself and we pulled over, left the car and hurried off to see what we could see. This turned out to be the inside of a cloud. A cloud which seemed very comfortable where it was and not at all inclined to move off and let us enjoy whatever view was beyond. Franz Josef, later in the day, would have to satisfy our remaining glacier craving. In the meantime, there was Lake Matheson.

Picture a serenely calm, tree fringed lake in which the snowy peaks of two jagged mountains (Mount Cook and Mount Tasman to be precise) are breathtakingly reflected. Now picture that scene on postcards, key-rings, calendars, tee shirts, chocolate boxes and in numerous other places designed to separate tourist from cash. That is Lake Matheson, an example of a kettle lake, formed from an iceberg orphaned by glacial retreat. (Note that a kettle lake is not a place where Kiwis dispose of old electrical equipment). On a normal day the lake can be reached from Fox Glacier (the village) by means of a short drive down Cook Flat Road. Sadly the day we chose to visit was an abnormal day. It was cow shifting day for the local farming community.

So it was that we found ourselves on the wrong side of a herd of cattle doing their level best not to be encouraged along by two farmers on quad bikes. Who had time to go forwards when there was a grass verge to be munched, dung to be deposited (didn't the farmer check that they'd all been before setting off?) enemies to be jostled and friends to be got friendly with? Some of the animals seemed to be getting extremely friendly with each other considering they were all girls.

The technique the farmers were using to clear the rapidly growing backlog of traffic was to tear along the side of the road making lots of cow startling noise to clear a path for two or three cars to follow. If any gap was left between the cars it was swiftly sealed by bovine bodies and the whole process began again. From our turn at running the gauntlet I learned that cattle regard a Mitsubishi Colt as an enemy (a point of view with which THB and I sympathised immensely) since the car suffered a prodigious amount of jostling during its passage. Did our insurance cover cow attack, I wondered?

The bonus of the cattle jam was that Lake Matheson was reasonably free of people when we arrived, allowing us to take a pleasant and peaceful walk from Café Lake Matheson, where we parked the car, down a well trodden path, through a small wood, to a viewing platform at the lake's edge.

Here our guide book let us down. It said quite clearly that in order to get the perfect view of snowy mountains reflected in a calm lake we would have to get up before breakfast. Note there was no stipulation about the time we should get up, just that we should not have breakfast before doing so. Having followed this instruction to the letter, and arrived at the lake around midday, we found all but the very bottoms of the mountains shrouded in cloud and the water's surface whipped by a persistent breeze. No chocolate box picture for us then, but there was another extraordinary sight to see.

As we stared down from our platform above the water's surface, a pair of beady eyes stared back from the murky depths. Eyes attached to a thick black body the size of a man's arm, lying perfectly still among the weeds. This was our first encounter with a giant eel in the wild, Kelly Tarlton in Auckland having provided an introduction to the species in captivity.

It was obviously the first eel experience for a lone American woman who joined us on the platform too. She peered down to see what we were looking at, failed to spot anything so she peered harder... then jumped backwards with a cry of, "Jeepers!" almost as if the creature had leapt from the water and taken her by the throat. "Did you see the eel?" we enquired innocently, as she sat down panting behind us.

A rash of tour buses at Café Lake Matheson, when THB and I returned to the car, suggested that the cattle had finally been mooved from Cook Flat Road, allowing us an easy escape. But should we head north to visit Franz Josef glacier or press on southwards towards Haast and Wanaka where our next hotel awaited us? No contest. Franz Josef it was, by a vote of three to nil. Even Jack Peterson's views count when they coincide with my own.

Franz Josef glacier used to be known as Victoria by those who knew it well until explorer and geologist Julius von Haast, evidently a fan of the Austro-Hungarian Emperor of the time, renamed it in the late eighteen hundreds. What prompted him to do so seems to be glossed over in accounts of the event. Did someone in authority actually say to him, "Hey Jules, if you're at a loose end for a while, can you rename our glacier for us?" Or did Frau von Haast simply get fed up with her husband saying, "I'm off to see Victoria, dear. Her upper reaches look particularly splendid in the early morning sunlight"?

The late eighteen hundreds were obviously a time when devising alternative names for icy geographical features was really in vogue. Or maybe it was just that royalty from the mother country had stopped being in vogue. Fox glacier ceased to be called Albert at around the same time, following a visit by prime minister William Fox.

Getting to see Franz Josef's face involved a similar tramp to that undertaken at Fox, across the rocky floor of a spectacular glacial valley. We started off enthusiastically, one of us keen for further evidence of the blueness of ice, the other keen to stare up at Mount Gunn, second choice location for filming the scenes in *The Return of the King* where a string of fiery beacons are lit to summon help for the people of Gondor from the people of Rohan. A fire ban ruled out the first choice filming location, further south near Queenstown.

Starting off and taking a few photographs of the distant glacier face was as far as we got. Do you remember me mentioning a 'you wait 'til you get out in the open somewhere and I'll chuck it down' threat from the sky early in the morning? Well we were now in the open. Accordingly the celestial threat became torrential reality. So it was back to the Colt (Beep! Beep! Beep! Let us in, you useless heap of junk, it's wet out here!) and off down State Highway 6 in an attempt to outrun the rain.

South of Fox Glacier the highway headed for the coast, flirted with it briefly at Bruce Bay, then wandered off into the mountains again. Every few minutes, or so it seemed, we passed a yellow on green sign attempting to entice us from the road with the siren song of a scenic reserve. We resisted, wary of a hundred and fifty kilometres of road still ahead of us and precipitation by the bucketload on our tail. Then the highway made a bid for the coast once more and our resolve crumbled at Lake Moeraki.

The lake itself was small, at least in comparison with the mighty Hawea, Wanaka, Wakatipu and Te Anau further south, and Pukaki and Tekapo to the east, but more than made up for that with its beautiful rainforest setting and the abundance of wildlife to be admired locally, including fur seals and the rare Hector's dolphin along the coast nearby. As we watched two people in a red canoe far off on the lake fighting to persuade their conveyance to travel in a straight line, we contemplated a walk down to Monroe Beach, home of the Fiordland crested penguin. But time was ticking by and sullen clouds were beginning to gather over our heads, so we made do with breathing in the lake's tranquil ambience for a few moments more before moving on. That was a bad move.

As we drove the short distance down State Highway 6 to the irresistible Knight's Point Lookout a tiny insect droned lazily about my head. It then droned lazily between the trusty road atlas, being waved about in my right hand, and the side window of the car. As a result of the laziness of its droning it ended up as a red smudge on the glass. Rather too much of a red smudge, in fact, for one small insect. Hey that was my blood. The bite on the back of my hand began itching shortly afterwards and didn't stop until a good two months after I returned to Britain. Welcome to the southern end of New Zealand's South Island.

Knights Point was a high point, both actually and figuratively, on the roller coaster coastal road between Lake Moeraki and Haast. It offered spectacular views of waves crashing onto rocks in bursts of white foam, the brilliant blues of the Tasman Sea deepening towards a distant horizon and white sandy beaches far below fringed with vegetation clinging to almost vertical rock walls. Seals could be seen basking on these beaches by those with binoculars or telescopic sight.

THB and I boasted neither so had to take the word of our fellow sightseers for that.

The parking area at the viewpoint was guarded by a strange creature the size of a man but covered in writhing white feathers. Could this be some ancient Maori spirit that we had to appease before being allowed to progress? No, as it turned out. The creature's plaintive cry gave the game away. "Get the buggers off me! Get them off!" We realised it was simply a tourist who had decided it would be fun to feed the gulls.

Knight's Point was named after one of the surveying team that worked on the road linking the West Coast of New Zealand's South Island to Otago further east. It is interesting to muse on what he might have said on first experiencing the wonderful views out to sea. "Wow!" perhaps, or "Look at those waves!" My money would be on neither of these possibilities. But then I have inside information. I would bet on a rank outsider, "Woof!" Knight was the dog of one of the human surveyors.

Further down the coast, where the Waita River ended its journey from mountaintop to sea, we stopped at a beautiful white sandy beach dotted with white bleached logs, of course, and tussocks of grass. I climbed a lookout tower for excellent views of the river's final meanderings between rainforest and sand while THB spurned the climb and settled for exploring the beach itself. Consequently THB provided lunch for the local sandfly population and I escaped unscathed to itch another day.

Vowing to smother ourselves in industrial strength insect repellent, currently hiding uselessly somewhere near the bottom of our luggage, before the next day's excursions, we continued down State Highway 6 towards Haast.

12: WANAKA

Making The Baby Elephant

A tired and hungry couple ride into the outskirts of an unfamiliar town aboard a silver Colt. The streets are deserted. Nothing stirs apart from a cardboard sign attached to a low corrugated iron building surrounded by a flock of plastic tables and chairs. The sign flutters in the stiffening breeze like a trapped bird desperate for flight. "Café" it reads "Open 9.00 am to 5.00 pm." At 4.15 pm precisely the couple secure the Colt at the side of the road, in between a Bronco and a Pony, and walk towards the café's weather beaten door.

A hatchet faced woman, half hidden behind a transparent cabinet displaying pastries, and an equally grim waitress stare at the strangers as they enter. The women say nothing but continue to watch with ill disguised contempt as the couple sit down and begin to examine the menu. The couple are unsure whether they should wait for service or approach the counter, so they wait for a while, then try the counter as old age begins to draw on. The waitress, they decide, is a loved one who has died and been stuffed by the café owners.

"Two steak pies and two seven ups, please," the man ventures.

Hatchet face thrusts her hand forward, palm upwards, in a gesture which suggests she would like to see the colour of the couple's money before deigning to provide refreshment. It turns out to be the same sort of silver and coppery colour adopted by most coinage. This is the point when she utters the only sound made during the couple's stay in her establishment.

"Uh."

The drinks are introduced to the couple's table with sufficient force to scare local birds into flight thinking they have heard a gunshot, but just insufficient force to break the glasses containing them. It is a practised performance, repeated with the pie dishes. Even the waitress is roused from her taxidermic slumber by the sharp reports and begins to upturn chairs and stack them loudly on tables. Hatchet face, ensconced once more behind her counter, watches every mouthful the couple take with mournful concentration, willing it to choke them.

Surprisingly the couple do not stay for dessert. At 4.38 pm precisely they leave the cafe and make for the Colt once more.

That was how THB and I were introduced to Haast, the collective noun for a triumvirate of settlements Haast Junction, Haast Beach and Haast Township gathered together under the name of Julius von Haast, the chap who thought that Victoria was not a suitable appellation for a glacier. Rumour has it that the town was relatively cut off from the rest of New Zealand up until the nineteen sixties when proper road and radio links finally conquered the Southern Alps. Proper customer service, alas, is still fighting its way through the mountains.

Leaving Haast behind, we followed State Highway 6 as it looped around the northern edge of Mount Aspiring National Park, home of the eponymous tallest peak outside Mount Cook National Park, before plunging south towards Wanaka. This route, the lowest crossing of the Southern Alps, was followed by ancient Maori in search of greenstone. It must have been a long trek. If I'd been an ancient Maori, I'd have sent the youngsters.

So who was the first non Maori to make the crossing? Are you thinking of the bloke who shares his first name with Ceasar? The one whose last name rhymes with fast? Yes, that's what Julius von Haast thought too when he modestly named the trail, 'Haast Pass' after using it to struggle his way west. Sadly for him a lone prospector called Charles Cameron had made the trip before him and buried his powder flask on the far side of the mountains to prove the fact. Sadly for the prospector the route was never renamed 'Cameron Pass'. It seems that Julius' word counts for a lot in this part of the world.

The good news is that there is a Mount Cameron and a Cameron Flat in Mount Aspiring National Park. I don't know if they are named after the pioneering prospector but if not they ought to have been. There is also a Mount Awful, a Mount Dispute, a Mount Dreadful and a Sombre Peak, all obviously discovered by an explorer who was having a very bad day.

While we are on the subject of what things are called, Haast Pass wins the Gisby award for the stretch of New Zealand road boasting the highest density of geographical features with names that sound as if they really belong in *Lord of the Rings*. "Having escaped from Burnt Top by swimming over Thunder Falls, the Hobbits found themselves in the shadow of Misty Peak, standing before The Gates of Haast." All of the place names in that sentence come from the Haast Pass page of our road atlas rather than from Tolkein's imagination.

As THB and I negotiated Haast Pass, the rainforest of the West Coast was gradually replaced by beech forest, then more open grassland as we approached Lakes Hawea and Wanaka, nestling together in the mountains like a giant blue letter H. The horizontal of the H was crossed by a thin strip of land known as The Neck, over which State Highway 6 climbed to present us with glorious views of snow topped mountains peering through a grey veil of cloud into still blue waters. These lakes were clearly different in character from the North Island's Taupo, brooding teenagers rather than a happy, smiling infant.

Pulling over to the side of the road, I deColted to fully appreciate the majesty of the view, our introduction to New Zealand's ruggedly beautiful south west. It didn't matter to me that the rain that had been chasing us all day had finally caught up, but it mattered to THB who refused to join me in the twenty or so metre walk from car door to view point, there being no yellow eye marked on the road map until much further south. As I stood and soaked up the atmosphere (while the atmosphere did its best to soak me) a second car pulled up beside the Colt. (This is a sufficiently rare occurrence on the South Island's empty roads to be noteworthy). It was slightly larger than the Colt. A Carthorse perhaps?

A woman emerged from the car and stomped over to join me, pausing now and again to beckon to a stubbornly stationary companion in its passenger seat. "He's afraid of getting wet," she announced as she reached the view point, just in time to witness the tentative appearance of a rainbow arching from lake shore to lake shore in the distance. Now both of us beckoned carwards, neither eliciting any response. So we made do with taking photographs of the scene to make our wussy partners jealous later on.

"What did she say?" asked THB as soon as I returned to the car.

"She suggested I elope with her, since we were clearly kindred spirits," I replied.

"And what did you say?" THB was almost but not absolutely sure I was joking.

"I said I couldn't bear to leave the delightful Mitsubishi Colt behind."

Now she was sure.

Having hugged the side of Lake Wanaka, State Highway 6 now switched over to Lake Hawea for a while to let it know it hadn't been forgotten. The gentle slopes and beaches at Wanaka's edge were replaced by Hawea's steep cliffs, a change of character brought about when its own beaches were submerged in the late nineteen fifties as the water rose by twenty metres following the construction of a dam. Set beneath threatening skies, with layers of cloud darkening into the distance, Lake Hawea was both beautiful and menacing. An ideal location for some *Lord of the Rings* scenes, you might think. If only Tolkein hadn't neglected to mention the deep blue glacial lake encountered by Frodo and Sam on the way to Mordor.

We parted from Lake Hawea at its southernmost tip, marked by the small and sleepy village of Hawea, before driving across the bottom of the watery H to the southernmost tip of Lake Wanaka, marked by the not quite so sleepy as Hawea (but not quite so jumping as Queenstown) town of Wanaka. Note that this name is pronounced as if enquiring whether someone would like a motor vehicle (wanna car?) rather then rhyming it with banker. The alternative pronunciation did keep us entertained for a while, in a juvenile sort of way, coming up with tag lines for the town. "Wanaka. No need to bring your friends," or "Wanaka. Paper tissue capital of New Zealand," for example.

Our home for the night was the *Edgewater Resort Hotel* which earned its name by being positioned in meticulously tended grounds on the edge of the southern shore of Lake Wanaka. We dined alfresco, enjoying views of rocky brown and verdant green peaks basking in the evening sunshine across the calm waters of Roys Bay. Then we enjoyed views of the same peaks disappearing into a grey ceiling of cloud. Finally we enjoyed views of a relentless and soul sapping drizzle, having retreated to our lakeside lodge. The rain had caught up with us again. Just like the Canadian mounties, wet weather on New Zealand's South Island always seems to get its man (and his Hobbit bothering wife).

There is general agreement among list makers that Lake Wanaka is New Zealand's fourth largest lake by surface area, trailing behind Lake Taupo of the North Island and Lakes Wakatipu and Te Anau further south. It is in awarding the accolade of New Zealand's fifth largest lake that arguments start.

In the red corner we have the holder of the title "New Zealand's second deepest lake", boasting a surface area of 142 square kilometres, hailing from the edge of Fiordland, give a warm welcome to Lake

Manapouri. And in the blue corner, we have the challenger, with a surface area of 181 square kilometres, hailing from just south of Christchurch, put your hands together for Te Waihora, also known as Lake Ellesmere. The judges' verdict would seem to be a forgone conclusion with the challenger taking the crown, or should that be belt? But wait. There is an objection!

Te Waihora, you see, only reaches the depth of a swimming pool and is separated from the sea by a thin gravel spit than can be bulldozed through to provide an outlet to the Canterbury Bight if rising water threatens its shores. So is it a REAL lake or a giant paddling pool? That is a puzzle indeed. Which brings us around to Stuart Landsborough.

Just outside Wanaka, where State Highway 6 interrupts its journey south with a right angled turn to follow the Clutha River, there is a clock tower balanced on one corner and leaning at a fifty five degree angle. (The famous tower in Pisa, for comparison, manages a less than impressive five and a half degree tilt). For good measure, the clock on the tower runs backwards.

"Ah," you might think, "I've known builders like that."

But in this case the tower was built correctly to its albeit eccentric design. The Leaning Tower of Wanaka, as it is called, is the lure to attract passing punters (assuming they haven't just crashed their car through lack of attention to the road) into an establishment boasting a three dimensional maze, illusion rooms and puzzle filled café. This is Stuart Landsborough's Puzzling World, Wanaka's fourth biggest attraction, after the obvious location, location, location.

The intriguing tower featured on a leaflet we discovered in the *Edgewater Resort Hotel* reception as we were checking out. That is how we came to be wandering around a maze on Christmas Eve morning instead of being half way down the road to Queenstown, making sure we arrived in time to book somewhere to eat our traditional Christmas dinner. The Englishman's meat and two veg. gene kicks in again.

THB and I tackled the illusions first, passing through a display of holograms to reach an eerie room lined with moulds of famous faces whose gaze seemed to stalk us wherever we went, like an army of overzealous store detectives watching a pair of suspicious shoppers. Next there was a room tilted at an angle just small enough not to trigger immediate alarm bells in our brains, but large enough to create illusions like a seat mounted on a rail appearing to glide uphill when we sat in it. THB's brain cottoned on to the scam half way along this disconcerting journey forcing her to beat a hasty retreat to non tilting normality before her breakfast made an unscheduled reappearance.

The final illusion was provided by the Ames Forced Perspective Room. This seemed like a perfectly normal chequerboard floored box when viewed through a window in one wall, but in fact was so twisted in shape that it made anyone entering seem 'head bumping on the ceiling' huge when visiting one corner and 'couldn't reach the ceiling even if stretching on tiptoe' tiny when visiting a neighbour. This we were assured was one of the many tricks used to establish the vertically challenged nature of Hobbits and Dwarves in *Lord of the Rings* scenes when interaction with other characters of more conventional height was necessary. Oh no. That wasn't Jack Peterson making his way across the Ames Room was it? Off to the maze!

The challenge in tackling this puzzle, built from wooden fencing with a few raised walkways giving tantalising but not quite helpful glimpses of the paths below, was to reach four differently coloured towers in a predefined order. People with low frustration thresholds (yes I have my hand in the air) were allowed to make the visits in any order on the understanding that the kudos gained when their task was finished would be somewhat diminished.

THB and I made lots of new friends as we encountered the same faces over and over again struggling along in the opposite direction and always offering the same advice in mournful tones, with a hangdog look, "It's not that way!" Some of them still write. I'm sure the rest will too when they eventually make it out into the real world again.

We kept our spirits up by pigeon holing our fellow lab. rats according to their different attitudes to the maze experience.

(1) The Big Brother/Sister
"*If I run really fast, then I'll lose my little sister / brother.*"
(2) The Little Sister / Brother
"*Waaaaah! I'm gonna tell mummy.*"
(3) The Teenager.
"*This is really, really, really, really, really lame.*"
(4) The Concerned Parent

"Have you seen a boy wearing an I Beat The Puzzling World Maze tee shirt?"
(5) The Unconcerned Parent
"Hey, there's an exit here. Just wait 'til the kids get around that corner."
(6) The Loving Couple
"Quick, there's nobody else around."
(7) The Un-Loving Couple
"I told you we should have turned right. I told you. Are you listening?"
(8) The Gardener
"Look at the quality of that fencing. I wonder where they buy it."
(9) The Lord of the Rings Fan
"I've seen Two Towers."
(10) The Maze Expert
"I've done this before. All you have to do is keep turning left."
(11) The Maze Expert At Closing Time
"I would have made it out eventually. No really I would."

With previous experience of the famed Hampton Court and Leeds Castle mazes in England we started off at ten, drifted towards eleven for a while, but staved that off by finishing our task in a rather tardy hour, having enjoyed a little six (yes that is a letter i) in the middle.

Our final stop was the café for some well deserved refreshment and more puzzles, this time of the table top variety. We watched a small boy attempting to transfer a set of wooden rings of various sizes from one pole in a line of three to another according to a series of rules outlined on a slip of paper. Eventually he gave up in frustration, allowing me to impress both him and THB by completing the puzzle in one attempt. I should say that this was not entirely due to perspicacity on my part. The fact that I'd seen it done before had a little to do with it.

"That was easy," I boasted, planning to retire from puzzling on this high note, but my audience had other ideas. They introduced me to a new challenge which involved arranging a series of coloured tiles of different shapes inside a square tray to reproduce a picture from a booklet. My assignment was an arrangement called 'baby elephant'.

Half an hour later THB had become bored and wandered off as I continued to shuffle tiles. My own patience was wearing thin, thoughts turning to the drive to Queenstown which ought to begin soon, but I couldn't just shrug my shoulders and walk away. What would the half of my audience which still remained think of me? I would NOT be beaten!

"Are you driving alung the Cardrona Villey Road?" enquired an irritatingly familiar voice as the clicking of tile upon table top continued unabated. Jack Peterson was all I needed.

"No!" I replied. "I'm trying to finish this blood..." (I remembered my diminutive spectator) "...this wretched puzzle."

"I mint are you tiking the mintain road to Queenstown?"

A drive through the Cardrona Valley, following one of New Zealand's highest roads, seemed a more exciting prospect than the longer loop of State Highway 6 between Wanaka and Queenstown through Cromwell. Of course we were taking that route.

"It's a viry twisty road," Peterson continued, "Ind yir wife is alriddy quizzy frim the tilting room."

"I'm sure she'll cope." I sounded more confident than I felt. We would have to schedule plenty of fresh air breaks, or if the worst came to the worst chunder breaks, during the journey.

"The ither road wud lit you see The Flight to The Ford and Pillars of the Kings. Rimimber why you are hir!"

These, I presumed, were sites where *Lord of the Rings* filming had taken place. I was about to point out that he had just sounded the death knell of State Highway 6 as a choice when two things happened.

Firstly my small companion (the real one) ran excitedly to his mother shouting, "Mama! Mama! That man has an imaginary friend just like Uncle Mikey." He was quickly ushered away by a worried parent.

Secondly THB reappeared with a face saving way out of my 'finish the puzzle or look like an idiot' dilemma. (I don't know why I was concerned about looking like an idiot in front of THB. If she hasn't realised after fourteen years of marriage that I am an idiot, she probably isn't ever going to, or doesn't care). She presented me with a copy of The Kaleidoscope Classic (the name of the puzzle I had been struggling with) bought from the Puzzling World gift shop. Now I wasn't giving up on the baby elephant challenge, I was just taking a breather while I drove to Queenstown, then on to Te Anau, Dunedin and Christchurch, flew back to London...

Reacquainting ourselves with the Colt, we drove out of the Puzzling World car park searching for signs to the Cardrona Valley Road. All right, I drove out of the Puzzling World car park searching for signs to the Cardrona Valley Road. My navigator picked up the road atlas, found the Wanaka page and advised, "Turn left here and we'll follow State Highway 6. There are two yellow eyes on the way to Queenstown." In the mirror I saw Jack Peterson dancing a jig of celebration along the top of the rear seats.

"Why did you swerve?" asked THB, adjusting her seat belt.

I said nothing, but in the rear view mirror I watched contentedly as Jack Peterson rubbed his head.

Outside Wanaka, State Highway 6 followed the course of New Zealand's most voluminous river, The Clutha, which was dammed in the nineteen nineties as part of a hydroelectric scheme, forming Lake Dunstan. It was to the north of this lake, in an area of tranquil pine forest, that The Flight to The Ford scene was filmed for *The Fellowship of the Ring*. In this scene Liv Tyler (playing the elf Arwen) aboard a barrel (playing a horse) carries an injured Frodo away from nine evil black riders to the sanctuary of Rivendell.

We certainly saw pine forests from State Highway 6 but the unsealed road allowing closest access to the filming site departed from State Highway 8 on the other side of The Clutha River. Rather than backtracking half way to Wanaka to take a detour to see pine forest like that in the film (the actual filming site is on private land) we made do with the pine forest like that in the film where we were, then pressed on to The Pillars of the Kings.

The Pillars of the Kings is the scene in *The Fellowship of the Ring* where The Fellowship travel in canoes down the mighty River Anduin passing into a rocky gorge guarded by two gigantic statues of ancient kings. The site where this was filmed on the Kawarau River was exactly as it appeared in the film. Minus the computer generated statues, of course. And minus the paddling actors and their canoes. And minus the view of a lake in the middle distance beyond the statues. And plus a few electricity pylons and a bungy jumping business. Maybe not exactly as it appeared in the film then.

The most striking feature of the real life scene was the brilliant turquoise blue of the river's water which certainly did not come across in the movie. I suspect it was toned down to match the more subdued colour of the mighty River Anduin filmed elsewhere. In reality a host of different rivers and lakes in New Zealand were stitched together to form the Anduin of Middle Earth.

Before (and I hazard a guess since) *The Lord of the Rings* movies, the site of The Pillars of the Kings was (and is) more famous as the location of the world's first bungy jumping business, set up by A J Hackett.

For those of you who find popular culture as unfathomable as a modern child finds a slide rule (You use it to do calculations? But where are the buttons?) I should explain that bungy jumping involves tying a length of stretchy cord to your ankles, attaching the other end to a bridge or tall building, then letting gravity do its worst. No, it's not an alternative to a custodial sentence, people do it for fun.

The original Hackett bungy experience involves jumping from a pretty red suspension bridge across the Kawarau gorge to touch the turquoise waters of the river below, before being yanked skywards again by the bungy cord. After several bounces you are lowered to the safety of a rescue boat and taken gibbering to the shore. You then try to encourage others to go through the same thing so you aren't the only one to look totally insane.

There was quite a queue while THB and I were there, which didn't seem to diminish much as we watched a series of jumpers get bound up and counted down by the friendly bungy staff before disappearing head first into the gorge. For the more reluctant participants two or three countdowns were required along with a fair amount of cajoling and a final reminder that they weren't any refunds. Even this failed to work for one shamefaced girl who had to be untied and returned to her loved ones via bridge rather than boat.

I know exactly how she felt. I remember pleading with my father, as a child, to take me on a helter-skelter at a fair. We climbed the winding stairs to get to the top of the tower and emerged to a stunning seaside view. We then climbed back down the same stairs, squeezing apologetically past people on their way up, when I couldn't find the courage to climb on the mat I'd been given and slide down.

I now know my limitations and bungy jumping is beyond them. Unless, of course, I could go straight to the front of the queue before fear had had a chance to team up with rational thought and subdue excitement, repelling the threat of shame. Then I might...

All I remember is being asked to reveal my weight so they could choose the right cord. Then a bearded man in shorts and a tee shirt invited me to hop onto a small platform high above the Kawarau river. A stiff breeze tugged at my hair. Terror tugged at my heart. Three. Two. One. And I was sailing through the air into a rocky canyon. Water rushed up to meet me. Shouldn't they have tied a cord to my ankles? Shiiiiiii...

I awoke from the nightmare in the *Novotel Gardens* hotel in Queenstown with THB holding my ankles to prevent me from falling out of bed.

Just in case you are wondering, six months later I still haven't completed the baby elephant. Well, I've been writing this book haven't I?

13: QUEENSTOWN, NEW ZEALAND

That's No Good, It's Australian

The largest town on the shores of Lake Hawea is named Hawea.
The largest town on the shores of Lake Wanaka is named Wanaka.
The largest town on the shores of Lake Te Anau is named Te Anau.
Do you see a pattern emerging here?
So the largest town on the shores of Lake Wakatipu is named...
If you said Queenstown, award yourself a gold star.

There should be a monument by the side of the road on entering Queenstown like the one in Ohakune. Not a gigantic root vegetable though. That would be inappropriate. No I'd recommend a giant plaster cast and crutch to indicate the town's position as Adventure Sports Capital of New Zealand, if not The World. If you have a yearning to jump off the side of a picturesque mountain with nothing more than a few yards of fabric or a stretchy cord to keep you from morphing into strawberry jam on the ground far below, then Queenstown is your kind of place.

Our guide book had described a synthetic settlement with an 'in your face' attitude to parting tourists from their cash. This bore no resemblance whatsoever to the laid back and friendly place in achingly beautiful surroundings that THB and I encountered. (If the guide book writer wants to experience the real hard sell he or she should walk the streets of Tenerife in the high season wearing a tee shirt bearing the legend "I want to buy a time-share". Come to think of it, the tee shirt isn't really necessary).

THB and I arrived at our hotel, on the waterfront of Lake Wakatipu, in the early evening of Christmas Eve to be greeted, not by the familiar "Win are you living?" but more by a kind of "Hwen air yur leeveeng?" The man behind the hotel desk came from Queenstown by way of Paris.

Once we'd completed the formalities of checking in we asked whether it would be possible to book Christmas lunch at the hotel. "Could we reserve a table for two?" I asked. The French receptionist looked horrified, muttered under his breath about, "Ze Ingleesh" assuming all Frenchmen were waiters, and called over a colleague. "Is restaurant!" the man barked like a Russian army officer and pointed up a flight of stairs.

At the top of the stairs a cheery waitress with an Irish accent (from Galway, THB discovered, always pleased to encounter a fellow countrywoman) allocated us a time slot for the next day and promised us some good craic. (This is not a reference to an illicit substance, but to fun in the Irish vernacular. No that is not the same thing). In the meantime a man of Oriental appearance had been given the keys to the Colt and told to take it away. Only as far as the hotel car park and not to the breakers yard we discovered later with some disappointment.

Then it was back to the lobby to be escorted to our room by a man with a down-under twang. (That is a mode of speech not something you have to see a doctor about). "You're Australian aren't you?" I asked. He seemed pleased not to be mistaken for a Kiwi. As pleased as Kiwis are when not mistaken for Aussies. "You ricignised the iccent?" he asked. "Not really," I replied. "It's just that this hotel seems to operate a no Kiwi policy."

Incidentally if you really want to tell if the person you are talking to is a Kiwi or an Aussie, there is a simple test. You ask them to repeat the following phrase "Australian rugby players are the best in the world." If they manage to do so they are undoubtedly an Aussie. If you wake up in hospital the next morning they were a Kiwi.

On Christmas morning, THB having been presented with her *The Return of the King* DVD and formulated a plan to purchase a portable DVD player at Christchurch airport so she could watch it on the flight home, we strolled along the sunny shores of Lake Wakatipu open mouthed with wonder at the majestic mountains all around, each peak wearing its very own wispy halo of cloud. We passed the landing stage for the Shotover River jet boat (the look in THB's eye said NO even before I asked) then wandered up through the compact and almost deserted town centre, more modern than most we'd encountered in New Zealand but still refreshingly low rise. Eventually we came upon the Skyline Gondola terminal at the bottom of Bob's Peak, looming over Queenstown like a doting parent watching a sleeping child.

On the scale of scary things to do in Queenstown a couple of minutes of dangling from a cable strung between pylons stretching like a zipper up the side of a hill is on a par with finding a small spider in the bath. But having experienced the Skyline Gondola, facing towards the hillside with THB enthusing over the stunning view revealing itself behind me that I dared not turn to see, I'd choose the spider any day.

From the Gondola terminal at the top of Bob's Peak (I could look now, the ground had stopped swaying) the panorama was spectacular. To the left a green isthmus stretched out into the blue waters of Lake Wakatipu like a frying pan on a hob. Beyond that, green and brown hills led up to the The Remarkables, a string of grey, craggy, snow capped peaks used as rent-a-range whenever a mountain backdrop was required in the *Lord of the Rings* movies. To the right, the lake shimmered into the distance, disappearing behind another series of rocky peaks, brown this time with green forested fringes close to the water.

The only sound that disturbed the tranquillity of the scene, apart from the clicks of camera shutters, was the occasional rustle of wind in a billowing canopy as a paraglider passed over our heads. Yes, there are people who choose to descend from Bob's peak by jumping off it dangling from a parachute strapped to a man who hopefully knows what he is doing. (If you think about it the chances that he does know what he is doing must be fairly slim since he is jumping off the side of a mountain). On Queenstown's scale of scary things to do this one rates alongside finding a crocodile in your bath. Never mind the small spider.

Another activity on Bob's peak, designed to prompt an impromptu evacuation of the lower reaches of your alimentary canal, is the luge. I'd seen this sport, where competitors tackle a bobsleigh run aboard a tin tray, in the winter Olympics and had half a mind to try it. But the other half a mind said, "Don't do it. You'll die a horrible death!" and that half won the day when push came to shove at the lower Gondola terminal where tickets were sold. When we saw the actual run, made from concrete rather than ice, it looked rather less likely to promote an early death than my imagination had suggested, but by then we were at the top of the peak and ticketless.

We made our way back to Queenstown by strolling down the peak's forested slopes. It was a pleasant walk at first, down a winding road dappled by sunlight filtering through the leafy canopy above, catching occasional glimpses of Lake Wakatipu and The Remarkables through the trees. The only cause for concern was the stream of people we met running (yes running) in the alternative uphill direction. At first we wondered what was chasing them and whether we should be walking towards it. Then we realised they were just Kiwis, following the sporty Kiwi code.

(1) Never walk when you can run.
(2) Never run downhill when you can run uphill.
(3) If you really have to go downhill, bungy. (Note that paragliding and zorbing are slowly becoming accepted as alternatives in more enlightened parts of the country).

We found that rule (3) was adhered to so rigidly that we weren't able to give the return halves of our Gondola tickets away at the top of Bob's Peak.

Just beyond a rather forlorn picnic table which provided a welcome rest on our journey back to ground level we were forced to make a decision. Should we continue on the road which looked as if it was heading away from Queenstown towards far off Glenorchy or should we take what looked like a mountain bike track that had fallen into disrepair but which at least seemed to be headed in the right direction?
I chose the track.
Note the use of the singular I rather than the plural We at this point. As our descent became harder, scrambling over wandering tree roots and sliding down crumbling banks in a rather undignified manner, THB reminded me that the decision to take the track rather than the road had been mine alone. Then she reminded me again in case I wasn't paying attention the first time. Then she reminded me again...
An act of contrition was called for.
"How would you like to spend all afternoon sitting in the sunshine?" I asked.
"Hmmm." The idea was obviously appealing.
"With beautiful mountain scenery drifting past your eyes?"
"Maybe." Slightly suspicious, but she was coming round.
"And a refreshing iced drink in your hand?"
"Okay." That clinched it. THB had agreed to a boat trip.
Did I neglect to mention that I was talking about cruising the waters of Lake Wakatipu aboard the ninety-four year old steamer TSS Earnslaw? Oh, sorry about that.

The TSS Earnslaw is a Queenstown institution, chugging out to

Walter Peak farm at the far western end of Lake Wakatipu several times a day at an age when most people would need a Zimmer frame to make it to the corner shop. Animal lovers and those seeking temporary relief from sea sickness can disembark to find out more than they ever wanted to know about sheep and sheep husbandry. Or simply to chunder. Note that the term sheep husbandry refers to the act of looking after sheep rather than the act of marrying them, despite the many jokes about the fondness of Kiwis for their woolly friends. More of them later. You didn't think I could go through a whole book on New Zealand without a few sheep jokes did you?

From the deck of the Earnslaw at the half way point on our cruise (THB had the end of the boat journey in her sights and didn't want to delay it by a sojourn on land) I wondered whether Walter Peak was a real working farm or a Disneyesque theme park. The answer was provided by an adaptation of the Monty Python method for recognising a medieval king. In *Monty Python and the Holy Grail*, peasant Michael Palin proclaims that the passing Graham Chapman must be a king because he isn't covered in shit. Similar reasoning suggested that Walter Peak with its pretty red roofed buildings and immaculate flower beds must be a theme park. Apologies to them if I simply couldn't see the big pile of shit out the back from where I was standing.

On the voyage back to Queenstown there was entertainment for everyone. As breathtaking mountain scenery slid gracefully by, those passengers turned on by pounding pistons (almost exclusively male) could disappear below deck to drool over the engines, religious passengers could sing Christmas carols around a piano (keeping God in a good mood and so the Earnslaw afloat), nervous sailors could hang over the rail and feed the fishes and the rest of us, THB surprisingly included in this rather than the previous category, could enjoy the cabaret.

The show began with an unexpected and ear shattering blast on the ship's whistle as the Earnslaw bid a temporary farewell to Walter Peak. A small boy hunkered down on the deck close to where THB and I were sitting made a valiant if involuntary attempt to achieve orbit. On returning to Earth he thrust a finger in each ear and adopted a 'my dog has just died' expression on his face.

When his mother had finished laughing she asked, rather unnecessarily in my opinion, "Ahhhh. Did that frighten you Tarquin?"

Tarquin said nothing and remained motionless apart from a slightly trembling bottom lip.

"You can take your fingers out of your ears now. It's not going to sound again," she cooed not really convincingly, the lack of evidence to back up her assertion all too evident.

Fingers remained firmly in Tarquin's ears and continued to remain so despite initial promises of good things to eat followed by threats of paternal intervention. (Father, it transpired, was a pounding piston fan but could be recalled from the Earnslaw's bowels as a last resort, if really necessary, once crowbars had been tried and failed). Finally Tarquin's pretty teenage sister was despatched to appeal to the ship's captain, begging him to take pity on her young brother and agree not to sound the whistle again. After what seemed a very long a time she returned, slightly flushed.

"Do you see the blonde one?" she said. All eyes turned to the bridge where one of the younger members of the crew could be seen waving. "I think he fancies me!"

"Did they agree not to blow the whistle?"

With a resigned, "I knew I had forgotten something" look, the girl turned around and trudged back to bridge, beginning her quest again.

When she hadn't returned after another very long time her mother set off on a search and rescue mission, leaving Tarquin in the care of grandma. Eventually, as the Earnslaw approached Queenstown once more, there was extra long blast on the ship's whistle. Grandma was ready and just managed to catch Tarquin before he left the ground.

Mother and daughter returned together shortly afterwards, slightly dishevelled, looking as if they had just come from a rather good party. Maybe they had.

"He let ME blow the whistle!" the older woman, shouted triumphantly to all aboard. Tarquin, fingers still rammed in his ears, looked betrayed.

In the final scene, once the ship had been tied up and its pistons had stopped pounding, Tarquin's father appeared. "Fingers out of your ears boy," he said. And Tarquin obeyed.

As we made our way back to the hotel for Christmas dinner I realised I'd left my sunglasses aboard the Earnslaw. So if you cruised on Lake Wakatipu on Christmas day 2004 and picked up an unattended pair of wrap around sunglasses in the style favoured by Aussie cricketers who wish to impress tipsy Sheilas in the crowd, they are mine. Put them in the post now! Unless, of course, your name is Tarquin. Then you can keep them. You need all the breaks you can get in life.

THB and I were surprised to find most shops in the centre of Queenstown, unlike those in British towns, open for business on Christmas day. This was to service the needs of tourists from Japan, for whom 25th December has no special significance, we were told by a chatty sales assistant in a shop that sold outdoorsy stuff like monsoon proof rainwear, seriously rugged tramping boots and ozone hole proof sunglasses. Ching. My lost shades were replaced. He may have been chatty because, if the lack of bodies around us was anything to go by, we were the only people he'd seen all day. Even the few establishments offering plastic Legolas figurines or "I did something life-threatening and stupid in Queenstown" tee shirts seemed to be doing more of a whispering than a roaring trade. Someone had obviously warned the Japanese that Queenstown might be closed on Christmas Day and they'd all gone off on a coach trip to Milford Sound instead.

Our Christmas Day shopping extravaganza also took us into a chemist's, with the aim of purchasing protection. Better safe than sorry, we thought, planning a romantic walk along the secluded shores of Lake Wakatipu later in the evening.

"This is what we have been using," THB explained to a brace of disinterested girls behind the chemist's counter. She waved a half empty packet in front of their eyes, adding, "but it doesn't seem to be working. Can you recommend anything else?" No response, so THB ventured, "What do you use?"

Disinterest became disdain as one girl examined the contents of THB's hand. "That's no good," she said. "It's Australian!" The last two words were uttered in the tone of voice that a mother uses for "It's dirty" when trying to persuade a toddler not to retrieve a toffee carelessly dropped into a cow pat. THB was quickly ushered up an aisle featuring the home produced article. "This is what you need!"

So we invested in insect repellent from New Zealand rather than from Australia and were spared the annoyance of itchy bites, well fresh ones anyway, for the rest of our trip. (Of course I was talking about insect repellent. What else did you think?) Mind you the torrential rain that unbeknown to us was just a few of days away might also have had something to do with keeping the blood suckers away.

Christmas dinner back at the hotel began with the presentation of a stylish menu promising seven sumptuous courses in a language about sixty percent English, thirty percent French and ten percent Italian. Normally an abundance of French on a restaurant's menu, unless you happen to be in France, indicates that you are likely to leave the establishment with an empty feeling in both stomach and wallet. Not this time. The meal featured traditional Christmas fare, but served with a light and imaginative twist. Turkey and ham with roast spuds and sprouts, for example, were replaced by *turkey breast wrapped in prosciutto, carved onto potato and cranberry rosti, with roasted pumpkin and beans hollandaise.* I only understood about half of that (*prosciutto* apparently is not a woman of ill repute and *rosti* is not an Italian footballer) but it tasted very good.

The first few courses were served in a cavernous room filled with seasonally decorated tables and chairs awaiting diners who, apart from THB and I, had failed to show up. Never have we had such attentive service, with an exclusive army of waiters and waitresses on hand to refill glasses, whisk empty plates off to the kitchen and be reassured at regular intervals that we were all right, the food was all right and we would not like anything else except maybe to be left in peace for a while.

By the third course a Japanese tour party had been installed and began tackling the strange foreign fare set before then with curiosity and a sense of adventure. The bravest among them even tackled their Western companions with the sort of awkward questions that they'd always wanted answered but been afraid to ask. So what was this Christmas thing all about? Was she really a virgin? How did the fat guy with the white beard and the red suit fit in? What was the significance of the pointy tree?

Having dealt ecumenically and reasonably successfully with the religious queries put our way and not able to think of a polite way of turning the tables by asking, "So what's the deal with Shinto then?" we left ourselves open to much sterner inquiry. Our fellow diners picked up a menu and asked "What is *prosciutto*?" and "What is *rosti*?"

Gourmet speak is a language only mastered after a long apprenticeship in a sweaty kitchen suffering hourly abuse from a cantankerous chef. But there is a language that demands even greater dedication and powers of endurance from those wishing to plumb its depths. You have to read and inwardly digest a rather fat book and watch three long films over and over again and again for a start. That language is *Lord of the Rings* speak.

"You are tiking two *Lord of the Rings* trups tumurrow," Jack Peterson said. Disconcertingly he was sporting a mortar board along with the usual baggy shorts. He was also carrying a short cane, which I hoped was for pointing at things like the blackboard behind him, rather than for hitting things, like soft parts of my anatomy. "I think I shud tich you abut sum of the plices you will suy."

I was about to point out, sleepily, "I have a wife who deals with that sort of thing," when the Hobbit bothering guru tapped his blackboard, pointed to some strange words he had chalked there, and barked.

"What is Lothlorien?"

"Isn't that the time travelling car in *Back to the Future*?"

"What is Isengard?"

"A device to prevent small children stealing pieces of the sugary coating from a newly decorated fruit cake."

"What is Ithillien?"

"That's what Ian's wife, who has a lisp, says to him when she discovers the budgie is poorly."

"What is the Ford of Bruinen?"

"Bruinen's motor vehicle."

I thought I was doing rather well, but Headmaster Peterson apparently didn't.

"You'll nivir hilp your wife if you don't tick this sirriusly," he muttered. "Hild out yur hind."

I awoke the next morning with numb fingers. THB must have been sleeping on my arm in the night.

14: QUEENSTOWN, MIDDLE EARTH

The Lord of the Rings Bathroom.

If you are heterosexual, male and on the pull in New Zealand you could do a lot worse than book a place on a 4WD (four wheel drive) *Lord of the Rings* tour. THB and I experienced four in all, one from Wellington, two from Queenstown and one from Christchurch, and the ratio of females to males cosily packed into the back of a lurching vehicle never dropped below two to one. Luckily my fumblings around shapely rear ends in search of the buckle to fasten my seat belt were never misinterpreted. Be warned, however, that to impress these females you will certainly have to know your Edoras from your Elrond. Unless of course you bear a striking resemblance to Orlando. Then your brain will not be required. Just an ability to run very fast if you value your life.

THB and I were picked up on Boxing Day morning for the first of two *Lord of the Rings* outings courtesy of Nomad Safaris. Nomad gained early bonus points for attention to detail by providing a 4WD with the registration plate B1LB0S but lost them again when THB and I were split up. Our fellow travellers, an Irish couple named Michael and Siobhan and two Aussie backpackers named Naomi and Kate, had already been collected from their hotels, leaving just one free seat in the back of the vehicle and one up front with our driver and guide, Greg. I gallantly volunteered to let THB have the front seat but for some reason she seemed adamant that I should be afforded that honour. Maybe it had something to do with the fact that the spare seat in the back nestled between Naomi and Kate.

As we headed out of Queenstown and up the winding and precarious road leading to the Remarkables Skifield, the girls commented on something that THB and I had also noticed while acquainting ourselves with New Zealand's roads. There was an awful lot of road kill to be seen. Was the poor quality of Kiwi drivers or the stupidity of Kiwi creatures to blame? Greg provided the answer. Kiwi drivers were good in that they managed to hit possums almost every time they saw one. And Kiwi creatures were intelligent, the stupid possums, mesmerised by oncoming headlights, being Australian imports. You may remember from Pukekura that possums do a tremendous amount of damage to local flora and fauna in New Zealand. Greg was a part of a nationwide campaign (or so it seemed) to redress the balance. "Possums are the only Australian we're allowed to kill within the law," he said with just a little too much relish.

Animal lovers should be reassured that no possums were killed in the research for this book. The same cannot be said of sandflies, mozzies and other biting insects. THB and I were both fairly ruthless when it came to them. But hey, they were after our blood.

It was a fairly strenuous walk from the end of the road (for want of a better description of the bumpy track we had driven along) at the Remarkables Skifield to Lake Alta, the surrounds of which became Dimrill Dale in *The Fellowship of the Ring*. This is the desolate and rocky place where The Fellowship minus Gandalf began their journey to Lothlorien where they met Galadriel. Gandalf was otherwise engaged in a wrestling match with the Balrog, a creature rather like a giant, fiery stick insect with menacing horns and a bad attitude. Our tour didn't stretch as far as Lake Alta but we were treated instead to spectacular views over Queenstown airport, the Kawarau River meandering towards Lake Wakatipu and a eight hundred metre high hump known as Deer Park Heights, reduced to a pimple from our Remarkables vantage point.

As cameras clicked, THB and I taking pictures of the scenery, Naomi and Kate taking pictures of each other and Michael taking a tongue lashing from Siobhan for forgetting to charge up their camera overnight, Greg provided a verbal tour of the landscape before us. Deer Park Heights, a serious contender for the 'most versatile *Lord of the Rings* location' award, appearing in a variety of guises in Peter Jackson's three films, was the star. Our guide regaled us with tales of ferocious Wargs, a tumbling dwarf and a Korean prison. (The latter was not from a *Lord of the Rings* film, THB has checked again and again, even in extended versions and Director's cuts). He also informed us that we would not be able to visit this Hobbit bothering gem since Deer Park was privately owned. Luckily your own guide has better information. For a bargain twenty New Zealand dollars THB and I were able to get up there and roam about the following day. More of that later.

Greg the possum lover's next stop was Arrowtown, a settlement with a past built upon the discovery of gold in the Arrow River and a present built upon the discovery of gold in the pockets of tourists on buses up for the day from Queenstown. Hey that was us! But we had no time for the famed Avenue of Trees, a row of fifty or more prettified cottages where miners once lived, now dwarfed by great oaks and sycamores planted in 1867. Our destination was a path beside the Arrow River lined by densely packed trees whose branches stretched low and almost horizontally overhead, banishing the sky from sight. This was the path upon which King Isildur was attacked by Orcs at the very beginning of *The Two Towers* and lost The Ring in the mighty River Arrow, sorry mighty River Anduin. So that's where the gold came from.

Arrowtown was originally called Foxes after an early prospector William Fox who managed to keep his glittering find secret for long enough to accumulate more than one hundred kilograms of gold. You'd have thought that with riches on that scale he'd have had the wherewithal to grease enough palms for the town to keep his name. Apparently not. Maybe Julius von Haast happened along one day and decided to rename the place as, we have found, he was wont to do. Or maybe the prospectors thought they'd do well to lose the name Foxes since that's where the world and his wife (come to think of it, probably not his wife) were heading to seek their fortune. "No mate," they would say, "This isn't Foxes. This is Arrowtown. You must want somewhere else." It's the sort of scheme a drunken and avaricious miner could easily come up with.

The Arrow River also doubled as The Anduin, or more specifically The Ford of Bruinen, where Arwen challenged a group of Black Rider punks lurking menacingly on the far bank to come on over and make her day. When they tried it they were swept away by a wall of water conjured up by the elf maiden. Even the mighty Clint couldn't top that.

As we sipped coffee and ate cake beside the Arrow (all part of the Nomad Safari package) Greg grabbed a large rubber dinner plate from the back of the 4WD and began a gold panning demonstration. "You can usually pick up a few flecks if you know where to look," he assured us. After half an hours worth of fruitless scraping and swirling we were convinced that he didn't know where to look. Perhaps all the precious metal had been sucked out of the water by the lazy man's panner, powered by a throbbing generator, in operation a short way upstream. I took a photograph of this contraption just as its operator decided to bend down, unwittingly illustrating the fact that cheap shorts are liable to become transparent when wet. Not my favourite picture from our New Zealand collection but surprisingly popular with many of THB's friends.

After elevenses we were whisked off to the Kawarau River gorge and shown how the The Pillars of the Kings looked before the effects people added giant stone statues and subtracted both electrical pylons and the A J Hackett bungy. An impressive sight even though THB and I had seen it before on the way down from Wanaka. It was good to have a Hobbit bothering commentary from Greg this time though, especially since it involved the story of one of The Fellowship actors tumbling out of his Elvish boat. Who? Let's just say that the Kuwarau Gorge would have been filled by the tears of teenage girls if he'd happened to drown. And the film *The Calcium Kid* might never have been made. Not all bad then.

Greg's final delight for his passengers was a climb towards the Coronet Peak Skifield, to the north east of Queenstown. As we approached the summit he stopped and pointed out a sign indicating that rental vehicles were prohibited from taking a twisty and perilous looking side track. To a Kiwi, of course, such a sign is nothing short of a challenge. So it was Skippers Road for us then, a dizzying drive up to a view point overlooking the grassy walled gorge of Skippers Canyon. Every spin of wheels upon dirt conjured up premonitions of an all too swift descent into the canyon and every hairpin turn made the contents of THB's stomach a little more restless. She had to sit up front on the way back down to calm the urge to chunder, leaving me tossed back and forth between Naomi and Kate (if you'll pardon the expression). This was not such a pleasant experience as you might think since both of the girls had very loud screams and were not afraid to use them in response to every change in speed, direction and number of wheels on the ground of our conveyance.

As other vehicles from Nomad's 4WD fleet were making the same journey we quickly learned the etiquette of meeting other vehicles safely on a poorly paved and precarious path.

(1) Any vehicle descending gets to go inside, away from the drop.
(2) Any vehicle going backwards gets to go inside, away from the drop. (There was no room to turn when we reached the end of

our journey, so Greg nonchalantly selected reverse gear and backwards we went).

(3) Any vehicle not mindful of the etiquette of meeting others safely had better have wings.

The river to be found in the depths of Skippers Canyon also features in some Ford of Bruinen scenes in *The Fellowship of the Ring*, but our tour did not venture that far. There is a special Skippers Canyon trip for Hobbit Botherers with stouter hearts than Michael, Siobhan, Naomi, Kate, THB and yours truly.

Back in Queenstown we were dropped outside Nomad's offices, a slice of heaven for THB in that they were packed with *Lord of the Rings* books, videos and games, Legolas, Frodo and Aragorn figurines and even specially designed armour and weapons to buy. Somehow I couldn't see us getting a sword past airport security on our way home, even if it was a shiny replica of Anduil, but THB did invest in a *Lord of the Rings Trivial Pursuit* game. It is a great triumph in my life that the first time we played this game I managed to defeat her, yes defeat The Mighty Hobbit Botherer, thanks to an abundance of multiple choice questions and a little inspired guesswork. It hasn't happened since.

On our second trip of the day, imaginatively named the "B" tour by Nomad Safaris to distinguish it from the "A" tour earlier on, we were taken along the shores of Lake Wakatipu to Glenorchy in a 4WD with the registration plate ARWEN. Ominously we were shadowed by another 4WD with the registration plate ORCS for most of the afternoon. At each sightseeing stop we expected it to disgorge a bunch of ugly creatures baying for our blood.

Our driver was an older and marginally less possumicidal version of Greg called Martin and our fellow passengers a father and daughter from New York, Paw and Jo (yes he really introduced himself as Paw) and a pair of elderly Scottish ladies who obviously thought it would be much too vulgar to be on first name terms with us so early in our acquaintanceship. Or at all really. Maybe not even with each other.

Before we had reached the outskirts of Queenstown we had stopped twice, first for Jo to buy something to drink and then for Jo to find a bathroom. For those unfamiliar with the American vernacular, I suspect she wanted to relieve herself rather than to take a bath, although it has to be admitted, she did take rather a long time about it. This seemed to annoy the Scots immensely. They erupted into fits of tut-tutting and tried to coax THB and me into joining an anti-American alliance. We refused, reflecting that if the poor woman had to pee it was better that she did it somewhere other than inside the 4WD. Particularly since I was sitting next to her.

Our first *Lord of the Rings* stop of the afternoon was a few kilometres outside Queenstown at Closeburn Bay. This was a location which offered glorious views over Lake Wakatipu but no tingle of déjà vu, despite being used for scenes at the end of *The Fellowship of the Ring* when a band of rampaging Orcs finally caught up with The Fellowship at *Amon Hen*. The problem was that the cinematic *Amon Hen* was a Frankenstein's monster stitched together from a number of component locations. Closeburn Bay was a mere kneecap.

The bolt through the neck of the *Amon Hen* monster, the bit everyone remembers, was lurking beyond the end of Lake Wakatipu along a seemingly endless gravel road stretching across river flats. When Martin finally brought the 4WD to a halt in a beautiful stand of beech forest, rays of sunshine filtering through the green canopy above to spotlight mossy stumps on the leafy floor below, he announced that this was (close to) where Sean Bean as Boromir had met his end. Well the end of an Uruk-hai arrow to be precise.

In the brief time set aside for arboreal admiration while sipping beverages provided by our driver, two couples set off to explore the forest while the other pair sat resolutely in the 4WD complaining that foreign tea didn't taste as good as it did back in Bonnie Scotland. (I hear that the tea terraces of Glasgow are a wonderful sight to behold, particularly at harvest time). When THB and I returned, with Jo and Paw still missing, tut-tutting was already in full swing.

Even my Death of Boromir tableau, with a stick playing the role of the fateful arrow shaft, didn't lighten their mood. It did amuse two Japanese girls though, passengers from ORCS which had arrived during our absence. (ORCS joining ARWEN at *Amon Hen* for an afternoon cuppa is one scene that never made it into the movies). I imagine a Japanese family some weeks later settling down to watch their daughter's holiday footage from New Zealand only to see a strange gaijin in red trousers messing about with a stick. I would have loved to have heard the daughter's commentary.

By the time our American friends returned, Martin had brought off the transfer coup of the century by swapping two huffy Scottish ladies, who would now ride in ORCS, for the friendly Japanese filmmakers, who would join us in ARWEN. I'm sure money must have changed hands as well.

Our return journey offered fleeting views of distant peaks, Misty Mountains during *Lord of the Rings* filming, and wooded foothills, also known as Fangorn Forest. These were quickly swallowed in billowing clouds of dust as ARWEN lumbered back down the unsealed road to Glenorchy. Martin said that Lothlorien, the woodland paradise where The Fellowship encountered the mysterious Galadriel, was also nearby. But we didn't pay the elf queen a visit. I think he was afraid we might get the tut-tutting Scots back if ORCS fetched up at the same time.

Instead of Lothlorien there was Ithilien, specifically the spot where Sam's taste buds moistened as he contemplated rabbit stew, his eyes moistened as he caught sight of oliphaunts and his underwear moistened as he and Frodo were captured by Faramir. In real life we had reached Twelve Mile Delta, just a few kilometres away from our first stop, at Closeburn Bay.

With Paw resting in the 4WD the Japanese girls, THB and I followed Martin on a meandering walk through dry scrubland until we finally came to the cliff from which oliphaunts had been sighted. Even without the beasts it was an 'I remember this from the movie' moment. Our oriental companions felt sufficiently moved to lay down and peer over the edge, just as Sam and Frodo had done. Then they got up to reveal a generous and tenacious coating of dust and grass on the front of their clothes. Now that's why THB and I didn't lay down.

As we wandered through the scrub wondering whether to revert to childhood and attempt a re-enactment of the battle between oliphaunt owning baddies and Faramir led goodies (the bit where Faramir captured the Hobbits was all a mistake really, they parted friends and still send each other Christmas cards) a scream jerked us back from Middle Earth.

"Stop! Stop!" was its simple message, grabbing the attention in the way that only a scream and a dentist's drill can. We looked around to see where it was coming from, and maybe to offer help, only to be told "Don't look! Don't look!" But we'd already seen. Jo's head was peeping out from a patch of scrub that would have been waist high had she been standing up. "Go the other way," she begged. "This is the *Lord of the Rings* bathroom."

It was time to return to Queenstown.

As we piled back into the 4WD, Martin enquired, "Has anyone been on the 'A' tour?"

THB and I said that we had, that very morning.

"Which one did you like best?"

I pitched in first with an answer. "This one went to the better movie locations." (Ever the diplomat). "But the one this morning was scarier with that narrow track on the way to Skipper's Canyon." (Ever the fool).

"Not scary enough for you, eh?"

Martin grinned and proceeded to give us an exhibition of just how steep an incline a 4WD can tackle going up... then coming down. Then how steep and high an incline a 4WD can tackle going up... then coming down. Then how steep, high and bumpy an incline a 4WD can tackle going up... then coming down. You get the idea.

Just as we thought the white knuckle ride had come to an end he made for the river. Maybe you've seen jet boats careering down narrow canyons, almost bouncing their passengers' heads off rocky walls, then doing the nautical equivalent of a handbrake turn in a shower of spray. This was Martin's next trick, only he was on four wheels... at least some of the time.

"Okay Martin, the afternoon tour was scarier."

The following day it was time for us to renew our acquaintance with State Highway 6 and the 2WD Colt to head off for Te Anau. But not before we had made one last Hobbit bothering visit in Queenstown, Middle Earth. That was to Deer Park Heights, the hotbed of *Lord of the Rings* (and other) filming locations we'd peered down on earlier from the road to the Remarkables Skifield.

Deer Park Heights was a wildlife park which boasted fiercely inquisitive goats and donkeys roaming freely as well as the eponymous deer in several varieties and more unexpected creatures such as bison, llamas and thar. (The thar is a kind of woolly mountain goat from the Himalayas famed for its sure footedness in precipitous terrain and the ability to ascend inclines that even Martin's 4WD couldn't tackle, thumbing its nose metaphorically at government sanctioned hunters with rifles who seek to keep its numbers down. It sits high up with the possum on the New Zealand hit list for crimes against indigenous flora).

But it was not to see the animals that we'd paid our twenty dollars at the tollgate and set the Colt on a winding climb, pleasant enough viewing though they were. One of us wanted to experience the promised panoramic views over the Queenstown area, Lake Wakatipu and the surrounding snow capped mountains. The other wanted to see where Legolas had fired arrows at the Warg, where Legolas had leapt athletically onto his horse before battling the Warg, where Aragorn had lazily tumbled over a cliff to go for a swim while Legolas continued in a heroic manner to turn Warg into ex-Warg and where Gimli had fallen from his horse with all the grace of a sack of carrots while Legolas rode on with effortless majesty. Did I mention that THB is a Legolas fan?

Even as a Hobbit bothering sceptic who can count the number of times he has seen *The Two Towers* on one hand with a thumb to spare, I have to admit that Deer Park Heights was something special. Fists of grey rock punched through a grassy hillside with jagged mountains climbing to watch from the shores of a turquoise blue lake below. From some spots there was no sign at all of buildings, roads or any stamp of modern living upon the landscape. The air was clean, the sky was vast, the terrain ripe for exploring on horseback. This was Rohan for us, at least until we visited Mount Potts Station later on.

Surprisingly we got to explore all this beauty almost alone, locals not being interested in anything but the physical challenge of a run to the top of the Heights and the occupants of passing tour buses not being allowed outside to play like we were. THB stood on the rocky outcrop where Legolas first sighted the Warg and I took her photograph. (This is one of my favourites since the camera lens embellished the scene with a vertical shaft of light immediately above THB's head, making her look as if she was in the process of being beamed up to the *Starship Enterprise*). I dived over the cliff where Aragorn was carried by a stampeding Warg and THB took my photograph. (Luckily it was only a couple of feet to a grassy landing. Special effects helped Aragorn to fall further horizontally than he did vertically as he landed in the Kawarau River, which we crossed on our way out of Queenstown). Then we both marvelled at and took photographs of the weedy edged mountain tarn which the refugees from Edoras passed on their way to Helms Deep, mirroring both blue sky and jagged topped Remarkables.

But *The Two Towers* is not the only film to use Deer Park Heights as a location. There is also that classic of the late nineteen eighties *The Rescue* in which, I'm reliably informed by the internet movie database, a group of kids spring their Navy Seal fathers from a North Korean prison. The prison set, a walled enclosure with a pagoda like building at one end decorated with a picture of an oriental gentleman who looks as if he suffers from constipation, was left in place for the *The Rescue II* which never materialised. Why? Maybe *The Rescue's* rating of 4.1 out of 10 on the internet movie database gives you a clue. Kevin Dillon (Matt's brother) was nominated for a 'best young actor in a motion picture (drama)' award for his performance as J J Merrill in *The Rescue* though. Inspired to greatness by the location, no doubt.

A piece of advice. As you pay your twenty dollars to enter Deer Park Heights, consider very carefully the small additional investment needed to acquire a nut tin. The place is very beautiful, but eventually you will have to leave, to eat, to sleep, to get on with your life, and the nuts will make this process so much easier.

As the Colt approached, a herd of donkeys milling about near the exit gate assembled themselves into a line across the road blocking our passage. We advanced slowly and they stood their ground with steely eyed determination, like policemen in riot gear, not that THB and I have first hand experience of policemen in riot gear, you understand. We beeped the horn, but still they refused to budge. We wound the window down to shout, "Could you please let us through?" and when that didn't work, "Clear off, you buggers!" but were still only rewarded by a face full of donkey slaver. They were used to receiving nuts from passing vehicles and didn't see why we should get away without paying our toll. In the end we edged forward trying to gently nudge the four legged extortionists out of the way, wondering whether, if we injured one, we'd be praised as if we'd dispatched a possum or jailed as if we'd murdered a kiwi (or even a Kiwi). Luckily we never had to find out. A tour bus appeared on the track behind us and the donkeys, sensing richer pickings, left us alone.

State Highway 6 hugs the shore of Lake Wakatipu's eastern arm, continuing beyond its fingertips towards the farming and fishing town of Lumsden. Just before Lumsden, State Highway 94 branches off to

Te Anau. Before we'd gone too far south THB and I stopped to enjoy a final view of the lake and to feast on sandwiches we'd bought before we left Queenstown. It was here that I heard a rustling in the undergrowth, presaging an encounter with a wild kiwi perhaps...

...then I heard a loud "Psst!"

It was Jack Peterson's strange headless chicken of a celebration dance that was causing all the noise. His grin was wider than I'd ever seen before.

"Yur imprission of Boromir nir Glenorchy was putticirly impressive," he said. "And yur ricreition of Aragorn's fall on Dir Purk Hights was inspured."

I couldn't quite see where he was going with this.

"But I remibur you lurfing at piple drissed as Hubbits and Ilves when we first mit."

Now I had a map.

"That was different. I was messing about. They were taking it sirri... sorry seriously!"

"It's only a mitter of tim. Only a mitter of tim. I'll ixpict you to driss up at the nixt mitting!"

The bugger. He wasn't trying to cure THB, he was trying to poison me... and I'd been happily sipping from his chalice.

All that would change now I'd been warned.

15: TE ANAU

Thousands Of Pinpricks Of Light.

The drive from Queenstown to Te Anau took us through a grassland wilderness designated a conservation area for red tussock, an odd name seeing as most of the stuff THB and I saw was orange or brown. Apparently it provides an excellent habitat for New Zealand's many unique species of bird including local speciality the takahe. You'll be introduced more formally later on.

Starkly beautiful though tussock grassland is, kilometre after kilometre of it can become a little wearisome on the eye. Suffering from lake, waterfall and *Lord of the Rings* withdrawal, THB scanned our road atlas and discovered three yellow eyes about forty kilometres up a metal road leading off from State Highway 94. Mavora Lakes, at the end of this road, and their tranquil surroundings, provided the real life location for the pile of dead Orcs on the fringes of Fangorn Forest, Nen Hithoel and the Silverlode River. I suspect all but the most dedicated Hobbit botherers will be scratching their heads at the last two, so some explanation may be required.

The junction of the Silverlode and the Anduin in Middle Earth is the point from which the Fellowship leave Lothlorien by boat bearing Galadriel's special gifts. After some paddling they pass the Pillars of the Kings, then land their boats on the shores of a lake to set off into the woods for Boromir's death scene. I suspect Boromir didn't know that was coming, otherwise he'd never have left the boat. That lake is Nen Hithoel. It is also where Sam rushed into the water to catch Frodo as The Fellowship finally broke up, actor Sean Astin having to be flown to hospital by helicopter after impaling his foot on a submerged piece of broken glass. Maybe he shouldn't have left the boat either.

As we pressed on down State Highway 94, THB spotted a sign for 'Lakes' supplemented by dire warnings about the state of the road beyond. Were they the correct lakes? Would the Colt survive the journey? Would it be dark by the time we drove back, so we'd hit a tree or kill some rare local beastie with no road sense? I managed to plant the seeds of doubt in THB's mind. In the end she consulted the map and said that if 'Lakes' was indeed the correct turn, there would be another one we could take a short distance down the road anyway.

So we drove on and on and on, passing no likely looking side road, and ended up in Te Anau.

Phew. That was one Hobbit bothering opportunity averted. It's your own fault for warning me, Peterson.

Te Anau was our third consecutive town on the shores of a beautiful lake, all different in character. Wanaka for those who want to view great scenery from a comfortable distance, Queenstown for those who want to jump off great scenery then return to a comfortable hotel and Te Anau for those who want to get out and amongst great scenery, sleep in camper vans or tents, wear muddy boots and muddier underwear and carry a dictionary to look up the word comfortable if they are asked what it means.

Fortunately for us, in addition to being a haven for outdoorsy trampers, Te Anau was also the gateway to Fiordland, an overnight stop for coach tours on their way to Milford Sound. So there were hotel rooms to be had. Instead of sleeping beneath the stars (or more probably rain clouds) we could enjoy the hospitality of the *Te Anau Hotel and Villas* for three nights. Although the name suggests this establishment was the only hotel in Te Anau, I'm sure there must have been others. The fact that I can't remember seeing any is probably a trick of my memory. But THB can't remember any either. Hmmm.

The hotel was a long, thin, low-rise affair with rooms leading out onto a well kept garden and swimming pool area along one side and upmarket rooms with a lake view (over a car park and main road) on the other. Our allocation on the downmarket side was eminently

com-fort-a-ble *adj. Providing physical comfort;*
producing feelings of ease or security.

The lake was low rise too compared to its northern cousins, the mountains surrounding it being more distant, not crowding in to dominate every view. Its shores were green and wooded with a pebbly beach nestling beside the road which passed in front of our hotel.

THB and I strolled along the beach in gathering gloom, breathing in the delicious aroma of hot and vinegary food from camper vans lining its edge. Somewhere nearby a take-away was bidding for the world chip frying record. We savoured the last few moments of dry weather we would experience for a while (though we didn't know it at the time) then it was off to the main drag for dinner, pausing only to photograph the giant moa sized replica of a pukeko, a colourful, flight-shy rather than flightless bird, mounted opposite the Te Anau visitor centre.

The plan for the evening was to eat, then watch a film, so having selected an Italian restaurant and made sure it had plenty of spare tables, we set off to find the Fiordland Cinema to pre-book tickets before our meal. (The concept of being able to book tickets is familiar to the locals of Te Anau, unlike those of Greymouth). On our return to the restaurant there was only one free table remaining. It was ours! By the time we'd finished our meal a queue extended out of the door and down the street. Wonderful food, but we never managed to get a table there again.

Finding the cinema wasn't easy either. THB and I weren't expecting a giant multiplex but we weren't quite prepared for just how small and understated the cinema building would be. No hint of flashing neon lights or giant posters to drag the punters in, just a glass fronted building that could have been the reception for an office complex until you got up really close. Twice we walked past it down the aptly named Wong Way (only missing an 'R') before finally cottoning on.

It was worth the trouble though. Fiordland Cinema provided the most sumptuous movie experience either of us had ever experienced. The sound was excellent, the screen large (much larger than you'd any right to expect from a mere fifty-two seater) and the seats were nothing short of amply padded armchairs. Sofas for two in the back row would have been the only possible improvement. This would be THE place to watch the *Lord of the Rings* trilogy all the way through without the accompaniment of a numb bum.

We watched a Kiwi film called *In My Father's Den* about a war journalist returning to New Zealand for his father's funeral who becomes a suspect when a young girl he has befriended disappears. It was shot at around the town of Roxburgh almost directly east from where we were sitting, and starred Miranda Otto, a good enough actress to prevent me thinking, "Hey that's Eowyn. Where are the Rohirrim?" whenever she appeared on screen.

Leaving the cinema in the dark we began the walk back to the hotel through the streets of Te Anau, well street really, deserted except for us and another couple walking in front. They were close enough for us to hear snippets of conversation...

"I wonder if the werewolf is out tonight."

"A bloke saw it down by the water last month. It was in the paper."

"Was he a tourist?"

"Yeah."

"They say it only goes for tourists."

...then they turned off in a different direction.

Not wishing to worry THB, I checked to see whether there was a full moon as furtively as I could. But it's not easy to scour the skies behind you (and the streets as well just in case) furtively.

"Is it a full moon?" THB asked. Nought out of ten for furtiveness then.

"I can't tell. It's too cloudy."

"Oh."

What THB should have been asking herself was could she run faster than me with a werewolf in tow? Judging by the tightness with which she held my hand as we quickened our steps back to the hotel, she had indeed asked herself that question and decided it would be best not to let me get away.

New Zealand, before man arrived and brought other mammals with him, was a haven for birds. They thrived in the absence of predators and the most bird-brained among them even abandoned flight so they could grow big and fill niches that mammals occupied elsewhere. The tall moa fitted into a giraffe sized hole in the eco-system, kiwi took the place of small insect eating mammals and the takahe, something like a blue and green turkey with a pink face like an embarrassed parrot, filled the wandering about and grazing role of sheep. It drew the line at being sheared though.

For over fifty years the takahe was thought to be extinct until in 1948 a determined ornithological detective by the name of Geoffrey Orbell tracked down a group in the Murchison Mountains. Since then a programme of culling animals such as deer, which compete with the takahe for food, combined with the hand rearing of chicks from eggs that would not be viable in the wild, has helped their numbers grow. As the hand reared chicks are destined for release back into the wild they must be fed using adult takahe puppets, to teach them who their friends are, and shown scary puppet shows with stuffed stoats cast as baddies, to teach them who their friends aren't. Just imagine being able to answer the question, "What did you do at work today Daddy?" with "I played the stoat in a puppet show for a takahe."

Much pioneering work on the hand rearing of takahe was carried out at the Te Anau Wildlife Centre just out of town on the road to Manapouri. (I imagine the stoat versus takahe script being honed to perfection during rehearsals with a harassed director shouting, "Hey you! Stoat! Act as if you mean it! We can weaselly get someone else in to do your job you know!") This was our first stop the morning after our lycanthropic scare.

The Wildlife Centre, on the shores of Lake Te Anau, was much more low key than I had expected given its importance in the takahe story. Entry was by payment of a dollar per person in an honesty box, this sum entitling us to view avaries containing parakeets, kaka and kea, (types of parrot) weka, (an aquatic bird) and tui (a song bird, probably THE song bird in New Zealand), along with a waterfowl enclosure and a central run containing takahe and its close relative, the able to fly but can't be bothered to that often, pukeko. That was the problem.

The pukeko is a chicken like bird with black and blue plumage and a red beak. The takahe, as I have mentioned, is a turkey like bird with dark green and blue plumage and a pink face. I cannot say that on the basis of that description I could convict in court a bird accused of being a takahe but claiming to be a pukeko. Maybe it is just my untrained northern hemisphere eye.

THB and I came up with five possible ways of deciding whether a bird was, in fact, a takahe or a pukeko. Sadly all of them had downsides which made them useless in practice.

(1) Ask it. (Unless your name is Doolittle and you have a medical qualification the chances of receiving a meaningful reply are small).

(2) Creep up behind it and say BOO loudly. If it is a pukeko it will take to flight. (A little cruel and possibly unreliable. You may just happen upon a plucky pukeko).

(3) Creep up behind it and poke it with a stick. If it is a pukeko it will take to flight. (Okay it's a variation of (2), but a bit more likely to catch a brave pukeko out).

(4) Introduce the bird to some boiling water and make a stew. If it is a takahe you will be offered a chance to spend some time

exploring the inside of a Kiwi jail. If the Kiwi constabulary throw a party for you it was a possum. In that case see an optician. (A non destructive test really would be a better option).
(5) Go back into town and purchase an illustrated guide to Kiwi birds (not just kiwi birds) in full colour. Compare the pictures with real life to help you in your decision. (The kindest option, but can you be bothered? Will knowing whether you have really seen a takahe improve your life that much?)

During our visit, THB and I encountered two birds strutting nonchalantly about the takahe/pukeko enclosure at the Te Anau Wildlife Centre, but we remain unsure whether we can actually claim a takahe sighting. Takahe or not takahe, that is the question, as William Shakespeare almost said. Wildlife centre staff, who surely would have been able to put us out of our misery, seemed to be in a worse state number wise than the takahe itself. From our experience they may already have been extinct. Or maybe they were just in the back of a hut somewhere deeply engaged in a breeding programme.

The last word on the takahe is that it is part of the rail family. Maybe that is why it is in such peril. People keep hanging clothes on it and running trains over the poor thing.

Little did I know that since our failed attempt to visit the *Lord of the Rings* filming locations at Mavora Lakes, THB had been hatching a plan. Probably with the help of Jack Peterson. She had found two more yellow eyes beside the road from Te Anau to Manapouri. How could she make certain that she would get to visit these Hobbit bothering havens?

"I'll drive," she said.

You may remember that my first experience with the Colt back in Picton was far from auspicious. THB did much better. Without the aid of a hire company employee she coaxed the machine ten kilometres or so down State Highway 95, only occasionally fumbling between the front seats for a non-existent gear stick. Then, nose pressed to windscreen and knuckles turning white on the steering wheel, she guided it down a rough gravel track leading (so her navigator maintained) to a bend in the Waiau River. This waterway was Hobbit botheringly famous for its day or two in the sun as the mighty River

Anduin (another one) during *Lord of the Rings* filming.

Finally THB spotted a flat piece of ground, obviously used as a viewing point by vehicles before us, and crunched to halt. We would walk the rest of the way then... if THB could walk. She emerged from the car rubber legged and sweating, like a bomb disposal expert who'd just cut the correct wire.

"You drive," she said.

So I retired from navigational duties, with a one hundred percent record in getting us where we wanted to go, to take up chauffeuring once again.

After a short walk through dusty scrubland dotted with wizened trees, we finally sighted the river. Its water was a greeny blue, fast flowing in a central channel and more sedate at the edges, with fallen trees basking in mid stream. The starkness of the near bank, cliffs of bare earth in the early stages of being colonised by vegetation, contrasted with the lushness of the far bank, trees crowding down to the water's edge, almost rising from the river itself. The place was so quiet, so peaceful, so beautiful. And we were the only ones there.

It occurred to me that without the *Lord of the Rings* movies we wouldn't have been there. Nor would we have been to the stunning Matamata, Kaitoke Regional Park or Deer Park Heights. Finally I was cottoning on. The *Lord of the Rings* movies were secret guides to Kiwi treasures that non Hobbit bothering tours would never unearth. Secret guides visible to all but understood by very few. A bit like books by Stephen Hawking. And I was lucky enough...

Good grief. Jack Peterson nearly had me there.

As THB and I stood admiring the scene before us and enjoying the perfect silence, we suddenly became aware of a very soft buzzing sound.

zzzzzzzzzzzzzzzz.... Probably a gnat.
zzzzzzzzzzzzzzzzz.... Or possibly a bluebottle.
zzzzzzzzzzzzzzzzzz.... Maybe even a bee.
ZZZZZZZZZZZZZZZZZZ... Surely not a lawnmower?
ZZZZZZZZZZZZZZZZZZZ... VVVVVVVVVROOM... SPLASH!

It was a bright yellow jet boat.

Although the peace had been shattered, we were compensated with the bonus of finding out exactly which *Lord of the Rings* scenes had been filmed at this location courtesy of the boat's very loud public address system. I suppose it had to be loud enough to be heard over the VVVVVVVVVVROOM.

THB's next Hobbit bothering stop was only a short drive away. At least the car park at Rainbow Reach (sounded attractive) was only a short drive away. The actual filming location for The Dead Marshes (sounded not quite so attractive) was separated from the car park by a considerable walk, starting with a swingbridge across the Waiau River and continuing along the Kepler Track, a famed sixty kilometre loop covering mountain tops, beech forest, lake edges and wetlands. The wetlands, we presumed, were what we were after.

The uncertainty of the length of walk required worried THB. The whole Kepler track would take three or four days according to our guide book and there wasn't really even one day to spare in our itinerary. The swingbridge worried me. It made the one back at Kaitoke Regional Park (which I had only just stopped revisiting nocturnally before waking up in a cold sweat) look almost welcoming. While we watched, a succession of happy trampers tackled it without a qualm. THB and I tramped back to the car and headed for Manapouri, a quiet and beautiful town, nestling at the eastern end of the lake which shares its name, where State Highway 95 finally gives up and surrenders to water, mountain and bush.

The name Manapouri was bestowed upon the lake, and so the town as well, by a less than professional European map maker who shoddily transcribed the Maori name Manawapora (or sorrowing heart) and then applied it to the wrong piece of water. The Maori names for the lake were Moturau (many islands) or Roto-ua (rainy lake). South Mavora was the real Manawapora.

THB and I drove along the quiet road which skirted the lake shore, marvelling at some handsome real estate lining it on our left and handsome views from said real estate, over the lake and bush covered islands (1 out of 2 for the Maori) to mountains beyond, on our right. As we stopped to take a walk along the stony beach at the lake's fringe it began to rain (2 out 2 for the Maori).

Arriving at half past eleven and allowing ourselves the rest of the morning to explore the town, we were ready to depart with ten minutes to spare. Manapouri is a picturesque town with a few hundred inhabitants according to our guide book, although town may be something of an overstatement. A few hundred of its inhabitants were apparently elsewhere on the day we visited. There wasn't even anyone to furnish us with a midday pie.

Although Manapouri is small (and seemingly deserted except for brief periods of activity when coach loads of tourists hit town on the first leg of their bus-boat-bus-cruise trip to Doubtful Sound) it does boast one amenity that many larger conurbations in other countries might regard with envious eyes. Like many collections of houses in New Zealand that dream of one day graduating to the status of hamlet, it has its own airport. Often, these airports are only open for limited times during the day, when the cows are in for milking and the field is clear, for example, but airports they still are. The Manapouri airport code is TEU, which the pedant might say really indicates its big brother Te Anau.

So lets recap what we know about Manapouri. It stole its name from South Mavora, somehow insisted than Te Anau's airport should be named after it and is competing to have its lake recognised as the fifth biggest in New Zealand at the expense of poor Lake Ellesmere. Feisty little place eh? Incidentally I'm very impressed if you remembered the Lake Ellesmere story from chapter twelve. There's not an exam at the end of this book you know.

As we left Manapouri, heading back towards Te Anau, THB noticed a track leading off the side of the road that looked as if it headed in the direction of The Dead Marshes. A Hobbit bothering walk had been averted but not a Hobbit bothering drive. For what seemed like an eternity we crunched our way down a winding gravel track hemmed in by trees on the sort of journey that always ends with an isolated cabin and a madman with an axe in the movies. Luckily we weren't in the movies (though generous offers for the movie rights to the work you are reading will of course be given due consideration) so all we discovered was a landing stage on the Lake Manapouri shore with an axeless man beside it trying to encourage a jet ski into, or should that be onto, the water. From the furtive glances he gave us, I would guess that either the jet ski wasn't his or he thought I was the mad axeman.

One day, back in the nineteen forties, a man called Lawson Burrows began to ponder the original Maori name for Te-Anau, Te Ana-au, which translates as the cave of swirling water. "Where is this mysterious cave?" he thought, then disappeared for three years to look for it, or possibly even to dig it. Given the devotion with which he stuck to the task I suspect that a wager was involved somewhere. Lawson's description of what he eventually found is reproduced in the visitor's guide to the Te Anau Glow-worm caves.

"It was a fantastic sight... it looked like a page out of a space fiction picture book, a weird place but not at all frightening. Now give me the hundred dollars you owe me."

Actually I made up the last bit.

The caves are now Te Anau's major paying attraction, reached, if you believe the advertising literature, by means of a thirty five minute scenic cruise. True, the view across the lake from the boat at the landing stage was scenic enough. People were almost fighting each other for positions up on deck as I muttered calming words to THB within the vessel's belly. Words like, "At least it's not a jet boat," and "The water can't be very deep, it only comes half way up that duck."

Then we set sail and it was as if the Kiwi fire department had turned their hoses on us. The boat was buffeted mercilessly for the complete journey and any hope of viewing spectacular scenery (I'm sure it was out there somewhere) disappeared in a white-out of spray. Very, very wet people who had been on deck a just few moments before fought each other for positions inside.

We disembarked with a cheer, which died when we realised we had to sail back again in an hour or two, then were shepherded into an auditorium to watch a film about the caves and their mysterious inhabitants. Cue a list of five things you didn't know about New Zealand glow-worms. Unless, of course, you are an entomologist or have visited a glow-worm grotto yourself.

(1) A glow-worm is not a worm but the larva of a fly called a fungus gnat. Basically it's a maggot with a good publicity man. After all, who'd travel for half an hour across a lumpy lake to see a bunch of maggots?
(2) Eventually the larva grows up to become a pupa, then an adult. But neither of those is capable of eating, so the larva must stuff

itself silly with enough nosh to last it for the rest of its life. You can understand why the stage of the beastie's life cycle after the larva is pronounced pooper.

(3) To attract flying insects, fine cuisine to a glow-worm, a bunch of larvae gather together on the roof of a dark cave, then each shines a bright light from its bum. (Neat trick if you can do it). Flying insects, not noted for their quick wittedness, think, "They must be stars, I'll fly towards them," then get caught on sticky fishing lines dangled for that very purpose.

(4) All that sounds well and good, but there is one thing that worries me. If the flying insects are so keen on light, why do they travel deep into the dark caves in the first place? Unless, of course the flying insects are adult fungus gnats. Are glow-worms cannibals? I think we should be told.

(5) The scientific name for the New Zealand glow-worm is *Arachnocampa luminosa* which sounds like a spell Harry Potter would use to set fire to a gay spider.

THB was dismayed to discover that our journey into the cave system where the glow-worms lurked was to be a made alternately on foot (which she expected) and aboard a punt, sailing serenely upon the waters of an underground stream (which was a not altogether pleasant surprise). The final glide into the famed glow-worm grotto took place in the absence of man made light and in total silence, for fear of disturbing the creatures we'd come to see, causing them to turn off their display. Not only would this be disappointing for us but it would be potentially fatal for them as a glow-worm that doesn't glow doesn't eat either.

Everytime our guide shifted his weight to change the boat's direction and the craft wobbled ever so slightly in compensation, THB's hand grasped mine tighter. I felt that she wanted to scream, but couldn't... with every passing minute there was more pent up panic... and I couldn't say anything to help, couldn't calm her down.

But in the end the sight that greeted us in the glow-worm grotto was worth it. Even THB agreed. Maybe in a moment of weakness, that she now strenuously denies ever happened, but believe me she did agree.

We sat with about eight other people, perfectly still, in perfect silence, deep in an underground cavern. There was no breath of wind, nothing but the eerie glow from thousands of pinpoints of bluey green light from the rocky walls around us and the roof above our heads. Our guide slowly twirled the punt around and they too performed a slow pirouette. It was the strangest feeling being surrounded by miniature lights and not knowing how close they were. One moment they were stars far, far away and the next at the end of a dangling fishing line that I fancied brushed my nose.

Like a page out of a space fiction book? Yes I'd go along with Lawson Burrows there.

On our first full day in Te Anau we had done the must do thing for anyone who stays there, we had visited the glow-worm caves.

On our second full day in Te Anau we did the must do thing for anyone passing through, we visited Milford Sound, in relentlessly pouring rain. I'm sure that if you've ever made the trek yourself you will agree that the last four words of that sentence are superfluous.

16: MILFORD SOUND

A Bird With A Rubber Fetish.

Just as with the West Coast glaciers, there is a Pakeha theory involving immense quantities of ice and long periods of time which describes how Fiordland's ruggedly beautiful landscape, probed by a host of finger-like inlets from the Tasman Sea, was carved. Then there is the Maori theory.

The Maori tell of a god named Tu-Te-Raki-Whanoa who used his giant digging stick to craft the fiords and lakes of the region, leaving two islands where his feet stood, Secretary Island at the entrance to Doubtful Sound and Resolution Island at the entrance to Dusky Sound. No doubt he took great care not to squash any takahe with his toes. His skill increased with practise, so the raggedy edges of the southern fiords gave way to crisper lines further north. His final masterpiece was Milford Sound.

Te Hine-nui-te-po, the goddess of death, was impressed with Tu-Te-Raki-Whanoa's handiwork, but fretted that he'd created such a wonderful landscape that people would want to come and live there forever. Then she'd be out of a job, and what is more, the place would look untidy. So to remind the masses of their mortality and discourage all but the most leathery skinned from moving in, she released swarms of sandflies, eager to bite, at a place now known as Sandfly Point. Personally I reckon she had a hand in the weather as well.

To say it was raining cats and dogs as THB and I left Te Anau for Milford Sound would be an understatement. It was raining blue whales and giant moas as we drove north along State Highway 94, known as the Milford Road to its friends, following the shores of Lake Te Anua for thirty minutes or so before breaking off into the Eglinton valley beyond Te Anau Downs.

Visibility was poor at first. The closest we got to seeing anything of interest for a while was the intermittent appearance of Maui, Kea, Tui and Kiwi looming large and white on the road before us. Maybe there is an entry in the dusty tomes of New Zealand law that insists camper van hire companies have to associate themselves with birds. Maui seems to be the odd one out, not being a bird as far as I know, but the company has managed to stave off the lawyers by incorporating something resembling a blue dolphin with wings in its logo. We saw lots of Maui, Kea and Tui during our New Zealand travels but only a few Kiwi. Maybe they only come out at night.

At Te Anau Downs, the deluge decided to downgrade itself temporarily to a drizzle and, as we progressed, forested mountains began to take form through the mist, climbing from a valley floor carpeted in pink and purple lupins that looked as if they'd been lifted from an Impressionist painting. Our first stop, to experience the scenery in its full glory rather than between windscreen wiper strokes, was at Mckay Creek. On a clear day this location promised really spectacular views of the lupin lined Eglinton River winding its way through tussock covered flats sandwiched between the Earl and Livingstone mountains. Marbled by patches of mist, thinner here and thicker there, the view that greeted us was merely spectacular.

The journey through the valley and into the mountains beyond was punctuated by a succession of signs tempting us from the road for yet another stunning view. 'Mirror Lakes', said one, promising a mini Lake Matheson experience with mountain tops reflected in tranquil waters, if you were able to see mountain tops in the first place, of course. 'Knobs Flat', said another, not indicating something a dose of *Viagra* would be necessary to cure but a region of stony mounds left behind by retreating glaciers (or maybe blows from Tu-Te-Raki-Whanoa's stick). THB and I resisted both.

"Let's press on," she said, reluctant to venture outside the car in the rain.

There was no argument from me. I was keen to reach Milford Sound and if the water there looked calm and at least one of the tourist boats looked reasonably steady perhaps I would be able to coax THB onto a cruise. You don't travel to Milford Sound and not go on a cruise do you? But I would really need to be in THB's good books to pull that one off.

"Yes dear," I replied. "Anything you say."

The road between Mirror Lakes and Knobs Flat is known as 'The Avenue of the Disappearing Mountain'. Why such a name? Well, there are two competing theories. The one you'll find in the guide books says that the road itself slopes very gently, giving the impression that distant peaks, viewed from a vehicle moving towards them, are sinking into the surrounding forest. The other is that the mountain is always disappearing, if not permanently disappeared, behind a veil of white mist. (Misty Mountains, now that would make a good name for a *Lord of the Rings* location).

Around the hour and a half mark we passed Lake Gunn, its blue-grey waters fed by cascades from forested peaks gathered along its far shore, their outlines just visible between layers of cloud stacked motionless in the air before us. Next it was the smaller Lake Fergus, beyond which a group of tour buses had gathered in a lay-by beside what was probably a burbling brook on fine and sunny day, now swollen to become an angry torrent. The passengers had obviously been cooped up inside for a very long time. Long enough, in fact, to turn to suicide, as evidenced by the carelessness with which they ambled out from behind parked buses and into the path of passing cars (yes I was driving one of those cars) and the recklessness with which they scrambled up onto slippery rocks to fill bottles from the gushing stream. I imagine the tour guides must have spun some yarn about the miraculous restorative properties of mountain water in order to empty their buses and gain a few moments of peace.

State Highway 94 performs an abrupt ninety degree turn, heading west instead of north, at a place known as The Divide. This is the lowest east to west crossing point of The Southern Alps and the proposed terminus for at least two new transport links, involving roads, monorails and electric gondolas, devised to enable tourists to get in and out of Milford Sound as quickly as possible without the need to go through the spectacular drive which THB and I were two thirds of the way through experiencing. Missing the point, don't you think? These plans have been shelved at the time of writing, since just about everyone but the cash hungry developers thinks they are a bad idea.

Now we were in the mountains, rugged walls of grey stone rising up into a ceiling of low cloud from the forest around us, streaked white by hundreds of impromptu waterfalls, by products of the day's incessant rain. For a while the Hollyford River raced along beside the road, tumbling headlong past moss covered rocks in a fury of white water, gorging on the bounty cascading from the mountains. A sunny day would have offered breathtaking views of forested valleys and jagged peaks, but the waterfalls would then have vanished. The Milford Road drive cries out to be experienced more than just once.

After about two hours we approached the Homer tunnel. To save you looking through your collection of *The Simpsons* DVDs to find the episode where Bart and Lisa'a father dug a path through the mountains to Milford Sound, I should point out that the tunnel was named after W H Homer, who discovered the Homer Saddle at the end of the Hollyford Valley in 1889 and came up with the idea of burrowing through the ridge below. What are the chances of that? A man called Homer discovering a geographical feature that shared his name. Spooky eh?

Work on the tunnel was started in 1935 by a few men with hand tools and a very optimistic outlook on life and continued for twenty years, with an intermission for World War II, until the first private vehicles were able to drive through in the mid fifties. It still has a roughly hewn, water streaming down the walls, take your life into your hands feel today that would probably see it closed in many European countries on health and safety grounds. For bungy jumping, white water rafting, zorbing Kiwis it all adds to the rich tapestry of life. THB and I are with them.

The tunnel is single track, which means that travellers can experience a fifteen or twenty minute wait for a green traffic light, as a convoy makes it way through in the opposite direction. (If you don't like it, the alternative is a pickaxe and twenty years of sweat. Suddenly a fifteen minute wait doesn't seem so bad). A parking area is provided for those wishing to stretch their legs, enjoy the view (mountains dotted with patches of grubby snow emerging intermittently from swirling mist when we were there) or run the gauntlet of the kea.

In addition to being a camper van hire company, the kea is a rather heavily built and camouflage fatigue coloured alpine parrot with a thin and curved bill for rooting out food and a very, very, very (there can't really be enough verys here) bold and inquisitive nature. They make the donkeys on Deer Park Heights seem shy and retiring.

With regard to food, the kea isn't fussy. It will eat vegetable matter like roots and bulbs dug from the ground but also scavenge from the carcases of farm animals such as sheep that have come off second best in the harsh environment. Some high country farmers tell tales of flocks of kea squawking gleefully as they drive sheep over cliffs then pick their bones clean. I reckon this says more about what the farmers were growing and how much of it they had smoked that it does about the kea.

Perhaps the kea's strangest quirk, and that which brings it into conflict with motorists waiting at the Homer Tunnel and numerous other tourist spots around New Zealand, is its apparent love for rubber, particularly that in the shape of windscreen wiper blades and car tyres. It will peck and tear at these delicacies until distracted with a handful of bread or maybe a small child thrown on the ground, buying the besieged car or camper van owner a precious few seconds to drive way. Given the amount of time it spends in close proximity to moving parts of motor vehicles, and its less than sprightly waddle and hop gait when on the ground, I'm surprised that many of them survive long enough to produce little kea. Maybe the protection offered by the government has something to with it. I imagine that a flock of them flew up to The Beehive one day and said, "We want a law passed to protect our species. If you don't cooperate immediately, we know where your cars are parked."

Our closest encounter with the rubber loving parrot came at the entrance to the Homer Tunnel as we waited our turn to go through. A group of five or six bedraggled specimens were picking over some culinary offerings from past victims, so THB sauntered over to take a photo. She crept slowly towards one that had nonchalantly edged away on its own... while its colleagues hopped away behind her in the direction of the Colt. If they had had lips they would have been licking them.

The engine was revving, wheels in motion, albeit slowly, and wipers waggling on their most frantic setting as THB jumped back into the car and we set off past the green light and into the tunnel.

On the far side we were still half an hour from Milford Sound, with magnificent views over the Cleddau Valley to enjoy if we waited a week or two until the mist departed, and a short walk to The Chasm (a deep ravine in which sponge like rock formations have been carved out by the Cleddau River) to tempt us. We might even have succumbed had the blue whales and giant moas not returned with a vengeance.

Our first impression of Milford Sound as we finally reached the town at the water's edge was one of awe. There was an eerie quiet, sound deadened by a pall of cloud engulfing the tops of the steep tree lined glacial walls down which a collection of waterfalls silently tumbled, the perennial Bowen Falls joined by other smaller cascades, just up for the day. Out into the fiord there was nothing but white, the cloud becoming thicker and lower, even blotting out Mitre Peak, the world's highest sea cliff, normally said to dominate the skyline. It was as if the town, maybe the whole fiord, was holding its breath and waiting for the rain to pass. Then the bustle of tour buses, trampers, camper vans and cars, light aircraft and helicopters, which we'd expected to see, could begin again.

Although the streets, for the most part, had been emptied by a combination of rain and sandfly activity (Te Hine-nui-te-po is still doing her best) the car park (singular) was full. Along with several other cars we circled and circled, like vultures waiting for a wounded animal to expire, willing a space to become free. Then a family appeared, on foot, from the direction of the boat terminal. They wandered about for a bit (now where did we leave the car?) then squeezed into a small hatchback, not unlike the infamous Colt. *On your marks.* An animated argument raged between parents in the front and kids in the back. *Still on your marks.* Which eventually resulted in the huffy securing of seat belts all around. *Get set.* And a tyre screeching, wheel spinning departure. *Go!* We were beaten to the vacant spot by a fat-arsed Maui (oh the shame) which couldn't fit into the limited space (oh the joy) and so we were finally able to stop, get out, and explore the destination we had worked so hard to reach.

First of all we strolled to the boat terminal, making use of a convenient covered walkway, to watch a few cruise ships sailing serenely into to dock. Once THB had had the sereneness carefully pointed out to her, I reasoned, she might be willing to take a trip, to see mountaintops, dolphins, seals, penguins... wait a minute. We couldn't see the other side of the fiord from where we stood. Nor could we see a returning cruise ship until it had almost tied up in front of us. And it was bright orange. What hope was there for mountaintops, dolphins, seals, penguins... unless they were wearing high visibility jackets?

We walked back to the café beside the car park for some well deserved sustenance in the form of pumpkin and kumara (not to forget carrot) soup, hoping for a break in the weather. That break never came.

On our list of the world's most spectacular drives, THB and I both put Australia's Great Ocean Road somewhere near the top along with that ribbon of tarmac which clings desperately to the cliffs of Italy's Amalfi Coast. (We experienced the latter in the back seat of a local bus packed with Italian schoolgirls, one of whom, a Queen fan, kept asking us over and over again, "Hava you seen the arse of Freddie Mercury?"

Eventually, to our relief, her friend offered clarification. "She wants to know if you have seen the house of Freddie Mercury." Apparently it is a tourist attraction in West Kensington). Even in the pouring rain, or maybe because of the spectacular waterfalls created by the incessant downpour, The Milford Road is up there with the two of them. Three cheers for State Highway 94. We must go back one day in the sunshine. The trouble is, there's no telling when that sunshiney day will be.

17: THE CATLINS

An Explorer With A Sense Of Humour.

During our three weeks of travelling in New Zealand THB had developed a navigational strategy which had served us well, a strategy based upon three simple rules.

(1) Look at the road atlas the night before.
(2) Identify the road between where we are and where we want to be that passes within 'stop off and see' distance of the largest number of yellow eyes.
(3) That's the way to go.

Thanks to Peter Jackson, that strategy was useless for getting from Te Anau to Dunedin unless we were prepared to backtrack through Queenstown. There were no *Lord of the Rings* filming locations further south than the ones we'd already investigated near Manapouri. (It's a mystery to me why not. The teeming rain at the battle of Helm's Deep seems a perfect match for New Zealand's Southland). So what were we to do?

Our road atlas offered two non Hobbit bothering alternatives, the fast track through Lumsden and Gore or the slower Southern Scenic Tourist Route through Invercargill and The Catlins. As tourists we were naturally inclined towards the latter, but we looked up Gore in our trusty guide book just to give it a chance. Gore is the country music capital of New Zealand, the book advised. So The Catlins it was. Yeee Ha!

We began by following the Waiau River south through what seemed to be logging country to Clifden, where we paused briefly to view a retired suspension bridge dating from 1899, before continuing to Tuatapere. Now this was a place I wanted to see. All through our trip I had been plagued by bland sausages at breakfast time. Could Kiwis not make a tasty sausage? Well Tuatapere was the Sausage Capital of New Zealand. This was the place to find out...

...at least that was what I had hoped. Sadly there was no indication in town why it had been given (or maybe just adopted) this magnificent epithet, beyond a hint that a local butcher might have once considered it a jolly good wheeze. But it had caught on. A large sign showing a slightly dozy looking cartoon sausage in a baseball cap had been erected to introduce visitors to the Sausage Capital concept and there was even evidence of a company called Sausage Shuttles offering 'Southern Transport with a Sizzle' to trampers bound for Lake Hauroko to the west.

Before we leave Tuatapere, the dozy sausage sign also made a few other claims which I feel ought to be contested.

(1) End of Highway 99?
Highway 99 runs north to Clifden and south to Riverton and Invercargill from Tuatapere according to our road atlas. This must be some strange meaning of the word 'end' that I don't understand.

(2) Most southwestern town?
The road atlas again shows Te Waewae (no sniggering at the back) as further south and further west. Maybe it's too small to be considered a town. But then Tuatapere is also pushing its luck in that regard.

(3) Access to Hauroko, New Zealand's deepest lake?
I'm willing to concede this one as it only says 'access'. But the best route would surely be north through Clifden which offers better 'access'.

(4) Midway on the Southern Scenic Route?
If only. THB and I were aiming to travel the complete length of this road in one day and we'd barely gone a quarter of the way at the home of the sausage.

As it turned out the mystery of the tasteless sausage was resolved to just a few days later when THB discovered the horrific truth during a chance encounter with a Kiwi cookery programme while searching for *X-Files* repeats on television. (THB leads an alternate life as MSS, or Mulder and Scully stalker, to gain occasional relief from Hobbit bothering. I've never actually witnessed the transformation between THB and MSS but I suspect it involves much whirling about on the spot as with Wonder Woman and a whispered incantation such as "The truth is out there" or "The Orcs are out there" depending on which way she wants to go).

Back to sausages. The programme which THB saw advised budding cooks that these comestibles needed to be boiled for a couple of hours (or was it days?) before consumption. That's what happens to the flavour. It's boiled out.

This preparation method seemed to be received wisdom, there was no attempt to explain why extended immersion in very hot water was necessary. My own theory is that Kiwis have become so accustomed to dealing with carrots that any food that is vaguely carrot shaped gets treated in a similar way.

Both the Waiau River and the Southern Scenic Tourist Route hit the sea at Te Waewae Bay on New Zealand's southern coast. While the river just sort of hangs about and mingles with the sea, the road wanders along the coast making its way to Riverton, past desolate beaches relentlessly pounded by surf and macrocarpa trees having a very bad hair day. We saw a number of stands of these trees permanently bent backwards to escape the salty blast of fearsome winds blowing up from the Antarctic.

Riverton itself, an old whaling settlement, was a pleasant enough place, if a little sleepy, a sort of scaled up Tuatapere with sausages replace by paua shells. Every town has to have its niche, I suppose, and whale oil and blubber are politically incorrect nowadays. THB and I weren't interested in paua though. We drove into town looking for Shell of a different sort. The Colt's tank was getting low on fuel.

Acquiring petrol in a foreign country always presents a problem. You are an outsider on someone else's patch, unfamiliar with the local brand of filling station etiquette. Do you fill it yourself or wait for service? If you fill it yourself you risk spending the evening as the guest of local law enforcement operatives enquiring with some insistence, "Go on, tell us one more time how you were going to pay." If you sit in your vehicle and wait, you may waste an awful lot of time while they take bets in the garage shop as to how long your patience will last. Then out will stride a man built like an American fridge on legs. As you cringe before him, he'll offer witticisms like, "Have you got superglue on that car seat mate?"

As we drove into a service station on Riverton's main street I looked around for clues. What were other people doing? (We were the only car around). Was there a happy, smiling gas jockey bounding towards us? (No). Was there a sign saying "self service". (No). Was I unsure what to do? (Yes).

Reasoning that the police would probably take their time getting to a small town like Riverton, during which time any misunderstandings could be ironed out, I went for the DIY option. Slowly, without making any sudden movements, I removed the petrol cap and inserted the nozzle. I stopped and listened. (No sirens). I pulled the trigger for fuel. (No fuel). I released and pulled again. (Still no fuel). I looked down the nozzle. (You are waiting for the fuel to come shooting out into my face aren't you. What do you think this is? A Tom and Jerry cartoon?)

Around that point a ten or eleven year old boy appeared from behind a pump somewhere, stared at me for a while, took pity, then said, "You after butcher car dinners lot."

This did not help.

"It's not working," I said, more in an attempt to elicit further advice than to tell the youngster something he didn't already know. When he spoke again it was in a slow, talking to foreigners, kind of voice.

"You... have... to... put... your... card... in... the... slot."

The light dawned. But there was still a problem.

"I want to pay cash," I said, waving a few notes in his direction to illustrate the point.

"You... have... to... put... your... card... in... the... slot."

"Can't I pay cash?"

"Daaaad!"

A distant sound of sawing that had been accompanying proceedings stopped abruptly and a man appeared from a shed on the far side of the forecourt. The boy ran over to him, there was a short animated discussion, then the boy ran back and into the garage shop. To fetch a shotgun maybe? Or the fridge on legs? Neither. He returned brandishing a dusty master card which allowed him to fill our tank.

Back in the shop I handed over my dollars and waited patiently for my change. Change which would have to come from the till. The till that the young boy was trying hard to open. Trying with increasing desperation.

"Daaaad!"

I like to think that I performed a public service in encouraging a Kiwi lad to try a little bit harder at school when he returned after the Christmas break, so that he wouldn't have to work in a filling station when he grew up and deal with customers like me.

When THB and I were planning our trip to New Zealand our travel agent mentioned Invercargill, the half(ish) way point on the Southern Scenic Tourist Route, to us. It was preceded by the words "You're not thinking of going to" and followed by "Are you?" as I remember.

Having been there, for at least half and hour, I reckon it gets an undeservedly bad press. Sure it was a rather sprawling, wet and windy place, but its centre seemed rich in both history and amenities (that may have been the adrenaline rush of returning to the big city after a spell in the wilds though) and its people happy and full of life.

They embraced us wholeheartedly, allowing us to party with them when the local weather finally got the better of the ticket machine in the car park we had chosen and it was free parking all around for the afternoon. The saving was only a dollar or two but the celebrations were mighty. Is this the right time to point out Invercargill's Scots heritage?

South of Invercargill, at the end of a hook of land curving out to sea, lies the town of Bluff. Before visiting Southland I would have said Bluff had two claims to fame.

(1) As the departure point for ferries to Stewart Island, New Zealand's often overlooked real South Island on the other side of the Foveaux Strait.
(2) As the southernmost point on New Zealand's South Island, which is really New Zealand's Middle Island.

In fact there is a desolate piece of land sandwiched between a sheep field and the ocean some 50 km east of Bluff (also 803 km from the South Pole and 5140 km from the equator according to a signpost erected there) that is the real owner of the second crown. Take a bow Slope Point.

Bluff is only half as interesting as I though it was then.

THB and I had toyed with the idea of a day trip to Stewart Island but the ferocity of the waves off the coast washed away what little enthusiasm THB had for such a venture. I wasn't too disappointed, considering we still had a long drive ahead of us, but it did no harm to remind THB that she still owed me a boat journey. I could now add "Remember Stewart Island" to "Remember Milford Sound" in my locker, ready for retrieval when the next opportunity for travel by water came our way.

Beyond Invercargill the Southern Scenic Tourist Route headed east towards a beautiful corner of New Zealand in which native rainforest rubbed shoulders with windswept scrubland, isolated farms and a rugged rocky coastline loved by seals, sealions, dolphins and penguins. This was The Catlins. So why were we driving through instead of staying a few days? Because, like most people, we'd never heard of it when we planned our itinerary. If only Peter Jackson had taken his travelling band of pointy eared thespians there, things might have been different.

The road between Fortrose and Balclutha (two towns on the Southern Scenic Tourist Route and not a legal firm) assaulted us with a barrage of signs designed to lure us away from thoughts of the distance to our destination with offers of spectacular viewpoints, deserted beaches, wildlife havens, waterfalls, blowholes and caves. The one that snared us was 'Niagara Falls'. Of course we knew we weren't in Canada (THB checked and it said New Zealand on the front of our road atlas) but the New Zealand version just had to be impressive to be bold enough to appropriate the famous name. Didn't it?

It didn't.

We followed one of the few paved side roads between Fortrose and Balclutha (actually it might have been one of the one) until we came to another more homespun sign for 'Niagara Falls' pointing us to a dirt car park where we stopped, stretched our legs and listened for the roar of falling water. Nothing apart from our hearts beating with excitement. Deciding the falls must be a little further away than we thought, we prepared for a tramp. (This generally involved a ritual exchange of phrases like "I'll sit in the car" and "Oh no you won't" or "My shoe has got a hole in it" and "Of course it has, that's where your foot goes").

This particular tramp began with a few steps up a grassy bank, beyond which a river tumbled past some shiny rocks, hardly bothering to create white water in the process. "Niagara Falls must be further upstream," I said, turning to see THB pointing to a yellow and blue sign. The sign read:

The Niagara Falls were named by a surveyor with an obvious sense of humour who had seen the large North American Falls, and named these small falls after them.

Small falls? I'd seen more impressive cascades running off my shed roof after a rain shower. Lunch was called for.

Almost opposite the turn off for the falls was a sort of rambling country cottage with a menu outside and llamas in its garden. After several abortive attempts to find the right door to enter the public part of the building rather than the private living quarters, we went inside. The staff were busy tidying the place after either a coach party or a small tornado had just left, but cheerfully took our order for warming pumpkin and kumara (and carrot) soup (that stuff was becoming addictive) and left us alone to peruse a newspaper left behind by a previous visitor.

The front page headline was, "World's Tallest Chicken Found In New Zealand" (or something along those lines) accompanied by a picture of a happy looking farmer holding a rather puzzled looking bird as if trying to encourage it to walk on tiptoe. (Isn't that cheating?) Looking at the creature I reckon it would have had a fair chance at "World's Widest Chicken" as well. The accompanying article told the chicken's life story, from humble beginnings as an egg to country wide fame in a few short years. Most of the information was provided courtesy of the farmer, of course, but the bird itself did have one personal message for its adoring public. Asked whether it put its success down to diet, exercise or just good fortune it replied succinctly, "Cluck."

I'm not making this stuff up you know. Well maybe just the last sentence.

On our way to Niagara Falls earlier on I had spotted a sign for 'Petrified Forest' pointing further down the side road we were already on. On the basis that you don't see one of them every day (and not quite knowing what to expect) we headed further down that road and away from our route to Dunedin.

After a pleasant drive along a pretty stretch of coastline looking over Waikawa harbour and passing through the village itself, a sprinkling of dwellings set with grim determination against everything Antarctica could send forth, we reached a car park accompanied by a small 'Petrified Forest' sign.

A huddle of oddly bent trees in an adjacent field certainly looked petrified, but in the teeth-chatteringly frightened sense of the word (the icy wind responsible for that) rather than the turned to stone one. To get to the real petrified forest there was a precipitous climb down a set of wooden stairs clinging to the face of a cliff. There was good news and bad news for those crazy enough to descend. The bad news was that there was a gale blowing. The good news was that at least it was blowing onshore, pinning them to the rock rather than tearing them away to their doom. Yes, we were among the crazy ones. Well THB was. I thought about making my own bid for the "World's Biggest Chicken" crown, but in the end decided to follow her.

The story behind the forest begins 180 million years ago in the middle Jurassic period when New Zealand played quite happily with places like South America, Africa, Antarctica and even Australia in one big supercontinent called Gondwana. Curio Bay, was a strapping forest back then, happily minding its own business until tragedy struck one day and it was buried by volcanic debris. Gamely it grew back and was promptly buried again. At this point you'd have thought it would have got the message but no, it had to be buried at least twice more before that happened.

Over the millions of years that followed, water seeping into the wood deposited minerals which effectively turned it to stone. On a global scale the continents that we recognise today suffered irreconcilable differences and began to drift apart. New Zealand left the Gondwana party about 80 million years ago saying something like "I'm off, and I want custody of the kiwis." Relentless battering by the sea brought Curio Bay to the coast, finally living up to its name, and eroded softer rocks above the fossilised forest, bringing it to the surface for the delectation of tourists at low tide.

From a cliff top viewpoint the forest looked like a muddy field dotted with puddles and patches of moss. Closer up, the piles of mud transformed firstly into rocks, then into fossilised tree stumps, fallen logs and delicate ferns. I was impressed but THB was left cold. (That icy wind again). I think she was expecting specimens that were upright and head high at least, not lazy layabouts of trees. She may even have been expecting to encounter the odd group of wood elves (is there any other kind of group?) lounging about sharpening each other's aural appendages. Hobbit bothering withdrawal was beginning to bite.

I'd like to be able to regale you with tales of encounters with

Hector's dolphins frolicking close to shore in Porpoise Bay, with lolloping sealions catching a few rays on white sandy beaches at Cannibal Bay and with penguins waddling home after a hard day's fishing around Nugget Point. I'd like to, but I can't. By the time we'd clambered back up the Curio Bay cliff it was getting late, we'd only completed just over half of our mileage for the day and something had to give. All that wildlife was it. We even passed up the reputedly impressive Cathedral Caves, towering Gothic arches leading to voluminous caverns carved by the pounding of the sea, all to leave time to visit Purakaunui Falls.

We were assured that these were the real deal by all the guide books and pamphlets we had to hand, New Zealand's most photographed falls. (I can only assume that on the way to Huka Falls on the North Island, New Zealand's most visited natural attraction, there is an sour faced official who confiscates people's cameras).

For once the hype was deserved. A ten minute walk through beech and podocarp forest took us from car park to view point, where water cascaded twenty metres down three wide rocky tiers, like that party trick with champagne and stacked wine glasses but scaled up a bit. There was even another Niagara at the bottom with water tumbling a few inches over a step. A pretty rather than jaw droppingly awesome sight but a fine way to bid farewell to The Catlins, a region that had turned what could have been a lengthy slog from Te Anau to Dunedin into a memorable sightseeing experience.

Before we were allowed back into the Purakaunui Falls car park we had to note down how many photographs we had taken in a visitors' book supplied by New Zealand's Department for the Verification of Exaggerated Claims. People who hadn't reached double figures had to go back and fulfil their quota.

The final leg of our Southern Scenic Tourist Route experience took us from Southland into Otago, through the farming and forestry towns of Balclutha and Milton. Milton's claim to fame is a strange kink in its main thoroughfare, Union Street, said to be the result of the two surveyors who set out the road, working in opposite directions and failing to meet in the middle. Not a big claim, I grant you.

We arrived in Dunedin as the evening before New Year's Eve had moved perilously close to becoming New Year's Eve itself. After a couple of tours of the city in search of the *Southern Cross Hotel* we began our better late than never check in.

"On urrr yirrr love 'un?" enquired the neatly suited receptionist.

You have to believe that after almost a month of practise I was coming to terms with the New Zealand accent. What's more, as a Englishmen, I can generally make a reasonable stab at understanding the Scottish accent, at least if recorded and played back at quarter speed. But an unholy combination of the two? I had no chance. Even when the question was repeated twice, my inquisitor adopting a broader grin each time, I could still do nothing but squirm.

In the end THB rescued me, her Gaelic blood giving her an unfair advantage.

"He said 'When are you leaving?'" she translated.

I should have guessed.

18: DUNEDIN

Get Your Albatross Here.

Have you ever spent days trying to remember who it was that made that record on the radio that the DJ was too self absorbed to back announce? (For younger readers the radio is a bit like MTV but without the pictures). That was the feeling I had with Dunedin. I was sure I ought to remember that name from somewhere, other than the road atlas and signposts on the way up from The Catlins, but just couldn't work out where.

"*Lord of the Rings,*" hinted THB, obviously enjoying my struggle.
"Was Dunedin the dwarf king who let the Balrog loose?"
"No. That was Durin."
"Was Dunedin that river that appears in just about every scene in *The Fellowship Of The Ring*?"
"No. That was the Anduin... Think of Aragorn."
"Son of Arathorn?" I offered, hopefully.
"And Chieftain of..."
"Dunedin?"
It was close enough. The sword swinging protector of Hobbits and reluctant king in waiting was in fact a Chieftain of the Dunedain, a race of men's men (and presumably a few men's women as well to keep the whole thing going) who gadded about doing serious and manly things and getting very little thanks for it. That was that sorted then.

I should add that as well as being spelt slightly differently Dunedain and Dunedin are pronounced differently as well. The former sounds like a small mound of sand about to expire (dune-a-dyin') and the latter like a loud noise in a toilet (dunny-din).

"Of course there is another New Zealand city with a strong *Lord of the Rings* connection in its name," I told THB. Now she was struggling. You could almost hear the cogwheels spinning in her brain. Finally I put her out of her misery.

"Orc-land," I said.

Dunedin was a pleasant city with a vibrant (possibly because it was New Year's Eve) and compact centre, looking as if it had been cut and pasted from Scotland leaving a gap where Edinburgh used to be. It's not tartan, bagpipes or shortbread for which Dunedin is famous though, it's for having the world's steepest street. Yes, I was surprised too.

I've seen movies featuring car chases through San Francisco, always with at least one vehicle taking to the air as it crosses a relatively flat intersection while hurtling down a very steep street. San Francisco would have got my vote, but its best shot at fame is in fact a gradient of only 31.5% compared with Baldwin Street, Dunedin at 38%. At least that's the figure that wormed its way into the *Guinness Book of Records* and stuck there, like chewing gum on the sole of a shoe, despite being questioned by many people including the man who made the measurement.

The uncertainty doesn't stop the sale of "I climbed Baldwin Street," tee shirts, the hosting of an annual Gutbuster run up the slope and a regular stream of foolhardy visitors determined to pit their cars and driving skills against the worlds steepest (perhaps) road... and coming off second best.

As THB and I stepped out of our hotel on our first morning in town, fortified by bowls of porridge beginning to set like concrete in our stomachs, we were greeted by a grey and overcast sky. This is what passes for reasonable weather in Dunedin. If you can see the sky, it can't be raining all that hard.

To ensure that we remained dry for a while we picked an indoor attraction to set us on our way, The Otago Settlers Museum. The bonus of visiting this record of the region's people through the ages was that it was housed in a splendid art deco building, some small compensation for missing out on Napier.

The museum staff were extremely friendly and helpful, although a little surprised, it seemed, to find that two people from the other side of the world were interested in their exhibition. When it wasn't even raining.

It should have been no surprise. The galleries were really enthralling, guiding visitors through the lives of the original Maori inhabitants of the area, Scottish pioneers and Chinese who worked in the goldfields. There was a mock up of the living quarters that immigrants wouldn't have enjoyed on the sea passage to their new land, a room in which every spare space on the walls was covered by portraits of early settlers and their descendants and a gallery tracing the development of businesses in Dunedin, including law firms.

New Zealand With a Hobbit Botherer

The family tree of law firms as they evolved through time spoke of births and deaths, friendships and vendettas and alliances forged, betrayed and remade as "Smith and Jones" became "Smith, Jones and Brown", then "Smith and Brown" and "Jones", then "Smith and Brown" and "Jones and Son", then "Smith" and "Jones and Son", then "Smith, Jones and Son". You get the idea. Note that names have been changed here just in case any of the old lawyers are still practising and in the mood for litigation.

The museum also boasted a transport section with vintage cars, motorcycles, caravans, trucks, trains, trams and bicycles, including a popular penny farthing that could be mounted for an amusing photograph if other visitors could be prised away from it for a moment. THB and I didn't have a crowbar so our photo album remains bereft of penny farthing images apart from those obtained on an earlier visit to Portmeirion, North Wales. But that is another story *Prisoner* fans.

The centre of life in Dunedin was the Octagon. What would have been an austere concrete square in the centre of many European cities was a cheery tree lined avenue through a mini park in Dunedin, supervised by Scots poet Robert Burns in statue form. A chap in a skirt struggling manfully with a set of a bagpipes was also a regular feature during our stay, but you can't have everything.

On the north west side of the Octagon was Dunedin's Visitor Centre, home to an aquarium and kiwi house and, as we were to find out later, purveyor of bum information to tourists. (Actually I'm fairly sure that the service is not just restricted to tourists. If locals really wanted to be sent running after undomesticated water fowl, I'm sure that they would be accommodated too). THB and I tried the aquarium first. It turned out to be a reasonable enough diversion for half an hour or so, enlivened by fish feeding in which a man in a wet suit climbed into the main tank to frolic with the flounders, but what everyone had really come to see were the kiwis.

Even though they lived in a building with 'Aquarium' written over the door, these birds were not specially evolved aquatic kiwis that could be seen swimming and diving. You may be getting confused with penguins. They were housed in a special tank with water replaced by a sprinkling of earth and a collection of plants from "Undergrowth 'R' Us". Before we could witness this, however, we had to wait for a minder to give us a briefing on the dos and don'ts of visiting kiwis, before accompanying us into the dimness of the bird's nocturnal world, to ensure that we had been paying attention. The advice given boiled down to "Don't bang loudly on the glass and shout 'Oi Kiwi! Over 'ere!' while taking it's photograph using a flash."

For the first part of our viewing two kiwis spent much of the time rummaging about for food with their snouts as we had seen others do before. Then one of them seemed to develop an overpowering interest in the other, culminating in a brief kiwi grand prix around the tank's walls and a game of piggy back just behind the glass in front of us.

Somehow it didn't seem quite right watching that sort of thing without David Attenborough's hushed voice explaining "The male mounts the female, pushing her up against the glass so he doesn't fall off before his job is complete," or Steve Irwin's more enthusiastic "Crikey! He's going at it like a steam hammer!" I suppose we were very privileged to witness such an event, but it felt a bit voyeuristic at the time. I know I would find it a little off putting to have a bunch of kiwis sitting at the bottom of the bed while I was... you know. Even more so if they were Kiwis.

Our main reason for coming to Dunedin was to see penguins. Rumour had it that there was a place close by where flightless bird fans could wander about inside a network of hides to spy on rare yellow eyed penguins as they came ashore after a day's fishing. "What was this place called?" we asked at the information desk in the Visitor's Centre. "Penguin Place," (correct so far) came the answer. Nothing if not direct, these Kiwis.

The eager information giver then continued to explain how said establishment was located on the Otago Peninsula, a finger of land jutting out into the Pacific Ocean from the south of Dunedin, (still correct) also home to the world's only mainland albatross colony (a hat-trick of corrects). Our appetites whetted, we asked if we should buy tickets for the albatross viewing before we made our way out to the peninsula or would we be able to get in on the door. After a quick check on the computer we were told, "There's only a few places booked already. You'll be able to choose whichever time is best when you get there." (Wrong!)

The road leading to the albatross colony clung to the edge of the Otago Peninsula, winding around a succession of picturesque bays each, so it seemed, accompanied by a pretty sandy beach and a small cluster of houses. On one side of us rolling green hills headed off towards the peninsula's spine. On the other, the waters of Otago Harbour reflected a perfect blue sky, sparkling in the sunshine which appeared as soon as we left the city centre. Grey clouds still lingered in the distance behind us. Note to whoever it was who cut and pasted Dunedin from Scotland. You should have left the weather behind.

The albatross colony sat at the very end of the peninsula, on Taiaroa Head, where the birds nested in a fenced off area to protect them from non native predators such as cats, dogs, ferrets and stoats as well as from over familiar human visitors They could be viewed from an observatory accessible on guided tours from the Royal Albatross Centre. That was where THB and I were headed, having left the Colt on a cliff top patch of grass which served as a car park. We chuckled as a couple of gulls immediately made their opinion of the vehicle clear in the form of white deposits on its roof. Much the same as our opinion then.

"Sorry," said the albatross man (not a superhero able to fly vast distances but an employee of the Royal Albatross Centre) "all of our tours are fully booked for today."

"But they said at the Dunedin Visitor's Centre that there would be plenty of places," I offered, hoping for a sympathy allocation.

"Sorry," he repeated. "We are fully booked." This time he accompanied the words with a consolation shrug to convey the sentiment, "I know that lot at the Visitor's Centre are a bunch of no-hopers but what can I do?"

I tried a different tack.

"Say Peter Jackson and Kiri Te Kanawa were to turn up today. Would you find places on a tour for them?"

"Of course!"

"Well they're not coming. Can we have those places please?"

We were shown the door. It was brown, wooden and very heavy to stop it blowing open in the wind.

So we had to make do with the red cap of Taiaroa Head's lighthouse, peering over the top of the headland where the albatross colony was located, as viewed from the cliff tops a little further around the coast. White seabirds took to the skies now and again, raising our hopes that we might get to see an albatross after all. But there was a problem. THB and I were pretty sure that we could tell the difference between an albatross waddling on the ground in front of us (should we see one) and a gull strutting beside it. But an albatross soaring in the distance and a medium sized gull on the wing a bit closer by? We weren't quite sure. In the end we had a few albagull moments (hey that's a alba... gull as it flies overhead) but not a single sure-fire albatross sighting. Thank you Dunedin Visitor's Centre.

Maybe we'd have better luck with the penguins.

The Penguin Place was only a few minutes drive from the Albatross Centre, a privately run conservation project dedicated to the protection of a colony of rare yellow eyed penguins and their nest sites. The penguins are called yellow eyed because of their yellow cat-like eyes rather than because of any *Lord of the Rings* connection. I thought that I'd better make that clear to prevent any Hobbit bothering disappointment. They also have a characteristic band of yellow feathers that disappears around the back of their heads, like a coronet that has slipped down over their eyes

A group of ten of us were driven the short distance to the fringes of the nesting area in a rather elderly but nevertheless functional bus, then guided towards a system of trenches covered with netting that would allow us to get and in amongst penguins without disturbing them. But we were caught before we got there. On our way down a grassy track to reach the trenches a lone black and white photo opportunity appeared over the brow of a sand dune, making its way in the opposite direction. It stopped from time to time, firstly to give us a dismissive once over, then to look around quizzically. "I know there was a burrow around here somewhere when I left this morning," it seemed to be thinking.

Inside the trenches a walkie-talkie carried by our guide provided up to the minute information on the best positions to see penguins, supplied by other guides elsewhere in the network of hides. Occasionally our paths crossed those of the other groups, some ecstatic following a recent penguin encounter, others downcast, beginning to doubt that there were any penguins anywhere to be encountered. It is just a matter of luck, or occasional bad luck. A month or so before our trip to New Zealand, a bacterial infection had claimed the lives of many young chicks born that year. As I write, it is fingers crossed for the following year's birds.

Our tour took place early in the evening, just too early for the penguin rush hour around dusk when birds that have been fishing all day return to shore. Luckily for us, though, we were able to see one early bird, clambering from the surf, then progressing towards us with a determined forward lean as if struggling against a high wind. As it crested a dune just in front of us, it stopped for a stretch, flippers held out wide in an impression of The Angel of the North. Just as my camera went click, it ducked down behind the dune again.

As we climbed back to rejoin the bus, more than an hour having passed and seeming like ten minutes, I turned to take a final photograph of the beach where the penguins would arrive. I did quite a good job, capturing white capped waves breaking upon a ribbon of pristine sand edged by tussocky grass. Only when I zoomed in on the image on my computer at home did I discover three blurry yellow-eyed penguins waddling up the beach. Aren't digital cameras wonderful?

On this final climb we also encountered a young bird lazing on the grass like a sunbather waiting for someone to rub oil into its back. That made an excellent photo which always elicits the same question when shown to patient friends who've made it that far through our eight hundred and fifty or so New Zealand snaps, "Was it dead?" The answer is no. I did check several times to make sure it was breathing.

Returning to our hotel, THB and I had the chance to go out and party in The Octagon, to see in the new year Dunedin style. We'd heard there was live music arranged, but we were afraid (very afraid) that the experience might involve either bagpipes or the sort of jumpy, twirly, hand clappy dancing that seems to filter down from Scotland to infect English TV as midnight approaches on the 31st of December. So we made do with a splendid evening meal in the restaurant adjacent to the hotel. Roast lamb with an accompaniment of kumara chips. I'm salivating just thinking about it.

As we checked out the next day, ready for a long drive to Christchurch, the hotel bill we were presented with seemed a little on the low side. Should we own up? *Sharp pang of conscience.* Yes, we should!

"Excuse me," I said, "I don't think you've charged us for yesterday's meal."

"Oh," said the receptionist examining our receipt, "What did you have?"

Over the next ten minutes or so we produced a detailed description of the dining experience, which she painstakingly noted down, ending with "...and to drink we had two mineral waters."

"Each?"

"No. One each."

"Oh."

She rummaged underneath the reception desk, then called a colleague and they rummaged together.

"We don't have a restaurant menu, so we can't work out the cost."

We stared at each other for a while, receptionist and guest, trying to think up a solution to the conundrum. Actually guest was waiting for receptionist to say, "Thank you for being so honest. We'll let you off this time as we know you are anxious to be on your way." But it never happened.

Eventually the receptionist's colleague was sent to find another colleague who might be able to lay their hands on a restaurant menu. Several colleagues later a menu appeared. The cost of the meal was totted up and a new bill offered... and snatched back before I could take it and pay.

"I've forgotten the mineral waters."

"I think they were a couple of dollars each," I said, trying to stave off a further search of the hotel for a drinks menu.

"We'll put down three dollars, just in case," said the receptionist.

I did mention Dunedin's Scots heritage didn't I?

THB's plan had been to take a Cadbury World chocolate factory tour (with free samples) before leaving Dunedin. But the Visitor's Centre, given a chance to redeem itself by telling us how to get there, had some sad news to relate. There had been a fire at the chocolate factory a few days before and tours had been severely curtailed. That knocked our plans on the head, but did explain the strange smell of burning chocolate that had haunted us since we arrived in Dunedin.

So it was off to Christchuch... after a consolation visit to the sweet counter of a nearby newsagent's.

19: AORAKI / MOUNT COOK

Flour And Water.

Even without sightseeing it promised to be a very long drive up the east coast of the South Island from Dunedin to Christchurch. Five hours according to our road atlas. Then THB announced that she had seen a yellow eye marked *Pelennor Fields* lurking somewhere near Twizel in the centre of the island. That diversion would make it eight hours, not allowing for time spent searching for the exact Hobbit bothering site. But there was more. If we were going to Twizel anyway, I reasoned, it would only add an extra hour and a half onto the journey to continue to Aoraki / Mount Cook. We couldn't miss New Zealand's highest peak. So it was to be nine and a half hour's of driving in all. We had to be off.

The first leg of the epic journey took us along the coast from Dunedin to Oamaru on State Highway 1. It took just over an hour, passing through Palmerston on the way, for us to be seduced by our first tourist sign. 'Moeraki Boulders', it said. It doesn't seem quite so enticing now, I have to admit. Maybe it was the way it said it.

The boulders were a sight to behold, large, grey, spherical rocks up to two metres in diameter scattered along a sandy beach like giant marbles in the middle of a game. At first it seemed they were very popular. The car park at the information centre and restaurant was packed with vehicles and we had to settle for one of those end of row, is it a bay or not, it is now, parking spots, next to a Maui. But the beach where the boulders lurked was almost empty when we reached it. Either each person had decided to bring two or three cars with them or the pumpkin and kumara (and carrot) soup in the restaurant was really, really good.

Just as with the Fox and Franz Josef glaciers there are three competing theories as to how the perfectly shaped boulders were formed. One of them is my own and can be summed up perfectly by the phrase, "Hey it's modern art!" Let's concentrate on the other two, shall we?

The Maori say that a great canoe once foundered on the Moeraki coast and the rocks are gourds from its cargo. The Pakeha theory relies on the gradual accumulation of minerals around a seed of plant material deep inside a sediment layer gathered on the ocean floor. The sediment eventually became soft mudstone, which was thrust to the surface as the Earth's crust shifted, then eroded by the sea to reveal the hidden septarian concretions. Yes that is their official scientific name. Have you noticed how Pakeha theories always take a little more time to tell and a lot more time to execute than Maori theories?

Having allowed THB to take a few photographs of yours truly in amongst the boulders (for the purposes of establishing scale) we climbed the cliffs behind them, via a set of steps I hasten to add, to return to the car park. This took us past an information board which emphasised that climbing on the boulders was forbidden. Apologies for the misdemeanour. We'd obviously followed the boulder trail in the wrong direction.

North of Moeraki, along State Highway 1, was the town of Oamaru famous for its two (yes two) penguin colonies and historic buildings built using a local creamy coloured limestone. The penguins were the more tempting of the two, but we didn't have the time to wait until dusk for them to put in an appearance. There was a Hobbit bothering battlefield and a mountain to be viewed and they were still far, far away.

Leaving the coast at Pukeuri we tracked the Waitaki river along State Highway 83 towards Lakes Waitaki, Aviemore and Benmore, eventually turning north along State Highway 8 and heading for the yellow eye of Twizel. But that's jumping ahead. Before we had encountered any of the lakes we were sidetracked by another sign, this one pointing to a limestone cliff resembling a huge slice of Swiss cheese at Takiroa. Inside caves at its base were ancient Maori rock paintings, stylised depictions of gods, men and beasts produced using a mixture of fat, charcoal and red ochre. A link fence prevented uncommissioned additions by more modern artists.

As we studied the drawings, which dated from 1000 to 1500 AD, pondering their meaning, another car drew up and we were joined by an enthusiastic man and a less than enthusiastic woman. You could tell from the 'I've got better things to do' way she stomped over to us that the stop hadn't been her idea. Together we contemplated what looked like a red snake with horns writhing across the creamy limestone, then the new arrival gave her verdict.

"Jeez. They weren't very good artists were they?"

In a hushed voice her companion explained how old the drawings were, how the materials available to the ancient Maori were limited, how it was all about symbolism, how you had to feel the spirit of the place, how you couldn't really expect the Mona Lisa. She listened patiently, taking it all in, waiting until he had finished.

"Yes, but they weren't very good were they?" she said.

Then she stomped back to the car.

While her back was turned the now not so enthusiastic man shrugged his shoulders resignedly as if to say, "I did my best."

And so it was on to the lakes.

Lakes Waitaki, Aviemore and Benmore are part of the vast Waitaki hydroelectric scheme along with three others, Ohau, Pukaki and Tekapo, a network of interconnecting canals and the majestic mountain ranges providing the run off to feed them all. Although we had encountered some beautiful lakes already on our trip, some sparkling in the sunshine, others brooding in the rain, nothing had prepared us for this particular collection and the brilliant, almost luminous, turquoise blue of their waters. On first sight we were gobsmacked. Even on second and subsequent sights our mouths were still painful. On double figures sight, showing the photographs to friends back at home, we were called liars for saying we hadn't used photo editing software to enhance the colours.

It's those glaciers again that are responsible for the brilliant colour of the lakes in this region. As they lumbered inexorably downhill rocks carried along with them ground against the valley floor producing a fine powder called glacial flour. It is this powder, suspended in their water, that turns the lakes turquoise.

Heading towards Twizel we entered Mackenzie Country, named after an immigrant from Scotland, James McKenzie, by people who couldn't spell. He was imprisoned for five years in the mid 1800s for stealing a thousand sheep (allegedly) but pardoned after nine months and three escape attempts. He has become a sort of folk hero, epitomising either the Kiwi's indefatigable spirit or the Kiwi's love of sheep depending who is telling the story. Strangely for a New Zealand folk hero he jumped on a ship for Australia as soon as he was released. Maybe he epitomises the Kiwi's love of travel as well.

New Zealand With a Hobbit Botherer

Twizel itself was a town constructed using a bicycle wheel design, with shops and recreation facilities sitting on the hub and residential streets leading off along the spokes. It's very easy for the unwary to drive along the ring road which circles the hub, thinking they are heading into town, and then end up completing several circuits before the onset of terminal déjà vu. Who would be so dozy as to do that? Can I put my hand down now?

The town was founded in the late nineteen-sixties to house the army of people required to turn blueprints for the Waitaki hydroelectric scheme into reality. It was due to be bulldozed when the project finished, but was saved by the love of its inhabitants and their tenacity in writing lots and lots of letters to government officials, both local and national. You only have to look around at the mountains and lakes to see why they were so keen to carry on living there.

THB and I enjoyed a mid morning something and carrot pie in Twizel's centre, there being no pumpkin and kumara soup on offer, then worked off the calories dodging skateboarders while searching for a tourist information office to dispense Hobbit bothering advice. Was there a tour we could join that would show us Pelennor Fields and regale us with *The Return of the King* trivia like the number of times Orlando Bloom fell off the oliphaunt while filming the famous climbing up the trunk and shooting it in the head scene? Yes and no.

Yes there was a tour. It was advertised on flyers stuck to a variety of vertical surfaces near where we had parked the Colt and discovered only when we finally gave up on the *i*-site search and returned to our petulant vehicle. (Beep! Beep! Beep! You didn't bring me back a pie!) No we couldn't join it. There were no contact details on the flyer. Someone had obviously slept in on the day they taught flyer design at business school.

Not to be discouraged that easily, we studied the position of the yellow eye on the road atlas carefully, then set off on a DIY tour. Curiously I was just as keen as THB on this endeavour. I'm sure it was the challenge of finding a real life location guided only by squiggles on a sheet of paper that attracted me, not the desire to stand on the spot where Orc number seventy two met the sharp end of Gimli's axe. I've always had a soft spot for orienteering. I really have. Peterson was NOT getting to me!

We took State Highway 6 north out of Twizel then turned off onto a gravel road alongside the stunning Ohau Canal, a milky turquoise down its centre tinged with pink towards its edges. No I didn't have my rose tinted spectacles on, I have the photographs to prove it. Then we searched for a river just beyond a side road leading away from the canal. There it was, winding its way through a clump of trees. That was the location of the yellow eye. We'd found Pelennor Fields, the open space in front of the white city of Minas Tirith where assorted good men and women, alive and dead (long story, don't ask) helped by the odd Hobbit, dwarf, elf and wizard defeat the combined forces of evil comprising Orcs, Uruk-hai, bad men and women, trolls, oliphaunts, Nazgul and fell beasts. Don't worry, I haven't given away the film's ending. There's still ages to go when you reach that point.

As we marvelled at the scene, a grassy plain giving way to gentle hills in the middle distance with snow capped mountains peering over the top of them, the silence was broken by the crunching approach of a 4WD. It stopped a few hundred metres away at the top of a shallow incline, disgorged its occupants for a short lecture by the driver, then, once everyone was back on board, moved off into a field and away. The 4WD had *Lord of the Rings* written on the side. Maybe we hadn't found the correct site after all.

But the yellow eye on the map straddled a river and only one river fitted the bill. We had to be right! THB had lost interest by now and wandered back to the car leaving me to rant about how the 'official tour' had got it wrong for a short while longer before I joined her for the drive to Aoraki / Mount Cook.

Incidentally we both got it right. A fair sized field was required to choreograph a battle scene featuring hundreds of strangely dressed and rubber masked extras, each trying to catch the director's eye with their desire for blood, while dodging a group of frisky horses set loose among them. THB and I had been viewing one part of that field and the tour had begun in another. Nevertheless I'm proud to say that the Gisby photo album contains a picture which matches almost exactly the one marked 'Pelennor Fields' in Ian Brodie's excellent *Lord of the Rings* location guidebook (yes we should have taken that with us to New Zealand) right down to individual trees. The only difference is that our vista is dotted with white fluffy sheep and boasts a set of power lines strung across it. Oh the influence that Peter Jackson has in New Zealand.

Jackson to locals: "Can I disconnect your electricity for a few weeks while I film a battle scene? The power lines are getting in the way."
Locals to Jackson: "We'd rather you didn't. We'll miss the TV."
Jackson to locals: "You can all have parts in the movie as Orcs ".
Locals to Jackson: "Where do we sign?"
A lone voice: "But I want to be an elf."
Jackson to wannabe elf: "You're already in the movie, Orlando."

Of course that is a completely imaginary scenario. No Kiwi would really complain about missing television. THB and I have experienced TV in New Zealand. It is the reason why Kiwis are so fond of outdoor pursuits.

Almost as soon as we returned to State Highway 8 we left it again, as it veered away to skirt the southern tip of Lake Pukaki and head off for Christchurch. We noted the turn for future reference (about two hours in the future) and continued north along State Highway 80 towards Aoraki / Mount Cook. This road followed the eastern edge of the lake for its complete length, offering beautiful views of mountains on the far shore, blue skies and cotton wool clouds reflected in still turquoise water. Of all the wonderful sights we photographed in New Zealand this was the one that became my screen saver. Hey, I'm writing this on my computer now, I'll show you. *Click. Minimise. Click. Maximise.* Wasn't that good?

Beyond the end of the lake, the road led across some rocky open ground, criss-crossed by the many strands of the braided Tasman River. Now a braided river was something neither THB nor I had encountered before visiting New Zealand. On our first few introduction to the phenomenon, by a Kiwi tour guide, we made the mistake of asking who the mysterious Mr Brady was and why the river had been named after him. When the guide had composed himself, and switched off his mobile phone after gleefully telling everyone he knew what we'd said, he explained that a braided river is simply an indecisive river, one that can't make up its mind which course to take. So it splits up and takes as many different courses as it can, looking like a mane of hair in serious need of a comb.

New Zealand With a Hobbit Botherer

The flats where the Tasman River meandered down to Lake Pukaki were the wide end of a funnel leading up into a narrower valley. There the surrounding mountains began to close in, swapping their green cloaks for white ones, sparkling in the sun. Ahead of us now was what we thought was Aoraki / Mount Cook itself, occupying more and more of the Colt's windscreen as we approached the end of the road at its base. It was easy to lose perspective when surveying the majestic peak, tempting to believe that you could reach out your hand and grab a clump of the brilliant white snow seemingly tumbling down its sides. But I couldn't. I tried.

A sprawling three dimensional model of the National Park in the visitor's centre at Mount Cook village eventually convinced us that the mountain we'd seen had been Mount Sefton all along and not Mount Cook after all. As we watched, its jagged top appeared briefly, now and again, through a sombrero of fluffy white cloud, always just after I had given up on the idea of capturing the perfect photograph and put my camera back in its case. Aoraki / Mount Cook more than lived up to its Maori name, which translates as 'cloud piercer'. Its peak never emerged at all.

We walked around the village of Aoraki / Mount Cook for a while, marvelling at the mountains, the snow, the peacefulness and the prices people were prepared to pay to stay at the famous Hermitage Hotel, then with a five hour drive to Christchurch ahead of us and white fluffy clouds above us turning distinctly grey, we began our journey back past Lake Pukaki to the turning we noted four paragraphs back.

Back on State Highway 8 we passed the southern tip of Lake Tekapo, a kind of mini Lake Pukaki with the same turquoise hue. Time didn't allow us to visit the Church of the Good Shepherd on its shore or the statue of a collie dog erected by local farmers in honour of the breed's services to sheep management, but we nevertheless got the message. This was sheep country. As we progressed through Fairlie, Geraldine and on to Ashburton the message was emphasised further when we encountered our first sheep jam. That's not bad going after almost a month driving around New Zealand.

The sheep jam technique appeared to be to stay put and let the beasts wander around you rather than to accelerate hell for leather past them when a gap appeared, as was the case with cattle. Maybe sheep break more easily than cows.

Anyway, as we wait for the baaing beasts to meander past, I'll tell you my favourite (clean) sheep joke.

A tramper walking across a field narrowly avoids falling down a sink hole. "Crikey," he says, (or words to that effect), "I wonder how deep that is." So he throws a small pebble down and waits for the noise of it hitting the bottom. He hears nothing. Intrigued he tries a larger pebble. Still nothing. How deep can it be? He searches for a while and eventually comes across a very large rock which he half lifts and half drags over to the hole. Over the edge it goes, but there is still no sound.

As he is just about to give up and walk away he sees a sheep careering towards him with its legs pumping madly and a surprised look on its face. Just as it reaches him it jumps, flies briefly through the air, then disappears down the hole. The tramper is shocked and reaches into his rucksack for a some water to calm himself down. While he is drinking a farmer appears and asks, "Have you seen my sheep?"

"Yes!" says the tramper, "It rushed past me, faster than I've ever seen a sheep move before, and jumped into that sink hole."

"That couldn't have been my sheep", said the farmer. "My sheep was tied to a big rock."

In describing the drive between Geraldine and Christchurch, the word tedious springs to mind. Maybe it was because the road was boringly straight for kilometre after kilometre. Maybe it was because we had been spoilt by day after day of mountains, lakes and waterfalls. Maybe it was because we had left the excitement of Geraldine, proud home of the world record for the largest home knitted jersey, behind. Or maybe it was just because we spent most of the time behind a very slow moving horse box. Never mind, there were two sights to make the journey memorable. A bridge and a billboard.

At regular intervals along the very first portion of the road we passed signs counting us down to the "longest bridge in New Zealand". As the reported distance to go shrunk, our anticipation grew. Would it be a great sweeping suspension bridge or a string of cantilevers? Would it be single track, like so many bridges in New Zealand, necessitating a game of chicken with vehicles approaching in the other direction? Would there be a queue to bungy jump off its side?

In the end it didn't quite live up to expectations. If you did try to bungy jump off its side, when your head hit the water (if you could find any in the braids of the Rakaia River) your feet would still be above bridge level. It looked as if it was made from pieces of decking laid end to end with a handrail along each side. Long it certainly was at 1757 metres, but a bridge? I had always thought that the very least one of them had to do was to get you off the ground.

The billboard was erected much closer to Christchurch and almost caused me to run into the back of the horse box as I did a double take. It showed a picture of a small silver car that looked much the same as every other small silver car on the road. Underneath the picture in large letters was written "Car of the Year" followed by the vehicle's name and make. What was that name and make? I'll give you a clue. "Beep! Beep! Beep!" I can only assume that there was some small print at the bottom of the poster which read, "We really had you going there!"

Finally we reached the pretty centre of Christchurch, having negotiated the not so pretty suburban sprawl surrounding it, and spied the last hotel of our journey, *Rydges* at the other end of a small road skirting Cathedral Square. A road with a no entry sign at what seemed to be its entrance. We followed the traffic around, treating ourselves to another tour of the sprawling suburbs, before being allowed back towards the centre and ending up in front of the same no entry sign once again. Having seen enough of the suburbs and with my, "Sorry officer, I'm a stranger in your wonderful country and I didn't see the sign", excuse ready, I drove straight through. It was late, we'd had a long day and there was no-one around to see. Hopefully.

When we reached our hotel room and walked across to close the curtains, to shut out the growing darkness outside, one thing caught our eye through the large picture window. It was shining big, bright and blue, right opposite the hotel. A sign that said POLICE.

Do you want another sheep joke? All right, a quick one.

A farmer drops his watch into the sheep dip and when he retrieves it he finds it's no longer working. No ticks.

Some people think that sheep, as a species, are intellectually challenged. Not so according to one of our *Lord of the Rings* tour guides, who told the following story, swearing it was true.

A farmer who owned a sheep paddock where *Lord of the Rings* filming had taken place wanted to allow paying tourists to get in but prevent his animals getting out. His first thought was a gate, but tourists would simply leave that open, so he came up with the idea of installing a cattle grid. For a few days things went well, then sheep began to escape. More and more of them each day. How could this be? He decided to set up a camera and record what was going on. When he examined the footage he'd obtained he was shocked to see the animals wandering up to the cattle grid, laying down beside it, then rolling over on their backs to get across and standing up on the other side. See. They just want us to think they are stupid. They are planning something...

20: CHRISTCHURCH

A Hillock In The Middle Of Nowhere.

Our trip to Christchurch started on a high. We had to return the beeping Colt to the hire company. This after filling it up with fuel and washing off a couple of weeks of accumulated dirt from New Zealand's metal roads. A petrol station was easy to find. A car wash, reachable with less than a day's knowledge of Christchurch's unfathomable road system, was less so. In the end THB and I reasoned that we'd probably lost our deposit anyway, courtesy of chips galore from flying gravel, and returned the car dirty.

The man in the hire car office seemed rather preoccupied with the woman in the hire car office when we pitched up, but reluctantly dragged himself away to deal with us. With a cursory glance out of the window to check that the vehicle still had at least two wheels (on the side he could see) he asked, "Have you filled her up?" We nodded and that was his inspection completed. A ream of papers was handed over indicating, rather verbosely, that our deposit was intact and we left with the alacrity of a magician's assistant during a vanishing trick.

Now we had two days of leisure to explore the delights Christchurch had to offer.

We began in Cathedral Square, much easier to negotiate on foot than in a car. It was a surprisingly quiet open space surrounded by hotels (and a police station) and paved in concrete with a sprinkling of trees. Saving it from the soullessness that that description might imply were two lofty constructions, one old and one new.

The old was the neo-Gothic cathedral itself, built in grey stone with creamy trimmings on its corners and around its doors and windows, with a tall pointy spire sheathed in weathered copper giving it a greenish tinge. (I'm sure there is a correct architectural term for fiddly bits on ancient churches but I don't know what it is so trimmings will have to do). In front of the cathedral was a photographer doing a roaring trade in taking pictures of tourists. Tourists with cameras hanging around their necks. Something didn't seem quite right there until I tried taking a photo of a smiling THB in the same position. To get the spire in I had to stand somewhere near Greymouth. Maybe the professional had a special lens.

The new was *Chalice*, a sculpture by a chap called Neil Dawson erected to celebrate the tick over from the year 1999 to the year 2000 as well as the hundred and fiftieth anniversary of the founding of Christchurch and Canterbury. It was an eighty metre high steel and aluminium lattice looking for all the world like a giant waste bin awaiting the insertion of a giant black plastic bin liner. Full marks to Christchurch for the imagination to try something other than a statue of a local dignitary wearing a white cap courtesy of the local bird life. And if hamburger restaurants ever start selling hundred pounders there will be somewhere to put the used wrappers.

From Cathedral Square we walked along Worcester Boulevard, shooed out of the way occasionally by approaching red and gold trams. This was the arts centre of Christchurch boasting an Arts Centre (of course) along with several galleries and a theatre where *The Rocky Horror Show* was playing. It was tempting, but I'd left my stockings and suspenders back at the hotel. At the end of the road were the Botanic Gardens and Hagley Park.

Hagley Park is a picturesque enclave of grass, trees and shrubs on the banks of the River Avon. If you have seen photographs in magazines which portray Chirstchurch as an idyllic corner of England transported down under, the chances are that Hagley Park is where those pictures were taken. There are two theories as to how such a beautiful green space came to be set aside in the centre of the city. Either it was a buffer zone negotiated by early arrivals, the Dean brothers, who hated the idea of a new city being built near them, or a buffer zone negotiated between English and Scottish settlers who simply hated each other. The Dean brothers theory is obviously correct. I can't imagine why there would be any animosity between the English and the Scots.

After a relaxing afternoon enjoying the gardens of New Zealand's 'Garden City' it was time for souvenir shopping. This is not an activity I would normally dwell on, but there was one item aimed squarely at the tourist market that caught my eye. It was brown, sold in plastic sachets and went by the enticing name of kiwi poo. What a gift for a young nephew or niece. What kudos would be earned by proudly munching on such a confectionary in the school playground. (I assumed it was chocolate, not real kiwi poo. The shelves were well stocked so if it was the real deal, there was a poor kiwi out the back somewhere working overtime). The gift was banned by THB on the grounds of being inappropriate. Ryan, Connor, Sol and Jude, I did try!

Back in our hotel room THB began a search for yellow eyes in our road atlas. We no longer had a hire car, but the chances were that if there was a *Lord of the Rings* filming site within travelling distance of Christchurch, there would be a company running a tour. That was her plan for our final day in New Zealand. Mine on the other hand was the Tranz Alpine rail journey through Arthur's Pass from the rich pastures of Canterbury to the rugged beauty of the West Coast... and Greymouth. Every silver lining has a cloud.

A shriek from THB a short while after her study began indicated that she'd either found a yellow eye or a spider on the floor. As she hadn't followed up the shriek by jumping onto a chair screaming for arachnid blood, I assumed it was a yellow eye. The *Lord of the Rings* site she had found was Mount Sunday, a hillock in the middle of nowhere used as the location for Edoras, capital of Rohan. It was a long drive away, almost back to Fox Glacier on the West Coast. Surely there wouldn't be a trip going all the way out there.

An intensive study of tourist literature gathered from a stand in the hotel's lobby, from the Christchurch visitor centre earlier in the day and from the comprehensive information pack provided on our first night in Auckland, revealed no trace of an Edoras tour. THB finally gave up. Arthur's Pass it was!

As I ruffled through the *i*-tag magazine for a few words about the Tranz Alpine rail journey, to stimulate THB's enthusiasm and take the edge off her disappointment, I saw it. An advertisement for a journey into Middle Earth with Hassle Free Tours that THB had missed. "Visit the location of Edoras from *Lord of the Rings*" it said. Moral dilemma. Should I tell or should I not?

I thought of the movies. Of brooding mountains, dusted with snow, bounding a vast plain. Of a plain bristling with tussock grass, probed by the tendrils of a braided river. Of Shadowfax's hooves splashing through the river's water as Gandalf left Edoras to warn Gondor of impending doom. Of a rocky hump rising from the plain like a whale surfacing for air from an infinite sea. Of a windswept Eowyn, and just about everyone else who ventured outside King Theoden's Hall, gazing enigmatically into the distance from the top of the hump. I wanted to be there and stare open mouthed too. I wanted to experience the wind... if you'll pardon the expression. I phoned Hassle Free and booked two places on a tour the following day.

So it was on to the evening's entertainment. Sadly there was a cinema directly opposite our hotel showing the film *Phantom of the Opera*. This was a movie that THB wanted to see and a movie that I had hoped would be released in New Zealand after we left having died a quick death in England while we were away. After sitting though almost two and a half hours of tedium one of us had changed our mind. And it wasn't me.

There was one piece of excitement to be had during the cinematic experience though. In a desperate attempt to attract obviously discerning Kiwi punters through the doors to see *Phantom* the cinema was running a raffle with one free entry for every ticket purchased. THB and I had a 1 in 5 chance, there being about ten people at the performance we attended. The winner was announced just before the opening credits... and we were unlucky. Ah well. We'd probably only have won free tickets for all our friends to see *Phantom of the Opera*. At least we've kept our friends.

We were picked up the following morning, our last in New Zealand, in a 4WD by Mark, our driver and guide for the Edoras trip. As an aperatif he took us on another tour of Christchurch's sprawling suburbs that we were coming to know so well. (I'm sure that Christchurch's road system was designed by a person whose previous job was working on the layout of one of those department stores where they make you walk past every display on every floor before allowing you to escape). This time we were searching for the backpacker's hostel where the next punter was to be collected.

Eventually Mark parked up and disappeared on foot to collect said punter, dragging them out of bed and through the shower first if necessary, leaving us in the company of Dave, who had been riding shotgun in the 4WD ever since our arrival. He was touring New Zealand with some friends who had a tendency to throw things at him whenever he started talking about *Lord of the Rings* (shame on them) so he was pleased to escape for a while and be among fellow aficionados.

After brief introductions, the serious business of establishing dominance began. You'll be pleased to know that this process among Hobbit botherers involves much more verbal jousting and much less genital sniffing than the corresponding one among dogs.

"I went on a *Lord of the Rings* tour in Wellington last week," opened Dave. *Fifteen-Love.*
"We've been on that one too," countered THB. *Fifteen-All.*
"I've also been on half-day tour in Queenstown." *Thirty-Fifteen.*
"We did the full day in Queenstown." *Thirty-All.*
"Did you go up to Deer Park Heights as well?" *Thirty-Forty.*
"Of course." *Deuce.*
"And have you visited Matamata?" *Advantage THB.*
"What's Matamata?" *Game, set and match to THB.*

At this point Mark returned with a tall Belgian backpacker called Maya who folded herself into the 4WD's back seat behind us. Maya's boyfriend was paying for her to travel around the world without him. (At this point my female readership sighs wistfully and asks "Where can I find a boyfriend like that?" My male readership nods world-wearily and says "Yeah, I've had girlfriends like that.")

Our final pick up was at a campground (where Maui, Kea, Tui and Kiwi go to spend the night) with a huge sign outside saying 'Top 10 Holiday Park'. I was mightily impressed, until I discovered that the sign didn't necessarily mean we were visiting the bees knees of campgrounds in New Zealand, it just meant we were visiting one of the fifty or so run by a company called 'Top 10'. Two Australian grandmothers who had spent the previous few days abseiling, kayaking, bungying, zorbing and generally doing all the scary things that THB and I had been studiously avoiding, completed the 4WDs complement and we headed off along State Highway 77 towards Mount Hutt.

Our first stop was at the Rakaia Gorge, where a bridge (a real one this time) carried the road across the braids of the Rakaia River. From the top of a steep bank, lined with trees, we surveyed the river's clean meandering waters and grey rocky braid bars, temporary islands separating its strands. Mark pointed out a jet boat operation running from a small pier somewhere below us and the two adrenaline junkie grannies suddenly reverted to five year olds.

"Can we? Can we? Can we? Can we? Can we? Can we? Can we? Pleeeease?"

Mark put it to the vote.

The grannies said, "YES! YES!" and I added my eager support, "YES!" It was looking very good until Dave came up with a firm "NO!" after enquiring "What does it cost?" THB abstained, torn between her fear of water and her fear of sending me off alone with the mad grannies. That left Maya.

"What is a jet boat?" she asked.

The answer to that question begins with the observation that rivers in New Zealand tend to be designed using a wide and shallow rather than narrow and deep template. Conventional boats work poorly in such waters since propellers are not at their most efficient when dragging along rocky river beds. Enter Bill Hamilton, who came up with the idea of using a pump to suck water in from underneath a boat, then spit it out at the rear, propelling the craft forwards. Jet boats designed along these lines are fast, manoeuvrable and capable of coming to a halt and reversing direction in a shorter time than it takes to write it down, a move known as a Hamilton turn.

"YES!" said Maya.

Four to one, with one abstention (who could be worked on if necessary) was only sufficient to coax a promise from our guide. "We'll see if it's open when we come back," he said.

As we progressed past a turn for the town of Methven, supplier of accommodation to winter skiers, summer trampers and the cast and crew of films about Middle Earth, the road became less travelled and more metal.

"I'll put on some music," said Mark.

It was Crowded House. On every tour we experienced in New Zealand, when the guide wanted to rest his vocal chords, it was Crowded House (local band made good) to the rescue. In deference to the nature of the tour, Mark also gave the *The Return of the King* soundtrack a brief outing on the 4WD's sound system closer to our destination.

Three quarters of the way from the Methven junction to Mount Sunday we turned off for a stop at scenic Lake Clearwater, one of a group of lakes huddled between the Rangitata and Ashburton Rivers. Shack like holiday homes or Bachs (pronounced "Batches" or with a

Kiwi accent something like "Bitches") and more upmarket (but only just) caravans formed a small settlement providing accommodation for anglers, rowers, windsurfers, birdwatchers, trampers and those who had taken a very wrong turn in the Christchurch traffic.

Motorised craft were forbidden on the lake for fear of endangering the rare Southern Black Crested Grebe, which nests there, even more than it is endangered already. As a result the lake was a tranquil place set in a swathe of open grassland, dotted with the hardiest of trees and surrounded by snow covered peaks. Mark encouraged us to stand together beside the 4WD for a group photograph with the lake in the background. I was expecting this image to appear on the Hassle Free Tours web site, but haven't seen it there yet. Which one of us was so ugly that the tour company thought they would drive customers away, I wonder?

Finally it was on to our Hobbit bothering destination, Mount Sunday on Mount Potts Station. The station was a sheep farm, not somewhere to wait for a train, although I have to admit that the simple phrase sheep farm doesn't quite do it justice. Think more like a tract of the Canterbury high country big enough to swallow several towns than a few barns with a field beside them.

Mount Sunday itself first came into view in the distance as a small hillock on an otherwise flat plain with the grey ribbon of a river emerging from a cleft in the mountains behind it. Mark stopped several times on the way in. At first the hillock was a blur, then a grassy hump took shape and finally the rocky flanks characteristic of Edoras in *The Two Towers* and *The Return of the King* emerged. Although King Theoden's Hall was gone, as was all of the set that took almost a year to build on top of Mount Sunday for just eight days filming, this was still Edoras. The rocky perch of Rohan's capital, the surrounding plain criss-crossed by a braided river and the snowy mountain backdrop, were all exactly as shown in the movies. Nature's own very special effects.

A Mordor of Hobbit botherers viewing the scene from the road at the entrance to Mount Potts station looked on jealously as Mark took the 4WD past them and on though boggy sheep paddock, over stony braid bars and across winding tributaries of the Rangitata River. A few hardy souls had begun the walk down to *Edoras*. Mark didn't rate their chances without waterproof underseal and four wheel drive legs. As we bumped our way onward, sheep scattered before us and cows gently mooved aside as we came close. All but one. She stood her ground with a determined look in her eye that said, "I didn't move for Gandalf and I'm not moving for you." We drove around.

To get things in perspective, just in case you haven't seen the *Lord of the Rings* movies, Mount Sunday is not a towering peak. It is an outcrop of rock adorned by grass in a Mohican style that rises less that fifty metres above the surrounding plain, So Mount is a rather grand appellation. The correct term is *roche moutoné* or a low, rounded hill moulded by glacial action. Let's stick with Mount shall we? The story goes that God fearing workers from the high country sheep stations used to congregate on the Mount each week on the day that comes just after Saturday and just before Monday. Hence the name. And I thought it was all because it was the shape of an ice cream dessert.

The 4WD came to rest in a sheltered hollow about half way up the spine of the Mount. Mark then guided us on a short climb to the top. Dave was away first, camera clicking in every direction, shortly followed by Maya. The grannies announced that they were off to find a quiet spot to relieve themselves, so no-one was to follow. Even in the wilderness, (or maybe especially in the wilderness) women pee in pairs. That left THB labouring up the incline, with me pushing behind her like a rugby second row forward.

The view from the top was tremendous. We were in a bowl formed by gently sloping mountains with their rougher, white topped cousins skulking behind in the distance. Tussock and clover covered the bowl's flat bottom along with the sparkling strands of a braided river, the one crossed by Gandalf and Pippin on their way from Edoras to Gondor. Far above us someone big was blowing on the bowl's contents to cool them down. At least that what it felt like. We were able to experience the very same incessant wind that tore the flag of Rohan from its fastenings in *The Two Towers* and ripped Peter Jackson's glasses from his face during filming. I can understand why Eowyn sneaked off to gaze into the distance from the top of Mount Sunday whenever she had the chance. So did we.

While we had been taking photographs that would never quite capture the majesty of the scene first hand, including snowy mountains reflected in a small tarn on the top of Mount Sunday and THB with splendidly horizontal hair, Mark had been setting out director's chairs and a champagne and strawberries picnic in a sheltered spot below us, beside the 4WD. So there THB and I dined, in the second most stunning spot we'd ever paused to consume a picnic. Even Edoras can't top the Grand Canyon!

The picnic conversation turned to *Lord of the Rings* (now there's a surprise) and in particular, as the champagne flowed down female throats, the relative merits of Frodo, Legolas and Aragorn as eye candy. Dave and I tried to introduce Eowyn the Rohan totty into the mix with only limited success, before he marched off to a place I could not follow, the world of *Xena Warrior Princess*, also filmed in New Zealand. I've never seen an episode of *Xena* and, sorry *Xena* fans, never really wanted to.

Talking of sword wielding warriors, one of them strode past as were sampling our strawberries on the grassy spine of Mount Sunday. He stopped for a moment nearby, used the weapon to indicate a few sights of interest to a wheezing companion, then marched off again. The companion gave our picnic a longing look then trudged gamely off in pursuit. THB and I congratulated each other on choosing the right tour.

Eventually we had to make our way back to Christchurch, travelling east to the rather inappropriate accompaniment of the haunting Annie Lennox song which closes *The Return of the King*. Oh all right non Hobbit botherers, it's called 'Into The West'.

As we sped along, Dave, who had been quietly staring out of the window at the wildlife beyond, suddenly came up with a innocent sounding question that would bring us to the brink of an international incident. "What kind of sheep are they?" he asked.

"They are Merinos," Mark replied. He should have left it there, but instead he went on rather wistfully, "You can always tell a Merino because it's an ugly sheep, stupid looking, with a long face and eyes peeping out from underneath a thick woolly fringe. Not like a Romney. Now that's a beautiful sheep. It's got a pleasant rounded face, a smiling mouth and eyes..."

He'd obviously just looked in his rear view mirror and seen five of his customers staring opened mouthed at him. The other one was staring from the seat beside him.

"So it's all true about Kiwis," the Aussie grannies shouted. Then the jokes began.

"A tourist out walking in New Zealand spotted a farmer standing behind a sheep with his trousers around his ankles. Curious as to what the farmer was doing, the tourist asked 'Are you shearing that sheep?'"

"'No!' shouted the farmer, 'Go away and find your own.'"

The riposte.

"How does an Aussie farmer find a sheep in the long grass? Very satisfying."

It was an entertaining ride back to the Rakaia Gorge, where the five year old grannies made another appearance. They hadn't forgotten the jet boat.

"Can we? Can we? Can we? Can we? Can we? Can we? Can We? Pleeeease?"

Mark took the 4WD down onto the pebbly banks of the Rakaia River where a man was busy packing away jet boating accoutrements for the evening.

We were too late... or were we?

Mark shouted, "Have you finished for the night?" and the man looked over. He paused for a moment to count the number of occupants of the 4WD, multiply that number by the cost of a jet boat trip and blink the dollar signs away from his eyes. Then he threw a few life jackets in our direction and unpacked the boat.

Another round of voting ensued.

YES! said the grannies. YES! said Maya (checking her purse as an afterthought to see if she could afford the ride) YES! said yours truly, whispering, "Go on. It'll be fun," in THB's ear. She still wasn't keen. Then came the clincher. Mark said, YES! (he hadn't been on a jet boat for years) leaving THB with the prospect of half an hour alone on the shore in Hobbit bothering combat with Dave. YES! said THB. Oh all right then, said Dave. The fellowship was complete.

After a brief scare that I might be left behind for the lack of a life jacket to fit (an ancient, dusty and above all large one was eventually found at the bottom of a storage locker) we were taken on the ride of our lives by the wrinkly and leather skinned boat owner who looked as if he'd spent most of his summers haring up and down the Rakaia River and had never ever heard of sun block. He introduced himself as Murray.

So on our last day in New Zealand THB and I experienced its wonderful scenery at closer quarters than we'd done in any of the previous twenty five. The rocky walls of the gorge passed centimetres away from my head (I had a prime seat at the side of the boat) and the rocky bed of the river just centimetres away from my backside, with the boat's hull, fortunately, in between. All this at breakneck speed, accompanied by the clatter of the hull upon gravel as we hit shallower spots and the throaty roar of the water pump propelling us on our way.

The highlights of the trip? Waving as we approached some kids on the river bank with the velocity of a flying mammal from a fiery pit. Watching them wave back. Seeing a devilish grin creep onto Murray's face as he half turned, raised his finger in the air then twirled it around. Realising what was coming. Realising the kids didn't know what was coming. Experiencing the famous Hamilton turn as the boat stopped dead, but the water in front of it didn't. Watching the water stop as it hit the waving (or was it drowning) kids.

It was a hot day and they took it well. Neither insults nor stones were hurled as we sped off down the river. Not loudly or forcefully enough to worry us, anyway.

Back on shore THB berated me for not being more forceful in my attempts to cajole her onto the Shotover Jet in Queenstown. She was a jet boat convert. All I have to do now is to find one in Britain.

That night I was visited by Jack Peterson for the final time in New Zealand. His mood was more sombre than I'd seen before. Was that a tear in his eye?

"Congritulations," he said. "It wus touch and go thur fur a while. You nirly pucked Arthur's Pass over Edoras. But you pussed the tist in the ind. You ire wun of us now!"

If I tell the truth, for all my non Hobbit bothering bluster, I think I'd been one of them since Matamata.

EPILOGUE: SOMEWHERE OVER THE ATLANTIC

Another Dream.

In homage to *The Return of the King*, which boasted at least half a dozen endings, I thought I'd produce more than one too.

THB and I were standing in our third or fourth queue at LAX when someone we assumed to be an airline official marched by shouting "Anyone for flight NZ0002 to London, go upstairs immediately." Hoping that this someone was indeed an airline official and not a random nutter who felt the need to order people about (well you never know in America) we went upstairs. There we found the Air New Zealand desk, conveniently located in front of an Air New Zealand check-in clerk. "You shouldn't have listened to the nutter downstairs," is what she should have said in order to provide an interesting punchline for this paragraph.

What she actually said was "NZ0002 has been overbooked. There are not enough seats for people who want to fly. We are looking for volunteers to go on tomorrow's flight." At this point a miserly offer of compensation is usually forthcoming from the airline. An offer which can sometimes be negotiated up to passable and on rare occasions to generous. "We will give you free hotel accommodation for the night, free meals and four hundred dollars each in compensation," was the opening gambit.

We conferred. A rare occasion, we thought. Plans were hatched for visits to the Hollywood sign, that stretch of pavement where film stars press bits of their anatomy into setting concrete and lastly the theme park run by giant mice. That would do for one day.

"Done!" we said.

We were presented with contracts to seal the deal, which we amended to feature ALL the promises that had been made to us verbally, then waited with a bucket of coffee (never order large in the USA) to discover whether we had been granted a bonus day in LA.

We hadn't.

Air New Zealand had managed to fit us on our planned flight after all, presenting us with boarding cards at a late enough stage to ensure a dash to reach the gate just in time to board... and be ushered onto the upper deck of the jumbo. A free upgrade for our trouble! Or maybe it was because I had made so many changes to their contract before signing it that they feared I was a member of the legal profession who'd better be kept sweet.

It was so quiet up there on the top deck, so roomy, so comfortable in those wonderful seats that fold back almost flat, just like beds, so sleepy, zzzzzzzzzz.

I find myself at a party dressed in dark breeches, a grey shirt and a cloak seemingly made from an old grey sack. Someone has stolen my shoes and my wedding ring has been etched with odd curvy letters by forces unknown. Embarrassingly I have also developed a strange "oh arr" kind of accent, half way between pirate and yokel, and a tendency to call anyone vertically challenged and boasting curly hair "Mister Frodo." So I'm not talking much.

THB is there too, having fared much better at the outfitters, dressed in a long white gown and silver coronet. There is something about her ears, though, that doesn't look quite right. She is busy supervising a queue of people waiting patiently to stare into a punch bowl. What can they see in there, I wonder? Punch probably.

As the sound of a horn brings the meeting to order, Jack Peterson skips into view, still sporting a tee shirt, shorts, spectacles and Hobbit hair.

"Welcome iviryone to Hubbit Botherer's Anonymous," he says in a New Zealand accent that has not become any easier to reproduce on the printed page as this book has progressed.

"Our latest mimber his retinned from his trivils."

I look around to catch a glimpse at the poor unfortunate who's been singled out and yes it's me again.

"He hus pussed the tist!"

A burst of excited applause fails to greet this announcement. But there are murmurings of "He's still only seen *The Return of the King* four times!" and "His cloak looks like an old sack!"

"He hus irned the right to tuckle the quistun of distuny."

Now the audience began to pay attention. Quizzes are always entertaining.

"If he inswers corrictly he kin luck into Gisbydriel's mirror."

All eyes turn to THB.

"Bit if he inswers incorrictly..."

All eyes turn to a group of Uruk-hai waving fire lighters.
"The quistun is..."
(just building anticipation here)
(and here)
"...Whut ire the first two litters of Orthanc?"
Groans and cries of, "Too easy!" from the back of the room.
"Oh Arr, Mister Frodo!" I say.
"Correct! But my nim is Pittersun."

So now I must gaze into the punch bowl. A punch bowl which (apparently) will show me my future, played out on the liquid's surface. Providing that the Hobbits have left any liquid in there, of course. And providing that I can see anything through the pipeweed fumes.

I move to the front of the queue (an advantage of having your wife run things) and gaze to the best of my ability.

"Whut do yu see?" asks Jack Peterson, expectantly.

I feel sorry to disappoint him, after travelling so far together, but the mirror obviously isn't working.

It shows me writing a book.

Fat chance of that.

A final thought.

THB has a friend called Kyp who loves to read the end of a book first to get an idea if it is worth bothering with the rest. I don't know if she'll ever get around to reading this one, but just in case she does...

Hello Kyp. You should see what I said about you earlier on in the book.

She'll have to read it now.

GLOSSARY

For People Who Think *Lord Of The Rings* Is An Aristocratic Jeweller.

Anduil	A sword reforged from the broken pieces of Isildur's weapon for use by...
Aragorn	A *Ranger* who reluctantly finds himself taking the lead in the fight of good against evil, in particular defending *Hobbits* from all comers. Eventually, of course, he becomes... you'll have to read or watch *The Return of the King* to find out. (I hope that hasn't given it away).
Arathorn	The man who has the right to say to Aragorn "Who's the daddy?"
Arwen	The (female) *elf* that Aragorn fancies, daughter of *Elrond*, who doesn't really approve. Daddy would much prefer her to go off Into The West with some nice *elf* lad and never see that *Aragorn* again.
Astin, Sean	The actor who played Sam in the *Lord of the Rings* movies.
Baggins, Bilbo	A Hobbit who believes strongly in the principle of finders keepers and so becomes owner of *the Ring* after *Gollum*, before passing it on to *Frodo*.
Balrog	A large fiery creature that lives deep underground and thinks it can kill a grey *wizard*. It later turns out that the *wizard* isn't in fact dead but is all white.
Bean, Sean	The actor who played *Boromir* in the *Lord of the Rings* movies. His fans are known as Beanstalkers.
Black Rider	One of the Nazgul on a horse. A black horse, of course.
Blanchett, Cate	The actress who played Galadriel in the *Lord of the Rings* movies.
Bloom, Orlando	If you've got a teenage daughter, go up to her bedroom (knock first!) and look on the walls. The chap in those posters is Orlando Bloom. If not you'll just have to make do with knowing he is the

	actor who played *Legolas* in the *Lord of the Rings* movies.
Bombadil, Tom	A mysterious character from *Lord of the Rings* (the book) that never made it into *Lord of the Rings* (the movies).
Boromir	Favourite son of the bloke put in charge of Gondor until *The Return of the King*. Dies heroically defending *Hobbits* from *Orcs* after succumbing briefly to a desire to snatch *the Ring* from *Frodo*.
Celtic	The other Glasgow football team. (See *Rangers*).
Dead, the	A bunch of dead blokes, as the name suggests, who once ran away from a fight and will only rest in peace when allowed to redeem themselves in battle by not running away again.
Dunedain	*Rangers* who live up north.
Durin	A dynasty of *dwarf* kings who mined too deep and got more than they bargained for when they unearthed the *Balrog*.
Dwarf	Diminutive creature, more warlike, avaricious and prone to face fungus than a *Hobbit*. Spends a lot of time underground in mines. Loves axes and hates elves.
Elf	A magical creature, tall and slender with pointy ears. Easily mistaken for a Vulcan by Star Trek fans. Loves lounging about in woods by waterfalls and sailing westward. Hates dwarfs.
Elrond	*Elf* who called the meeting where *The Fellowship of the Ring* was formed. I reckon the decision to take it to Mount Doom was really a plot to get *Aragorn* killed so he couldn't chase *Arwen* any more. Eventually *Elrond* went off to become Agent Smith in *The Matrix*.
Ent	A protector of trees. Has a trunk like a tree. Has branches like a tree. Has bark like a tree. But talks, unlike a tree.
Eomer	A horsey warrior who comes away from even the fiercest battles unscathed. Rohan's very own version of *Aragorn*. Nephew of King *Theoden*.
Eowyn	*Eomer*'s tomboy sister with a penchant for

	swordplay and staring into the distance. Also has a penchant for *Aragorn* but has to make do with...
Faramir	Boromir's younger and more cerebral sibling who can never live up to his elder brother in their father's eyes. What does he care? He gets Eowyn.
Farmer Maggot	A carrot grower.
Fell beast	The preferred mode of transport of the Nazgul. Big screechy dragon like creatures. Black, of course.
Fellowship of the Ring the,	First part of the *Lord of the Rings* trilogy. Also the group of nine mates (*Frodo, Sam, Merry, Pippin, Gandalf, Legolas, Gimli, Aragorn, Boromir*) who set out to destroy *the Ring* before its rightful owner *Sauron* works out they have it.
Frodo	The occasionally doe eyed and occasionally demented *Hobbit* entrusted with *the Ring* and the job of taking it to its destruction at Mount Doom.
Galadriel	Beautiful elf queen who lives in the forest, bewitches dwarfs (I thought they liked their women bearded) and encourages people to stare into bird baths to see their future.
Gandalf	A grandfatherly *wizard* fond of pointy hats, pipeweed and fireworks. His party trick is to summon up giant eagles at opportune moments. Well they're not much good at inopportune moments are they?
Gollum	A version of the *Hobbit*-like Smeagol corrupted by prolonged exposure to *the Ring* and turned into a spindly, bald CGI character that can't remember its own name. Responsible for the catchphrase that everyone remembers, my preciousssss.
Gondor, Man of	A bloke who comes from Gondor. Isn't it obvious?
Gondorian	Another name for a bloke who comes from Gondor.
Gimli	A dwarf who competes gamely with *Legloas* to kill the most baddies despite having to wait until they are on top of him (sometimes literally) to use his axe. Legolas has a bow and a limitless supply of arrows. That's cheating.
Hobbit	Diminutive curly haired, pointy eared, long lived creature that lives in burrows and spends its life

	enjoying wine, women and song. Actually you can probably substitute root vegetables and pipeweed for women.
Isildur	Early king who broke his sword hacking *the Ring* from *Sauron*'s finger then spurned the chance to destroy it in Mount Doom, much to *Elrond*'s disgust. Yes *Elrond* was around then too.
Jackson, Peter	The director of the *Lord of the Rings* movies. We are not worthy!
Legolas	A blonde haired, acrobatic elvish killing machine. Gimli's straight man, beloved of teenage and not so teenage girls.
Lord of the Rings	A book about the struggle between good and evil in a mythical land, originally published in three parts due to a paper shortage.
Merry	A *Hobbit*, best mate of *Pippin*, who after experimenting with carrot stealing and *Ent* climbing gets carted off to battle by Eowyn who has disguised herself as a man.
Mortensen, Viggo	The actor who played Aragorn in the *Lord of the Rings* movies. Eye candy for women who've grown too old to fancy Orlando and too tall to fancy Elijah. Upstaged by a horse in *Hidalgo*.
Nazgul	What remains of nine ancient kings corrupted by evil and now servants of *Sauron*. Also called Ringwraiths and *Black Riders*, when on horseback.
Oliphaunt	A beast like an elephant only with an O instead of an E and an extra U.
Orc	Someone has to do Sauron's fighting for him and the Orcs are that someone. Evil and twisted creatures that were once elves.
Otto, Miranda	The actress who played Eowyn in the *Lord of the Rings* movies. Eye candy for the blokes.
Pippin	A *Hobbit* with a Scottish accent, best mate of *Merry*, who after experimenting with carrot stealing and *Ent* climbing rises high in the *Gondorian* army wearing *Faramir*'s cast offs.
Rangers	Sword wielding nomads who live lonely lives wandering about keeping nasties like *Orc*s at bay

	and being unappreciated by everyone. Either that or a Glasgow football team.
Ring, the	A nasty piece of work that turns you invisible when you wear it. It also has the tendency to make you murder your friends, forget your name and fixate on the word precious. Also a rather good Japanese horror flick.
Rohirrim	Horsey people who come from Rohan, with the hillock in the middle of nowhere, Edoras, as their capital.
Return of the King, the	Third part of the *Lord of the Rings* trilogy.
Sam	The down to earth (being a gardener) *Hobbit* companion of *Frodo* on the journey to Mount Doom. The one with the yokel accent.
Sauraman	A turncoat of a *wizard* who used to be *Gandalf's* chum but gave that up to become a sidekick of Sauron, then a kebab. (Watch the extended edition of *The Return of the King*).
Sauron	The evil baddie who wants to destroy the world. There's always one. Appears in the guise of a not quite all seeing eye.
Serkis, Andy	The poor bloke who had to prance about wearing a full-body white condom acting as *Gollum* only to be CGIed out of the movies except for a brief appearance as *Smeagol* in *The Return of The King*. Never mind, he has a Las Vegas hotel named after him. (Serkis, Serkis).
Smeagol	Gollum before *the Ring* got to him.
Tyler, Liv	The actress who played Arwen in the *Lord of the Rings* movies after helping Bruce Willis to save the earth from destruction by comet.
Theoden	King of Rohan. The lucky bugger who got to build his house on Mount Sunday, alias Edoras.
Theodred	Theoden's son, who turns up almost dead in a river in his first scene, completely dead in Theoden's Great Hall in his second scene and buried in his third. Blink and you missed him.
Tolkein J R R	The man who wrote *Lord of the Rings*. You didn't

	know that? Do they breathe air on your planet like we do on ours?
Two Towers, the	Second part of the *Lord of the Rings* trilogy.
Uruk-Hai	A kind of super *Orc* with a white handprint on its head bred by *Sauraman* to serve *Sauron*. Not super enough to defeat *Aragorn* and company though.
Warg	A big ferocious hairy creature ridden into battle by *Orc*s. Not to be confused with the small ferocious hairy creature called *Gimli*.
Wizard	Magical creature, generally older and more wrinkly than an *elf* and more likely to produce arm waving, bangs and flashes type tricks. If killed, likely to turn up later, unscathed, in different coloured clothing.
Wood, Elijah	The actor who played Frodo in the *Lord of the Rings* movies. Eye candy for women reluctant to jump on the *Orlando* band wagon but who feel that *Viggo* might not take too kindly to being mothered.

SOURCES OF REFERENCE

THE OBVIOUS ONES

Lord of the Rings by J R R Tolkien
The Lord of the Rings: The Fellowship of the Ring (2001)
The Lord of the Rings: The Two Towers (2002)
The Lord of the Rings: The Return of the King (2003)
   (All three movies directed by Peter Jackson).

THE NOT SO OBVIOUS ONES

The web sites listed below were used for reference during the conception and gestation of *New Zealand with a Hobbit Botherer*. The author is not responsible for their maintenance or content in any way.

abeltasmanmarahaucamp.co.nz/map.html
   Map of Abel Tasman National Park.
www.albatross.org.nz/colony.htm
   The Taiaroa Head albatross colony, Dunedin.
www.angelfire.com/mo2/animals1/fly/nzfg.html
   The New Zealand fungus gnat or glow-worm.
www.atoz-nz.com
   A to Z of New Zealand, where S is for Southern Scenic Route.
www.catlins-nz.com
   The Catlins site, lots about scenery, little about activities.
www.destination.co.nz
   New Zealand travel and tourism directory.
www.doc.govt.nz/Conservation
   Department of Conservation (DOC) hit list of animal pests.
www.doc.govt.nz/explore
   National Parks and walking trails (DOC)
www.great-towers.com
   The World Federation of Great Towers (WFGT).
www.fiordland.org.nz
   Fiordland travel information site.
www.fourcorners.co.nz/new-zealand
   General New Zealand travel information

www.gateshead.gov.uk/angel/pics2.htm
  The Angel of the North.
www.geographylists.com
  Steepest streets of the world... and other geographical lists.
www.gns.cri.nz/what/earthact/earthquakes
  Earthquakes (Institute of Geological and Nuclear Sciences).
www.harlequin.co.nz/nelsonbays/activities/naturelandzoo
  Natureland Zoological Park, Nelson.
www.hasslefree.co.nz
  Trip to Mount Sunday (Edoras) with Hassle-free Tours.
www.hobbitontours.com
  Tours of the Hobbiton site at Matamata.
homepages.ihug.co.nz/~sarah/content/slang.html
  Excellent compilation of New Zealand slang.
homepages.paradise.net.nz/wmg
  Quirky Kiwi site, with a *"Do you think like a sheep?"* quiz.
www.imdb.com
  For all movie related information (Internet Movie Database).
www.kcc.org.nz/factsheets.asp
  Tuatara and other creatures (Kiwi Conservation Club).
www.lakevista.co.nz/deer_park.htm
  Deer Park Heights, Queenstown.
library.christchurch.org.nz/Childrens/NZDisasters/Edgecumbe.asp
  Edgecumbe earthquake and flying cow. No I didn't make it up.
www.lulu.com
  So you thought this book was great?
  Why not buy another copy for your best friend?
  So you thought it was rubbish?
  Why not buy another copy for your worst enemy?
www.nomadsafaris.co.nz
  Lord of the Rings tours from Queenstown.
www.nzine.co.nz
  On-line magazine about New Zealand
www.nzmaori.co.nz
  Whakarewarewa geothermal area and Maori culture shows.
www.nzmaritime.co.nz/wahine.htm
  Everything you want to know about the ship *The Wahine*.
www.nzti.com/cruise-milford/gettingthere.htm
  Milford Road drive, New Zealand Travel Information Network

onenews.nzoom.com/onenews_detail/0,1227,164476-1-5,00.html
   Is Baldwin Street, Dunedin, really the world's steepest?
www.parrotsociety.org.au/articles/art_010.htm
   Parrots of New Zealand, including the kea.
www.penguin.net.nz/news/archive/0412.html
   Virus threatening yellow-eyed penguin chicks.
www.penguin-place.co.nz
   Penguin Place, Otago Peninsula, Dunedin.
www.pukekura.co.nz
   The town of Pukekura, population two, and possum pie.
www.sixofone.org.uk
   All about *The Prisoner* and its penny-farthing connection.
www.rockyhorror.com
   Puzzled by the mention of stockings in chapter twenty?
   This may explain.
www.teara.govt.nz/1966
   An encyclopaedia about New Zealand... as it was in 1966.
www.terranature.org/flightlessbirds.htm
   New Zealand's flightless birds. Takahe, kiwi and more.
www.tramper.co.nz
   Route guides for trampers by trampers.
translator.kedri.info
   Maori to English word translator.
www.travellink.co.nz
   What to see, what to do and where to stay in Fiordland.
www.truenz.co.nz/kayaking/listings/westcoast/westcoast.html
   Dragon's Cave rafting in Greymouth, New Zealand's G-spot.
www.twizel.com
   Yes, Twizel has a web site.
www.wcl.govt.nz/wellington/wahine.html
   The sinking of *The Wahine*.
www.wellingtonrover.co.nz
   Rover Rings Tour from Wellington
www.yellow-eyedpenguin.org.nz
   Yellow-eyed penguin trust.
Also:
The Vikings and the Eskimos by S. M. Wilson,
Natural History, February 1992, pages 18-21.
   How Greenland got its name.

Silent Screams
By Annette Gisby
ISBN: 1-4116-2306-1

Not all monsters are under the bed...

Jessica Miller is a young woman with secrets, secrets that she feels she can't tell. Referred to a psychiatrist after a failed suicide attempt, she is reluctant to reveal the reasons why.

Over the course of several sessions, it soon becomes clear that Jessica isn't the only one with secrets. Some of them should have remained buried...

"Silent Screams is one of those thrillers that pulls you in by your emotions, then leads you on a path so scary that you want to close your eyes, yet can't because you have to keep reading!"
Elizabeth A. Merz, author of *The Last Gate* fantasy series.

"From the beginning it captivated me with the reality of the conflicts that face so many families today. The author deals with issues that come 'too close to home' for many people, but I believe it will help people with being able to confront the monsters in their own lives, and enjoy a spellbinding read in the process."
Janet Elaine Smith, author of *Monday Knight, House Call to the Past, Dunnottar* and more.

**Silent Screams is available from Lulu.com
& online bookstores.**

Shadows of the Rose
By Annette Gisby
ISBN: 1-4116-4324-0

A book of twelve tales, different genres, different characters, but all with one thing in common; an ending with a twist. Here is just a taster:

The Witch Hunter - a young girl accused of sorcery, but the man sent to condemn her is not as he seems...

Baby Blues - a dark future where family planning is controlled by the state and it is illegal to make love...

The Glass Guitar - Meg thinks a haunted guitar would be just the gift for her musician boyfriend...

Shadows of the Rose - a lovers' tryst in a ruined abbey, but something is not quite right. What's that, there, hidden in the *Shadows of the Rose*?

"I was also impressed with Gisby's ability to successfully integrate romance and eroticism into her suspense stories. This is indeed an art that, at the hands of a less skilled writer, might appear awkward or forced. Gisby manages the task with ease and grace."
Karen Mueller Bryson, award winning playwright and author of the novels, *Hey, Dorothy, You're not in Kansas Anymore* and *Where is Wonderland, Anyway?*

"I'm not fond of short stories, but every now and then I come across a writer who handles this format so well that my enjoyment surprises me. Annette Gisby is such a writer, because her collection of suspense tales whose endings I could NOT see coming the proverbial "mile away") had me gulping it down in a single evening."
Nina M. Osier, author of *Mistworld, Rough Rider* and other SF and mainstream novels.

Shadows of the Rose is available from Lulu.com
& online bookstores.

New Zealand With a Hobbit Botherer

1441544R0

Printed in Great Britain by
Amazon.co.uk, Ltd.,
Marston Gate.